Tora Study Bible - Book of Exodus

By
Zev Bitman

©2018
Feb 13, 2018

About This Book

Tōra Study Bible is a modern English reality-based non-literal rendition of the Jewish Bible. Interpretations and footnotes contain information taken from other sources, mainly:
The Living Torah by Aryeh Kaplan (1981) and
The Soncino Chumash by A. Cohen (1947, copyrighted in 1983).

The rendition and notes in Tōra Study Bible are based on traditional commentators such as Ibn Ezra, Rashbam, Rambam (Maimonides), Ramban (Nachmanides), Siforno, Rashē, and other sages. Each chapter is a section (alēya) as read for the weekly Bible portion on Shabat (Sabbath). To be fully prepared for the upcoming shabat service, read one section a day of the upcoming weekly portion.
The table of contents provides a quick yet comprehensive list of all important events, facts and commandments in each section of each portion.

Tōra Study Bible is intended as a starting point for further Tōra study. Every effort has been made to keep the language simple and appropriate for young readers.

Names are transliterated.
Long vowels are noted by a vowel with a bar above it, namely: ā, ē, ī, ō, ū.
"Y" is not used as a vowel.
The letter "ź" denotes the "tz" sound, as pronounced in the word pizza.
The letter "ĥ" denotes the guttural sound similar to the Russian letter "x."
See Transliteration Guide for a complete list of symbols.

Five Books of Mōshe, along with their Amazon print (& Kindle) IDs:
Brāshēt (At First)   - Genesis   ISBN 9781521446850 (B00I2CQXZO)
Shimōt (Names)   - Exodus   ISBN 9781520794860 (B00I53KBQC)
Vayikra (He Called) - Leviticus ISBN 9781521308400 (B00K1SVO1A)
Bamidbar   - Numbers   ISBN 9781521770450 (B00MO3H720)
    (In The Wilderness)
Divarim (Words)   - Deuteronomy ISBN 9781549504013 (B016J12NSK)

©2018 William Bitman

Table of Contents

Transliteration Guidelines												p. 26

Sources																		p. 27

Table 1. Letter, word, verse, and commandment counts						p. 30
Table 2. Chronology from Avraham to Mōshe									p. 31
Table 3. Boundaries of the land of Israel									p. 35
Table 4. The first six days at Mount Sēnī									p. 36
Table 5. Events during first year-and-a-half after exodus					p. 37
Table 6. Comparison of verses about the Stone Slabs							p. 38
Table 7. Calendar: Revelation until Day of Atonement						p. 41
Table 8. Universal Commandments												p. 44

Map of regions in the Mideast												p. 46

Essays:
Essay 1. Tōra																p. 47
Essay 2. G-d																p. 48
Essay 3. The Chosen People													p. 51
Essay 4. Serving G-d														p. 52
Essay 5. Jewish Identity													p. 56
Essay 6. The Land of Israel													p. 61
Essay 7. Prayer																p. 64
Essay 8. Commandments														p. 66

Table of Contents

Shimōt - Section 1   - 17 verses   (Total: 124 verses)   p. 67
Sons Of Yaakōv
That Generation Ends
Population Expands
Pharaoh Is Fearful
Taskmasters
Jewish Population Continues To Increase Despite Pharaoh's Evil Efforts
The Work Increases
Midwives Disobey Pharaoh

Shimōt - Section 2   - 13 verses
Midwives Fear G-d
Pharaoh Decrees Against Jewish Boy Babies
The Savior Is Born
The Baby's Mother Places Him In a Basket On the River
Daughter of Pharaoh Retrieves The Baby
Miryam Arranges For The Baby's Mother To Nurse The Baby
Pharaoh's Daughter Names The Baby: Mōshe

Shimōt - Section 3   - 15 verses
Mōshe Grows Up And Realizes That He Is Jewish
Mōshe Identifies With His People
Mōshe Leaves His Birthplace
Mōshe Marries Źēpōra, Daughter of Yitrō
Gârshōm, Mōshe's Firstborn Son

Table of Contents

Shimōt - Section 4   - 15 verses   p. 84
The Burning Bush
G-d Reveals Himself to Mōshe
G-d Appoints Mōshe To Confront Pharaoh and Lead The Jewish People
Mōshe's Negative Response 1: Do I Have The Ability To Succeed?
Mōshe's Negative Response 2: Are The Jewish People Worthy?
G-d's Answer 1: I Will Be With You
G-d's Answer 2: Jewish People Will Become Worthy
Mōshe's Negative Response 3: Why Should The Jewish People Believe Me?
G-d's Answer 3: The Password
G-d's Concealed Name

Shimōt - Section 5   - 24 verses
G-d Commands Mōshe To Convene The Jewish Leaders To Address Pharaoh
Pharaoh Will Not Give Permission Unless He Is Pressured
G-d Plans To Pressure Pharaoh
The People of Egypt Will Give Their Valuables To The Jewish People
Mōshe's Negative Response 4: Jewish People Will Doubt Me As Prophet
G-d's Answer 4: Wondrous Acts
G-d Transforms Mōshe's Staff Into A Snake
G-d Transforms The Snake Back To A Staff
G-d Turns The Skin Of Mōshe's Hand White
G-d Turns The Skin Of Mōshe's Hand Back To Normal
G-d Communicates About Turning Water To Blood
Mōshe's Negative Response 5: I Am Not A Fluent Eloquent Speaker
G-d's Answer 5: G-d Promises To Guide Mōshe
Mōshe's Negative Response 6: Appoint Someone Else
G-d Becomes Angry With Mōshe; Aharōn Will Do The Speaking

Table of Contents

Shimōt - Section 6   - 14 verses   p. 100
Mōshe Asks For, And Receives Permission From Yitrō To Return To Egypt
Żēpōra Circumcises Their Newborn Son
Aharōn Meets Mōshe At The Mountain Of G-d
Mōshe Relates G-d's Commands To Aharōn
Mōshe and Aharōn Convene The Jewish Leaders
Aharōn Performs The Wonders For The Jewish Leaders

Shimōt - Section 7   - 21 + 3 verses
Mōshe and Aharōn State Their Request To Pharaoh
Pharaoh Refuses
Pharaoh Increases The Burdens Of The Jewish People
Jewish Overseers Bring Their Complaint To Pharaoh
Pharaoh Confirms His Evil Edict
The Overseers Blame Mōshe and Aharōn For The Troubles Of The Jewish
         People
Mōshe Asks G-d: Why?
G-d Replies: Now You Will See

Table of Contents

Vaāra - Section 1 - 12 verses (Total: 121 verses) p. 111
G-d Explains His Strategy
Mōshe Relates G-d's Message To The Jewish People, But They Do Not Believe

Vaāra - Section 2 - 15 verses
Partial Genealogy
Riūvān
Shimōn
Lāvē – Lived To Be 137
Gârshōn
Kihat - Lived to be 133
Mirarē
Amram – Lived to be 137
Yiżhar
Ūzēâl
Aharōn
Kōraĥ
Elazar

Vaāra - Section 3 - 9 verses
- Summary Study Note on verse 7:3: Stubborn Heart of the King
Mōshe Is 80, And Aharōn Is 83 Years Old

Vaāra - Section 4 - 28 verses
G-d Instructs: Be Prepared To Transform Your Staff Into A Snake
Mōshe And Aharōn Confront Pharaoh
Aharōn's Staff Swallows The Other Snakes
Pharaoh's Heart Is Stubborn
Plague 1: Blood: G-d Instructs To Tell Pharaoh Why He Is Being Punished
Plague 1: Aharōn Performs
Plague 1: Pharaoh Refuses
Plague 2: Frogs: Mōshe Gives Pharaoh Opportunity
Plague 2: Aharōn Performs
Plague 2: Pharaoh Promises

Table of Contents

Vaāra - Section 5   - 12 verses   p. 132
Plague 2: Frogs Are Removed
Plague 2: Pharaoh Refuses
Plague 3: Lice: G-d Instructs Mōshe And Aharōn
Plague 3: Mōshe And Aharōn Perform
Plague 3: Pharaoh Refuses
Plague 4: Mosquitoes: Mōshe Gives Pharaoh Opportunity

Vaāra - Section 6   - 26 verses
Plague 4: Mōshe Continues to Warn Pharaoh
Plague 4: G-d Performs
Plague 4: Pharaoh Pleads and Promises
Plague 4: Mōshe Prays and the Plague Stops
Plague 4: Pharaoh Refuses
Plague 5: Fatal Animal Disease: Mōshe Gives Pharaoh Opportunity
Plague 5: G-d Performs
Plague 5: Pharaoh Refuses
Plague 6: Blisters: G-d Instructs Mōshe And Aharōn
Plague 6: Mōshe And Aharōn Perform
Plague 6: Pharaoh Refuses
Plague 7: Hail: Mōshe Gives Pharaoh Opportunity

Vaāra - Section 7   - 15 + 3 verses
Plague 7: Mōshe Performs
Plague 7: Pharaoh Refuses

Table of Contents

Bō - Section 1   - 11 verses   (Total 106 verses)   p. 145
Tell Your Children About The Miracles
Plague 8: Locusts: Pharaoh Can Choose To Avoid Disaster
Plague 8: Pharaoh Reconsiders
Plague 8: Pharaoh Refuses

Bō –Section 2   - 12 verses
Plague 8: Mōshe Performs
Plague 8: G-d Removes The Locusts
Plague 8: G-d Causes Pharaoh's Heart To Be Stubborn
Plague 9: Darkness: G-d Instructs Mōshe
Plague 9: Mōshe Performs

Bō – Section 3   - 8 verses
Plague 9: Pharaoh Refuses
Plague 10: Death Of The First Born: G-d Informs Mōshe

Bō – Section 4   - 27 verses
Commandment 3: Court Calculate The Start of Each New Month
Commandment 4: Slaughter The Pesaĥ Offering On Nēsan 14
Commandment 5: Eat The Pesaĥ Offering With Maźa And Bitters
Commandment 6: Do Not Boil The Pesaĥ Offering, But It Cannot Be Raw
Commandment 7: Do Not Leave Pesaĥ Offering Past Sunrise
Commandment 8: Destroy Leavened Food On Nēsan 14
Commandment 9: Eat Matźa On The First Night Of Pesaĥ
Commandment 10: Do Not Have Leavened Food On Your Property
Commandment 11: Do Not Eat Foods That Are Partial Leaven

Bō – Section 5   - 8 verses
Mōshe Instructs The Jewish People: G-d Will Pass Over Your Houses
Children Will Ask: Why Observe All These Rules Of Pesaĥ?

Table of Contents

Bō – Section 6   - 23 verses   **p. 165**
Plague 10: G-d Performs
Pharaoh Forces the Jewish People To Leave Immediately
Their Dough Is Not Fermented
Travel From Ramsās to Sūkōt; About 600,000 Men
Other Peoples Left With The Jewish People
Pesaĥ Night Is a Night of Divine Protection
Commandment 12: Only Jewish People May Partake Of The Pesaĥ Offering
Commandment 13: Hired Servants Must Not Partake Of The Pesaĥ Offering
Commandment 14: Do Not Move Pesaĥ Offering Out Of The Building
Commandment 15: Do Not Break Bones Of The Pesaĥ Offering
Commandment 16: If Not Circumcised, Must Not Eat Pesaĥ Offering
Commandment 17: If Priest Is Not Circumcised, Must Not Eat Trūma

Bō – Section 7   - 13 + 3 verses
Commandment 18: Do Not Eat Leavened Food On The Pesaĥ Festival
Commandment 19: Do Not Have Leavened Food During The Pesaĥ Festival
Commandment 20: Tell The Exodus Story On The First Night Of Pesaĥ
Commandment 21: Offer Your Firstborn Animals
Commandment 22: Redeem Your Firstborn Donkey
Commandment 23: Put Down A Firstborn Donkey If You Decide Not To Redeem
If Your Child Asks: What Is This About?

Table of Contents

Bishalaĥ - Section 1 - 14 verses   (Total: 116 verses)   p. 177
The Jewish People Travel Out Of Egypt
Mōshe Takes Along The Bones Of Yōsef
The People Reach Ātam, The Edge Of The Wilderness
G-d Leads The People Via Cloud Pillar During The Day And Fire Pillar At
    Night
The Jewish People Camp At Freedom Valley (Pē Haĥērōt) Along The
    Reed Sea
The Enemy Decides To Chase And Recapture The Jewish People

Bishalaĥ - Section 2   - 6 verses
The Enemy Catches Up
Jewish People Are Gripped With Fear
Jewish People Complain
Mōshe Reassures The Jewish People

Bishalaĥ - Section 3   - 11 verses
G-d Informs Mōshe Of His Divine Plan
G-d Uses The Pillars To Hold The Enemy Behind And Away From The
    Jewish People
The Jewish People Cross The Sea At Night By The Light Of The Divine
    Fire Pillar
Mōshe Acts And The Water Parts
The Jewish People Start To Cross
The Army Chases Them

Bishalaĥ - Section 4   - 32 verses
Enemy Is Drowned
Mōshe Sings
Miryam Sings
The Jewish People Stay In Shùr: No Water For 3 Days
Jewish People Arrive At Marata: Lake Of Bitter Water
G-d Instructs Mōshe: Sweeten The Lake Water With A Certain Plant
G-d Instructs The People: Be Law-Abiding And Ethical

Table of Contents

Bishalaĥ - Section 5   - 11 verses   p. 201
The People Arrive At Ālim Oasis
The People Reside In Źin
People Complain About Lack Of Food
G-d Promises Food
Each Person Must Collect Twice As Much On Friday
The Glory Of G-d Appears

Bishalaĥ - Section 6   - 26 verses
Food: Birds And Honey Wafers (Män)
Non-Believers Try To Save Some Food For The Next Day
Sabbath: Day Of Rest
Non-Believers Look For Food On Sabbath
Commandment 24: Do Not Go Outside Of The Boundary On The Sabbath
All People Now Accept The Sabbath
The People Name The Honey Wafers: Män

Bishalaĥ - Section 7   - 13 + 3 verses
The People Traveled To Rifēdim: No Water
Water From Rock
Amalāk Attacks
Yihōshūa Leads Army Against The Enemy
Instruction: Eradicate The Memory Of Amalāk

Table of Contents

Yitrō - Section 1 - 12 verses (Total: 75 verses) p. 214
Yitrō Prepares To Travel To Mōshe
Yitrō Travels To Mōshe And Brings Mōshe's Wife And Sons
Mōshe Travels To Meet Yitrō
Yitrō's Offerings To G-d

Yitrō - Section 2 - 11 verses
Mōshe Presides As Judge
Yitrō Advises To Appoint Judges

Yitrō - Section 3   - 4 verses
Mōshe Follows Yitrō's Advice
Yitrō Travels Back To His Home

Yitrō - Section 4   - 6 verses
The Jewish People Arrive At Mount Sēnī
Mōshe's First Ascent Up Mount Sēnī
Wings Of Eagles

Yitrō - Section 5   - 13 verses
Mōshe's First Descent Down Mount Sēnī
Elders: We Will Obey
Mōshe's Second Ascent Up Mount Sēnī
Mōshe Descends Mount Sēnī

Table of Contents

Yitrō - Section 6   - 20 verses   p. 232
Mōshe Ascends Mount Sēnī
Mōshe Descends Mount Sēnī
Commandment 25: Know That There Is G-d
Commandment 26: Do Not Believe That There Are Other Deities
Commandment 27: Do Not Form Idols
Commandment 28: Do Not Worship Idols In Their Manner
Commandment 29: Do Not Worship Idols The Way Jewish People
          Worship G-d
Commandment 30: Do Not Speak G-d's Name Unnecessarily
Commandment 31: Sanctify The Sabbath By Reciting Blessings
Commandment 32: Do Not Perform Forbidden Activities On The Sabbath
Commandment 33: Honor Your Father And Mother
Commandment 34: Do Not Murder A Human Being
Do Not Have Intimate Relations With Another Man's Wife
Commandment 35: Do Not Kidnap A Human Being
Commandment 36: Do Not Lie
Commandment 37: Do Not Scheme to Take Other People's Property

Yitrō - Section 7   - 4 + 5 verses
Commandment 38: Do Not Form Human Statues, Even Just For
          Decoration
Commandment 39: Do Not Use Metal Tools When Building An Altar
Commandment 40: Do Not Have Steps Leading To The Top Of An Altar

Table of Contents

Mishpatim - Section 1 - 19 verses (Total: 118 verses) p. 244
All Jewish Laws Are Divinely Given
Commandment 41: Properly Purchase A Jewish Man Servant
If A Father Arranges For His Young Daughter To Be A Ward
Commandment 42: Redeem A Jewish Maidservant
Commandment 43: Betroth A Jewish Maidservant
Commandment 44: Do Not Sell A Jewish Maidservant
Commandment 45: Do Not Withhold Your Obligations From Your Wife.
An Intentional Assault That Results In Death
Accidental Death
Premeditated Murder
Commandment 46: Do Not Hit Your Father Or Mother
Kidnapping
Commandment 47: Do Not Curse Your Father Or Mother
Commandment 48: Court Must Litigate Against Injury And Damages

Mishpatim - Section 2   - 21 verses
Commandment 49: Court Must Carry Out Capital Punishment By Sword
If A Master Injures A Gentile Servant
Commandment 50: Do Not Oppress Weak People
If Brawling Men Injure A Pregnant Woman
Compensation For Injury
If A Master Causes Serious Injury To A Gentile Servant
Commandment 51: Do Not Benefit From A Condemned Animal
Commandment 52: Court Must Assess Damages Caused By A Goring Animal
Commandment 53: Court Must Assess Damages Caused By A Pit In Public Area
If An Animal Kills Someone's Animal
Commandment 54: Court Must Judge A Thief
If Someone Steals Ox Or Sheep And Kills Or Sells It
If Self-Defense Results In A Person Being Killed
Causing Death When Not Mortally Threatened
Laws Of Theft

Table of Contents

Mishpatim - Section 3   - 23 verses   p. 255
Commandment 55: Court Must Assess Damage By A Grazing Animal
Commandment 56: Court Must Assess Damage By Fire
Commandment 57: Court Must Judge Cases Of An Unpaid Guard
Commandment 58: Court Must Judge Cases Of Plaintiff
Commandment 59: Court Must Judge Cases Of Hired Worker And Guard
Commandment 60: Court Must Judge Cases Of Borrower
Commandment 61: Court Must Judge Cases Of Seduction
Commandment 62: Court Must Judge Cases Of Indulging In Witchcraft
Commandment 63: Do Not Cheat A Convert
Commandment 64: Do Not Insult Or Harm A Convert
Commandment 65: Lend Money To Jewish People Who Need Funds
Commandment 66: Do Not Demand Repayment From Someone Who Is Poor
Commandment 67: Do Not Be Involved In An Interest Loan Among Jewish People

Mishpatim – Section 4   - 9 verses
Commandment 68: Do Not Blaspheme
Commandment 69: Do Not Curse Judges
Commandment 70: Do Not Curse Leaders
Commandment 71: Set Aside Tithes In The Proper Sequence
Commandment 72: Do Not Consume Meat From An Injured Animal
Commandment 73: Do Not Listen To Claims Unless All Parties Are Present
Commandment 74: Do Not Accept Testimony From Someone Who Is A Sinner
Commandment 75: Decide Court Cases By Majority Vote
Commandment 76: Do Not Decide Capital Cases By Majority Of Only 1 Vote
Commandment 77: A Judge Must Not Change His Verdict To Convict Once He Has Acquitted The Defendant
Commandment 78: Help Unburden An Animal

Table of Contents

Mishpatim – Section 5 - 14 verses   p. 264
Commandment 79: Do Not Disfavor A Habitual Offender
Commandment 80: Do Not Base A Capital Case On Circumstantial
    Evidence
Commandment 81: A Judge Must Not Accept Any Gifts
Commandment 82: Allow The Land To Re-fertilize During Year 7
Commandment 83: Rest On The Sabbath
Commandment 84: Do Not Lead A City's Population To Worship Idols
Commandment 85: Do not Take An Oath In The Name Of An Idol
Commandment 86: Celebrate The 3 Holy Festivals: Pesaĥ, Shavūōt, and
    Sūkōt
Commandment 87: Do Not Offer The Pesaĥ Offering Until All Leaven Is
    Gone
Commandment 88: Do Not Leave Leftovers Of Pesaĥ Offering Overnight
Commandment 89: Set Aside The First Fruits Of The 7 Types Of Produce
Commandment 90: Do Not Ingest Meat And Dairy Products Together

Mishpatim - Section 6   - 6 verses
Commandment 91: Pray To G-d Daily

Mishpatim – Section 7   - 23 + 3 verses
Commandment 92: Do Not Allow Idol Worshipers To Live In The Land
    Of Israel
The Jewish People Proclaim: "We Will Obey"
Mōshe Builds An Altar And 12 Columns
Mōshe Reads The Book Of The Covenant To The People
The Jewish People Respond: "We Will Obey And Listen"
Mōshe Stays On Mount Sēnī For Forty Days

Table of Contents

Trūma - Section 1   - 16 verses (Total: 96 verses)   p. 281
Donations For The Tabernacle
Commandment 93: Build A Sanctuary
Sacred Box
Commandment 94: Do Not Remove The Rods From The Sacred Box

Trūma - Section 2   - 14 verses
Lid Of The Sacred Box
Table
Dishes For The Table
Commandment 95: Prepare The Showbread

Trūma - Section 3   - 24 verses
Candelabra Menōra
Roof

Trūma - Section 4   - 16 verses
Walls

Trūma - Section 5   - 7 verses
Curtain At The Entrance Of The Holiest Room
Sacred Box Resides In The Holiest Room
Placing The Lid On The Sacred Box
Positioning The Table And The Candelabra
Front Entrance Curtain
Columns At The Entrance

Trūma - Section 6   - 8 verses
Outer Altar
Instruments Of The Outer Altar
Screen Around The Outer Altar
Poles For Carrying The Outer Altar

Trūma - Section 7   - 11 verses
Courtyard Enclosure
Entrance

Table of Contents

Tiżave - Section 1   - 14 verses   (Total 101 verses)   p. 302
Oil For The Lamp
Commandment 96: Light The Candelabra Lamps Every Day
Designating Who Will Be The Priests
Commandment 97: Priests Must Wear Priestly Clothes For The Service
Apron
Engraved Stones On The Apron

Tiżave - Section 2   - 18 verses
Breastplate
Stones On The Breastplate
Attaching The Breastplate To The Apron
Attaching The Bottom Of The Breastplate
Commandment 98: Do Not Loosen The Breastplate From The Apron
Names On The Breatsplate
Holy Name

Tiżave - Section 3   - 13 verses
Robe
Commandment 99: Do Not Tear The Priestly Clothes
High Priest Must Wear Holy Clothes When Entering The Sanctuary
Headband
Tunic, Hat, Belt
Clothes For Regular Priests
Anointing Priests
Short Pants

Tiżave - Section 4   - 18 verses
Sanctifying The Priests
Offering The Male Cow
Offering The First Ram

Table of Contents

Tiżave - Section 5   **- 19 verses**   **p. 315**
Offering The Second Ram
Commandment 100: Priests Should Eat The Offerings For Them
Commandment 101: Non-Priests Must Not Eat Holy Offerings

Tiżave - Section 6   **- 9 verses**
Morning and Late Afternoon Daily Offering

Tiżave - Section 7   **- 7 + 3 verses**
Incense Altar
Commandment 102: Burn Incense Every Day
Commandment 103: Do Not Burn Anything But Incense On The Gold
      Altar

Table of Contents

Kē Tēsa - Section 1 - 45 verses   (Total: 139 verses)   p. 321
Commandment 104: Give A Half-Shekel Every Year
Washing Basin
Commandment 105: Priests Must Wash Before Service
Ingredients For The Annointing Oil
Commandment 106: Prepare Anointing Oil
Commandment 107: Do Not Duplicate Anointing Oil
Commandment 108: Do Not Use Anointing Oil For Personal Use
Ingredients of Incense
Commandment 109: Do Not Duplicate Incense
Biźalel And Ahalēav, Head Craftsmen For The Tabernacle
Sabbath

Kē Tēsa - Section 2 - 47 verses
G-d Gives Mōshe The Stone Slabs
Some People Demand Aharōn To Fashion a Form
Gold Statue
G-d Orders Mōshe To Walk Back To The People
G-d Wants To Start Over
Mōshe Prays For The Welfare Of The Jewish People
G-d Agrees
Yihōshūa And Mōshe Hear The Noise Of Wild Celebration
Mōshe Throws Down The Stone Slabs And They Shatter
Mōshe Calls For The Faithful To Act
The Tribe Of Lāvē Respond
Mōshe Returns To G-d To Obtain Atonement For The Jewish People
G-d Communicates That A Divine Agent Will Accompany The People
The People Stop Wearing Jewelry
Mōshe Relocates His Tent Outside The Camp
The Jewish People Show Respect To Mōshe

Kē Tēsa - Section 3 - 5 verses
Mōshe Asks To Understand The Ways Of G-d

Table of Contents

Kē Tēsa - Section 4   - 7 verses   p. 344
G-d Agrees To Reveal Divine Behavior To Mōshe
Mōshe Asks To Experience The Glory Of G-d

Kē Tēsa - Section 5   - 9 verses
Mōshe Forms The Second Slabs, And Carries Them Up The Mountain
The 13 Attributes of Divine Mercy
Mōshe Bows And Prays
Mōshe Requests That G-d Stay With The Jewish People

Kē Tēsa - Section 6   - 17 verses
G-d Agrees To The Request To Lead The Jewish People
Do Not Intermarry
Passover Holy Festival
Firstborn Kosher Animals
Firstborn Donkeys
Commandment 110: Rest During Year 7
Sabbath And Sabbatical Year
Shavūōt And Sūkōt Holy Festivals
Come To The Central Location of Worship Three Times A Year
The Land of Israel Will Be Too Large To Come Every Day
Observe the Laws of Passover
Commandment 111: Do Not Cook Mixtures Of Meat And Dairy

Kē Tēsa - Section 7   - 6 + 3 verses
40 Days Without Food Or Drink
Decaloge On The Second Pair Of Stone Slabs
Majestic Splendor Of Mōshe's Face
Mōshe Wears A Veil

Table of Contents

Vayakhâl - Section 1 - 19 verses (Total: 122 verses)   p. 359
Sabbath
Commandment 112: Court Must Not Punish On Sabbath
Materials For The Tabernacle
Craftsmen

Vayakhâl - Section 2   - 10 verses
The People Donate
Skilled Women
The Leaders Donate The Precious Stones, Spices, And Oil

Vayakhâl - Section 3   - 13 verses
Biżalel
Ahalēav
The Jewish People Bring More Than Enough Material For The Tabernacle

Vayakhâl - Section 4   - 12 verses
Wall Curtains
Roof Cloth

Vayakhâl - Section 5   - 35 verses
Walls
The Entrance
Sacred Box
Lid
Statues On The Lid
Table

Vayakhâl - Section 6   - 13 verses
Menōra
Incense Altar
Anointing Oil And Incense

Table of Contents

Vayakhâl - Section 7   - 17 + 3 verses   p. 372
Animal-Offering Altar
Water Basin
Courtyard Enclosure – South Side
Courtyard Enclosure – North Side
Courtyard Enclosure – West Side
Courtyard Enclosure – East Side, With Entrance

Table of Contents

Pikūdā - Section 1 - 12 verses (Total: 92 verses)   **p. 373**
Total Amounts of Gold, Silver, and Copper

Pikūdā - Section 2   - 20 verses
Apron of the High Priest
Breastplate

Pikūdā - Section 3   - 11 verses
Robe
Tunic, Turban, Hat, Pants, Belt
Headplate
Completion of The Work

Pikūdā - Section 4   - 11 verses
Thirty Nine Items Fashioned
Mōshe Blesses the Jewish People

Pikūdā - Section 5   - 16 verses
Instruction To Assemble And Anoint The Tabernacle
Instruction For Priests To Prepare For Installation

Pikūdā - Section 6   - 11 verses
Tabernacle Is Assembled
Assembling and Positioning the Holy Box with Stone Slabs Inside
Positioning the Table
Positioning the Menora
Positioning the Incense Altar

Pikūdā - Section 7   - 6 + 5 verses
Hanging the Drapes
Positioning the Altar For Animal Offerings
Setting Up the Courtyard Walls
Construction Is Complete
Cloud Covers the Tabernacle
When the Cloud Rose, The Jewish People Travel
A Fire Above the Tabernacle At Night

Transliteration Guidelines

Proper nouns, names, do not have translations. Although some Hebrew names have common counterparts in English, Tōra Study Bible transliterates the Hebrew name. For more common names, the English equivalent is given in parenthesis the first time it occurs in a book chapter.

Long vowels have a bar above them. Vowels with no symbol have the standard short sound. Various phonetic symbols denote the other short vowel sounds. The letter "y" is never used as a vowel. The symbol "ĥ" has the guttural sound of the Russian letter "x." Note: If Ĥ is difficult to pronounce, say a strong "H" sound. The symbol "ź" has the sound of a double "zz" as is in word pizza (i.e., tz). There are many variants of Hebrew pronunciation, such as variants of European (Ashkenaz), Middle Eastern (Sefard), and Israeli pronunciation. A basic Israeli pronunciation is adopted in Tōra Study Bible.

A a Ä ä - ah, father, are, farther, pot (, aunt)
Ă ă - an, pat
Â â - air, care, ale, bear, lair, ant, ere
Ā ā - ate, pay, neigh, grey
E e Ĕ ĕ - pet, error
Ê ê - ear, beer
Ē ē - eat, eve, be, bee, rec<u>ei</u>ve, suite
Ĥ ĥ - pronounced like the Russian letter "X."
I I Ĭ ĭ - it
Ī ī - I, pie, by, sigh, buy
O o Ŏ ŏ - on
Ô ô - or, oar, more, all, saw, awe, caught
Ő ő - out, ouch, how, house, our, hour, ab<u>ou</u>t
Ơ ơ - oy, noise
Ō ō - own, toe
Sh sh - sh
U u Ŭ ŭ - uh, us, cut, won, one, <u>a</u>bout
Û û - urge, term, word, heard. firm, fir
Ú ú - took, put, <u>a</u>bout
ù - lure, moor
Ū ū - boot, glue, suit, cute, ewe, you, mule
Ź ź - the sound "tz" or "ts," as in "pizza"

Sources

Bibliography

- Broyde, Michael J., 2009. Hair Covering and Jewish Law, Tradition, 42:3, pp. 96-179.

- Cohen, A.: <u>The Soncino Chumash,</u> (1947. Copyrighted in 1983). Soncino Press. ISBN: 0-900689-24-2.

- Kaplan, Aryeh: <u>The Living Torah</u> (1981). Maznaim Publishering Corporation, NY. ISBN: 0-940118-29-7.

- Holzer, David: The Rav Thinking Aloud on the Parsha Sefer Shemos – Transcripts of shiurim from Rabbi Joseph B. Soloveitchik (2011). LAOR Press, Jerusalem.
  ISBN 978-0-9821310-2-2

- Holzer, David: The Rav Thinking Aloud on the Parsha Sefer Bamidbar – Transcripts of shiurim from Rabbi Joseph B. Soloveitchik (2013). LAOR Press, Jerusalem.
  ISBN 978-0-9821310-3-9

- Lustiger, A. <u>Chumash Mesoras Harav Sefer Shemos: Commentary Based On The Teachings Of Rabbi Joseph B. Soloveitchik</u> (2014). OU Press. ISBN 978-0-9891246-1-4.

- Miller, Chaim: <u>Chumash: The Five Books Of The Torah</u> (2003). Kol Menachem Publisher, NY. ISBN 1-934152-01-3.

- Scherman, Nosson: <u>The Chumash: The Stone Edition</u> (1993). Mesorah Publications, NY. ISBN: 0-89906-014-5.

- Wax, Dovid: <u>The Encyclopedia of the Taryag Mitzvoth: Volume 1</u> (2008). Old City Press, Jerusalem.

Traditional Sources

The following are traditional sources used to guide the rendition and are referenced in the study notes:

Book of Jubilees – Sefer HaYōvlōt - Written in 110 B.C.E. (Before the Common Era)

Ibn Ezra (1089-1164) – Avraham Ibn Ezra. Running commentary on the Tōra.

Klē Yakar – Beautiful Vessel by Rabbi Efrīyim son of Aharōn (1550-1619.

Midrash – Includes about two dozen different collections of homiletic commentaries, including "Midrash Raba" (Great Midrash), which includes Shimōt Raba."

Radak – (1160-1235) Rabbi David Kimchi.

Rambam (1135-1204) Also known as Moses Maimonides.

Ramban (1194-1270) Also known as Nachmanides. Running commentary on the Tōra.

Rashē (1040-1105) Shlōmō Yitzĥkē. Running commentary on the Tōra.

"Septuagint" – Written about 200 B.C.E. Translation into Greek by 70 rabbis, at the request of King Ptolemy II for inclusion into the great library of Alexandria.

Siforno – (1475-1550) Ovadya Siforno. Running commentary on the Tōra.

Joseph B. Soloveitchik (1903-1993) – Professor of Jewish Studies at Yeshiva University.

Books of Midrash Homiletics

One of the reasons that Tōra Study Bible de-emphasizes midrash is that there are so many midrash stories that give differing, often conflicting, accounts of the same event described in Tōra verses. This partial list of the more common collections of midrash that were written during a period spanning 200 to 1000 C.E. gives the reader an idea of the diversity of homiletic interpretation:

    Avōt (Principles) of Rabbi Natan
    Midrash Raba, which is made up of various volumes: Brāshēt Raba, Shimōt Raba, Vayikra Raba, Bamidbar Raba, Divarim Raba, Āĥa (Lamentations) Raba, Kōhelet (Ecclesiastes) Raba, Esther Raba.
    Midrash of Rabbi Tanĥūma
    Midrash Shmūel
    Midrash Tehilim (Psalms)
    Miĥlta on Divarim
    Miĥlta of Rabbi Shimōn on Shimōt
    Pesikta of Rabbi Kahana
    Pirkā (Chapters) of Rabbi Elēezer
    Seder Ōlam
    Sefer HaYashar (Book of the Righteous)
    Sifra on Vayikra
    Sifrē on Bamidbar
    Tōrat Kōhanim on Vayikra
    Yalkūt Shimōnē.

Table 1

Table 1. Letter, word, verse, and commandment counts for the Five Books of Moses.

	Letter	Word	Verse	Commandment count according to Rambam
Brāshēt	78,064	20,512	1,533	2
Shimōt	63,529	16,723	1,210	110
Vayikra	44,790	11,950	859	243
Bamidbar	63,530	16,368	1,288	57
Diavarim	54,892	14,294	956	201
Totals:	**304,805**	**79,847**	**5,846**	**613**

See Essay 8 on Commandments.

Table 2. Chronology from Avraham to Mōshe. See notes below.						
Note #	Event	Tōra Year	BCE Year	Pharaoh	Reign (BCE)
				Middle Kingdom	2050-1650
1	Avraham is born (3,828 years ago)	1948	1812	(Hammurabi: 1810-1750)	
2	Avraham in Egypt	2023	1738	Sheshi: Canaanite king east of Nile Delta	1745-1705
3	G-d foretells freedom	2018	1732		
4	Yiẑhak is born	2048	1712		
5	Yaakōv is born	2108	1652		
6	Avraham passes	2123	1637	**Intermediate Period**	1650-1550
7	Lāvē is born	2195	1565		
8	Yōsef is born	2199	1561		
				New Kingdom	1550-1069
9	Yōsef brought to Egypt	2216	1545	Ahmosis	1550-1541
10	Yiẑhak passes	2228	1532	Amenhotep I	1541-1520
11	Yōsef becomes viceroy	2229	1531		
12	Famine starts	2236	1525		
13	Yaakōv comes to Egypt	2238	1523		
14	Yaakōv passes	2255	1505	Thutmose I	1520-1492
				Thutmose II	1492-1479
15	Yōsef passes	2309	1451	Thutmose III	1479-1425
16	Lāvē passes	2332	1428		
17	Slavery starts	2335	1425	**Amenhotep II**	1425-1400
18	Mōshe is born	2397	1363	Amenhotep III	1390-1352
19	Mōshe flees Egypt	2415	1345	Amenhotep IV	1352-1334
				Ankeperure	1334-1333
				Tutankamun	1333-1324
				Keperkeperure	1324-1320
				Horemheb	1320-1292
				Dynasty 19	
				Ramesses I	1292-1290
20	Mōshe confronts Pharaoh	2477	1283	Seti I	1290-1279
21	Exodus	2478	1282		
22	People refuse to enter Israel	2479	1281		
23	Mōshe passes	2517	1243	Ramesses II	1279-1213

Notes on Table 2. Chronology from Avraham to Mōshe

Row 1. Brāshēt 5:3-32 and 11:10-26 state the years of birth relative to each previous generation, for the first 19 generations of people (see chart in Scherman, 1993, p.199).

Row 2. Brāshēt 12:4 states that Avraham was 75 years old when traveled to the land of Kinaan. Soon after, there was a famine such that Avraham traveled to Egypt. At that time Egypt was divided into 3 parts: a Canaanite rulership east of the Nile Delta; the Egyptian king who ruled in Thebes in the south; and a Hyksos rulership west of the Nile Delta. Avraham may well have found food in the closest of the 3 kingdoms.

Row 3. Brāshēt 15:13 relates that G-d communicated to Avraham that the first 400 years of his descendants' lives would be in a land that does not belong to them and that they would be enslaved. Brāshēt 15:14 states that the Jewish people would leave the country of their enslavement with wealth. This fits with the story of the exodus (Shimōt 3:22, 11:2, and 12:35). Ramban states that this 400-year number is a rounded down approximation. Shimōt 12:40 states that it was actually 430 years. See note 18.

Row 4. Brāshēt 21:5 states that Avraham was 100 years old when his son Yiźĥak was born.

Row 5. Brāshēt 25:26 states that Yiźĥak was 60 years old when his son Yaakōv was born.

Row 6. Brāshēt 25:7 states that Avraham lived to be 175 years old.

Row 7. Brāshēt 29:34 records that Lāvē is Lāa's third child. Yaakōv had 4 wives. His first 12 children were born within 7 years, as is evident from Brāshēt 29:27 and 30:25. As soon as Yōsef was born, the 7-year work agreement was up and Yaakōv made arrangements to leave. Lāvē most likely had been born about 4 years before Yōsef.

Row 8. Brāshēt 47:9 states that Yaakōv was 130 years old when he arrived in Egypt. Yōsef was 39 at that time, as evident from Brāshēt 41:46 (where Yōsef was 30), 41:53 (7 years of plenty had elapsed), and 45:6 (2 years of famine had elapsed). Therefore, Yaakōv was 91 when Yōsef was born.

Notes on Table 2 - continued

Row 9. Brāshēt 37:2 states that Yōsef was 17 years old when he had been brought to Egypt.

Row 10. Brāshēt 35:28 states that Yiżĥak lived to be 180 years old.

Row 11. Brāshēt 41:46 states that Yōsef was 30 when he was appointed viceroy of Egypt.

Row 12. After Yōsef became viceroy, there were 7 years of plenty. Then the famine began.

Row 13. After two years of famine, Yōsef's brothers come to Egypt to buy food. Yaakōv and his entire family relocate to Egypt soon thereafter.

Row 14. Brāshēt 47:28 states that Yaakōv lived to be 147 years old.

Brāshēt 50:4 states that Yōsef asks the advisors of Pharaoh to intercede with Pharaoh on his behalf to allow Yōsef to bury his deceased father in the land of Israel. Yōsef had been on a first name basis with Pharaoh. But Thutmose I was the new Pharaoh when Yaakōv passed away. Yōsef was not on a first name basis with the new Pharaoh.

Row 15. Brāshēt 50:26 states that Yōsef lived to be 110 years old.

Row 16. Shimōt 6:16 states that Lāvē lived to be 137 years old.

Row 17. Shimōt 1:8 states that once there was a king who did not know Yōsef, he enacted laws of persecution against them and enslaved them. Thutmose III was the last Pharaoh who knew Yōsef. A few years after the last of the brothers passed away, Amenhotep II became the ruler.

Row 18. At this point in Jewish history, there are only a few instances of year data given in Tōra. Using these data points we can derive the years indicated in rows 18-23 in the table. The main information is that Shimōt 12:40 states that the Jewish people were freed after 430 years. Ramban states that the 430 years starts from the birth of Yiżĥak (see notes on rows 2 & 3). Thus know that the exodus occurred in Tōra year 2478. Tōra also states that Mōshe was 80 years old when he confronted Pharaoh (Shimōt 7:7). Subtracting this from the year of exodus tells us when Mōshe was born.

Row 19. There are a number of opinions as to when Mōshe went out to his people, which resulted in a royal order for his arrest and execution. These include:
    a. Shimōt Raba Chapter 5: he was 12 years old.
    b. Sefer HaYashar: he was 18. This is the year used here.
    c. Shimōt Raba Chapter 1: he was 20.
    d. Bamidbar Raba Chapter 14: he was 32.

Row 20. From the time Mōshe confronted Pharaoh and performed the 10 plagues, about one year had elapsed. Therefore, subtract one year from the year in row 21.

    In a similar vein as explained in the note on row 17, here too a historical fact elucidates a verse. In verse Shimōt 4:19, G-d communicates to Mōshe that he can return to Egypt because the people who had wanted to execute him are no longer alive. The above table shows that the eighteenth Egyptian dynasty had ended and now, during the nineteenth dynasty, all previous edicts were nullified, thus making it safe for Mōshe to return to Egypt and confront Pharaoh.

Row 21. Exodus took place 430 years after the birth of Yiźĥak. Mōshe was 80 years old when he came back to Egypt and confronted Pharaoh. Exodus occurred within a year.

Row 22. A little over a year after leaving Egypt and experiencing divine revelation at Mount Sēnī, the Jewish people were poised to enter the land of Israel. But they asked to have scouts sent to report on the land. The scouts intimidated the people into thinking that it was not possible to successfully enter and settle the land (Bamidbar chapters 13 & 14).

Row. 23. Mōshe lived to be 120 years old (Divarim 31:2 and 34:7). There were 14 different Pharaohs from the time Yōsef came to Egypt until the exodus. The average length of reign is 18 years. The longest reign during this period was Thutmose III who reigned for 54 years.

| Table 3. Boundaries of the land of Israel. ||||||
Verse -> /Border	Brāshēt 15:18	Shimōt 23:31	Bamidbar 34:2-15	Divarim 1:7 and 11:24
South	-	Reed Sea (Eilat /Aqaba)	Negev Desert	Negev Desert
West	Wadi El Arish	Mediterranean Sea	Mediterranean Sea	Mediterranean Sea
North	-	wilderness	Lebanese mountains	Lebanon
East	Euphrates River	Euphrates River	Jordan River plus land east of Jordan River	Euphrates River

In four of the five descriptions of the boundaries of the land of Israel, the Euphrates River is identified as the east boundary.

Table 4. First 6 days at Sēnī according to Rashē, who asserts that Shimōt 24:1-9 and 20:1-17 are out of order. Items in braces are derived from implications in the verses. Day is date in the month of Sēvan.

	Verse	Day	Event	Up/down
1	19:1	1	Jewish people arrived at Sēnī.	
2	19:3		Mōshe walked up the mountain.	Up 1
3	19:7	{2}	Mōshe walked down the mountain.	Down 1
4			People: "We will obey."	
5	19:8		Mōshe walked up the mountain.	Up 2
6		{3}	Mōshe conveyed the words of the people.	
7			{Mōshe walked down the mountain.}	{Down 2}
8	19:9		{Mōshe walked up the mountain.}	{Up 3}
9			Mōshe conveyed {the people's request}	
10	19:10		G-d: "Go to the people	
11			"make them ready today and tomorrow	
12	19:11		"be prepared on the 3rd day (=Sēvan 6)"	
13	19:14	{4}	Mōshe walked down the mountain.	Down {3}
14	24:1		G-d: "Go up the mtn. Aharōn will come up part way."	
15	24:3		Mōshe taught the people laws.	
16			People: "We will obey."	
17	24:4		Mōshe wrote down G-d's words.	
18			Mōshe built altar and 12 stones. Offerings.	
19	24:7		Mōshe read Book of the Covenant to the people.	
20		{5}	People: "We will obey and study."	
21	24:9		Mōshe, Aharōn, etc. went up	Up {4}
22			{They went down.}	{Down 4}
23	19:16		Thunder, lightening, cloud, shofar sound.	
24	19:17		Mōshe brought the people out of their tents, to the foot of the mountain. (Also stated in 20:15 & 18.)	
25	19:20		G-d: "Come up." Mōshe walked up.	Up {5}
26	19:21		G-d: "Go down."	
27	19:24		G-d: "Go down. Then come all the way up."	
28	19:25	(6)	Mōshe walked down the mountain.	Down {5}
29	20:15-17		Thunder, etc. People trembled.	
30	20:1-14		G-d communicated the Decaloge	
31	24:12		G-d: "Come up."	
32	24:15		Mōshe walked up the mountain.	Up {6}
33	24:18		First day of the 40 days on the mountain.	

Table 5. Events during the first year-and-a-half after exodus.

	Verse	Date	Event	Days After Exodus
1	Shimōt 12:37 & 13:17	Nēsan 15	Exodus (Tōra year 2478) (1282 BCE)	0
2	Shimōt 14:16 Divarim 11:4	Nēsan 21	Reed Sea splits.	7
3	Shimōt 19:1	Sēvan 1	Arrival at Mount Sēnī.	45
4	Shimōt 20:1 Divarim 4:13 & 5:6-18	Sēvan 7	Divine Revelation at Sēnī. Afterward, Mōshe stays on mountain for the first 40-day period.	51
5	Shimōt 33:19 Divarim 9:17	Tamūz 17	Mōshe descends and breaks the stone slabs.	91
6	Shimōt 33:31 Divarim 9:18-29	Tamūz 18 – Av 30	Mōshe prays during the second 40-day period.	
7	Shimōt 34:2 Divarim 10:10	Elūl 1	Mōshe ascends Mount Sēnī and stays for the third 40- day period. Census: 603,550 adult men.	135
8	Shimōt 34:29 Divarim 10:5	Tishrā 10	Mōshe descends with the second pair of stone slabs.	175
9	Shimōt 40:17 Bamidbar 7:1	Nēsan 1	Tabernacle is anointed.	339
10	Vayikra 9:1	Nēsan 8	Installation of the priests.	347
11	Bamidbar 1:1	Ēyar 1 *	Census: 603,550 adult men of the 11 tribes, plus 22,300 Levite boys and men.	369
12	Bamidbar 13:21 Divarim 1:22	Tamūz 1	Scouts start their mission.	429
13	Bamidbar 13:25-14:12 Divarim 1:27	Av 9	People believe the negative report of the scouts.	469

Notes: Verses in Divarim are Mōshe recalling the event.
* Assumes that the year of exodus was not a leap year.

	Table 6a. Comparison of verses in Shimōt and Divarim concerning the stone slabs.	
	Verses in Shimōt	**Verses in Divarim**
1	31:18 G-d gives Mōshe the stone slabs.	5:19, 9:10 & 11 Mōshe received the slabs.
2	32:1 On Tamūz 16, people demand that Aharōn fashion a statue.	9:8 You angered G-d at Ĥōrev by sinning.
3	32:2-5 Aharōn forms a statue & builds an altar.	
4	32:6 On Tamūz 17, the people celebrate.	9:8 G-d wanted to destroy the Jewish people.
5	32:7-9 G-d: "People sinned. Go down."	9:12 G-d: "People had made a gold statue."
6	32:11-16 Mōshe prays. G-d accepts his prayer.	
7	32:17-18 Mōshe and Yihōshūa hear the noise.	9:15 Mōshe walked down. He saw they sinned.
8	32:19 Mōshe throws down the slabs.	9:17 Mōshe threw down the slabs.
9	32:20 Mōshe melts & pulverizes the gold statue.	9:21 Mōshe melted and pulverized the gold statue.
10	32:21 Mōshe asks Aharōn: "Why?"	9:20 G-d was angry at Aharōn. Mōshe prayed for him.
11	32:22-24 Aharōn explains that he was forced.	
12	32:25 Mōshe sees the people are out of control.	
13	32:26-30 Mōshe asks the faithful to follow him. The tribe of Lāvē, along with others, respond.	10:8 G-d selected the tribe of Lāvē.
	Continued on Table 6b.	

Table 6b. Comparison of verses in Shimōt and Divarim concerning the stone slabs.			
	Verses in Shimōt	**Verses in Divarim**
14	32:31-33 Mōshe prays for atonement for them: he admits the sin and asks for forgiveness via his merit. G-d responds: each person must be judged on his or her own merits and actions.	9:18 Mōshe prayed for 40 days. 9:19 Mōshe prayed that G-d not destroy the Jewish people. G-d listened to Mōshe's prayer. 9:25-29 Mōshe prayed for another 40 days and nights.
15	32:34-35 – 33:1-3 G-d informs that a divine agent will lead the Jewish people.	
18	33:12-13 Mōshe asks G-d who the agent will be.	
19	33:14-17 G-d agrees that His presence will lead the people.	
20	33:18 Mōshe asks to see the glory of G-d.	
21	33:19-23 G-d instructs that He will enable Mōshe to experience His glory.	
22	34:1-4 G-d instructs Mōshe to carve 2 slabs, walk up the mountain on Elul 1. {no mention of a box}	10:1-3 G-d instructed Mōshe to carve slabs, and also to construct a wooden box for the slabs.
23	34:5-8 G-d communicates His 13 divine attributes of mercy. Mōshe bows & prays.	
	Continued on Table 6c.	

Table 6c. Comparison of verses in Shimōt and Divarim concerning the stone slabs.

	Verses in Shimōt	**Verses in Divarim**
24	34:9-10 Mōshe asks that G-d Himself lead them and pardon them. G-d agrees.	
25	34:27 G-d requires the people to renew their acceptance of Tōra.	
26	34:28 Mōshe stays on the mount for 40 days and nights. Mōshe engraves the second pair of slabs.	10:10 Mōshe stayed on the mount for 40 days and nights
27	34:29 Mōshe walks down the mountain with the 2 slabs on Tishrā 10 – Day of Atonement. His face is radiant.	10:5 Mōshe walked down the mount with the slabs and placed them in the box.

Table 7a. Month of Sēvan in Tōra year 2478 (year of the exodus). Numbers in braces, which start at divine revelation, trace the 40 days that Mōshe spent on Mount Sēnī.							
Sun	Mon	Tue	Wed	Thur	Fri	Shabat
	1 – Arrived at Sēnī.	2	3	4	5 Fiftieth day after exodus.	6 Divine revelation {1}
7 {2}	8	9	10	11	12	13
14 {9}	15	16	17	18	19	20
21 {16}	22	23	24	25	26	27
28 {23}	29 {24}					
Note: Divine revelation took place 51 days after the exodus. This was on Sēvan 6. During that year, according to the opinion of the sages, Nēsan and Ēyar were both 30-day months. Today's Jewish calendar is set as a 30-day Nēsan and a 29-day Ēyar, so that the festival of Shavūōt occurs on Sēvan 6. However, this is only 50 days after the first day of Passover, as is specified by Tōra.						

Table 7b. Month of Tamūz in Tōra year 2478 (year of the exodus). Numbers in braces before Tamūz 17 are the 40 days Mōshe spent on the mountain. Today, Tamūz 17 is a fast day. Numbers in braces after Tamūz 17 are the days until Elūl 1.

Sun	Mon	Tue	Wed	Thur	Fri	Shabat
		1 {25}	2	3	4	5
6 {30}	7	8	9	10	11	12
13 {37}	14	15	16 People think Mōshe will never return. {40}	17 Mōshe descends and smashes the stone slabs.	18 Mōshe prays for 40 days. {1}	19
20 {3}	21	22	23	24	25	26
27 {10}	28	29				

Table 7c. Month of Av in Tōra year 2478 (year of the exodus). Numbers in braces show that there are at least 40 days from Tamūz 17 until Elūl 1.

Sun	Mon	Tue	Wed	Thur	Fri	Shabat
			1 {13}	2	3	4
5 {17}	6	7	8	9	10	11
12 {24}	13	14	15	16	17	18
19 {31}	20	21	22	23	24	25
26 {38}	27	28	29	30 {42}		

Table 7d. Month of Elūl in Tōra year 2478 (year of the exodus).

Sun	Mon	Tue	Wed	Thur	Fri	Shabat
					1 Mōshe ascends Mount Sēnī.	2
3	4	5	6	7	8	9
10	11	12	13	14	15	16
17	18	19	20	21	22	23
24	25	26	27	28	29	30

Although Elūl today is set as a 29-day month, it had been a 30-day month during the year of the exodus.

Table 7e. Month of Tishrā in Tōra year 2478 (year of the exodus). Numbers in braces show that the Day of Atonement (Yōm Kipur) occurred 40 days after Mōshe had ascended Mount Sēnī.

Sun	Mon	Tue	Wed	Thur	Fri	Shabat
1 {31}	2	3	4	5	6	7
8 {38}	9	10 Mōshe descends the mountain with the second pair of stone slabs. {40} Day of Atonement	11	12	13	14
15	16	17	18	19	20	21
22	23	24	25	26	27	28
29	30					

Table 8a. Universal Commandments Compared to Jewish Commandments.

Universal Commandment	Jewish Commandment	Verse
1 Justice Brāshēt 9:6	489 Appoint judges.	Divarim 16:18
2 Do Not Speak Blasphemy	68 Do not curse G-d.	Shimōt 22:27
3 Do Not Worship Idols	27 Do not form an idol.	Shimōt 20:4
	28 Do not worship idols in their manner.	Shimōt 20:5
	29 Do not worship idols in way G-d should be worshipped.	Shimōt 20:5
	85 Do not swear in the name of an idol.	Shimōt 23:13
	214 Do not study idolatry.	Vayikra 19:4
	215 Do not form an idol for other people.	Vayikra 19:4
4 Do Not Commit Adultery	208 Do not commit adultery.	Vayikra 18:20
5 Do Not Murder Brāshēt 9:6	35 Do not commit murder.	Shimōt 20:13
6 Do Not Steal	129 Return a stolen object.	Vayikra 5:23
	227 Do not steal secretly.	Vayikra 19:11
	229 Do not steal openly.	Vayikra 19:13
	519 Do not steal someone's land.	Divarim 19:14
7 Do not eat a limb of a living animal Brāshēt 9:4	450 An animal must be dead before eating any part of it.	Divarim 12:23
8 Procreate Brāshēt 9:7	208 Do not commit adultery.	Vayikra 18:20
9 Suicide Brāshēt 9:5	35 Do not commit murder.	Shimōt 20:13

Table 8b. Universal Commandments Found in Ancient Legal Codes.

	Hammurabi Code	Ancient Hittite Code	Ancient Assyrian Code
1 Do Not Murder	Included	Included	Included
2 Do Not Commit Adultery	Included	Included	Included
3 Do Not Steal	Included	Included	Included
4 Court System	Included	Included	Included
5 Do Not Assault		Included	
6 Do Not Commit Blasphemy			Included

Regions and locations in the Mideast

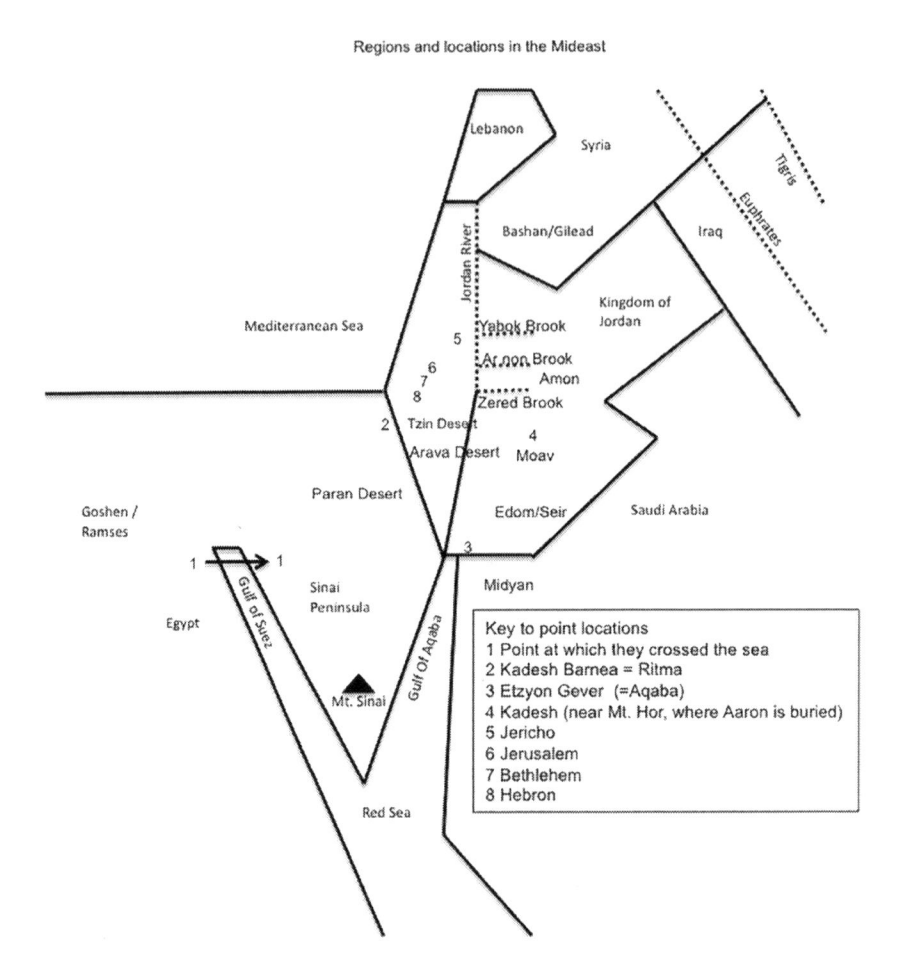

Key to point locations
1 Point at which they crossed the sea
2 Kadesh Barnea = Ritma
3 Etzyon Gever (=Aqaba)
4 Kadesh (near Mt. Hor, where Aaron is buried)
5 Jericho
6 Jerusalem
7 Bethlehem
8 Hebron

Essay 1. Tōra

The Bible as given to the Jewish people does not have a title. The word "tōra" (or a derived form of the word "tōra") is found in:
  Shimōt (Exodus) 18:16,
  Shimōt 24:12,
  Vayikra (Leviticus) 26:46,
  Bamidbar (Numbers) 15:16,
  and Divarim (Deuteronomy) chapters 28, 30, and 31.

The term Tōra is a noun that means "teaching." Many commentators take this word to be the name of the Jewish Bible. The collection of five books in Hebrew is also called *Ĥamēshā Ĥumshā Tōra* – The Five Fifths of Tōra. It is commonly written in English simply as "Chumash" (Ĥumash).

In actuality, the name Tōra includes all the Five Books of Moses, plus all the books of the Prophets, and all the books of the Writings (such as Psalms). Tōra also includes all the oral tradition that explains the written books and details the commandments, laws, and moral teachings given by G-d to Mōshe (Moses), and handed down by the sages through the ages. Today, the oral Tōra is embodied in the Talmud. In Tōra Study Bible, the word Tōra can have the specific meaning of Ĥumash, or, depending on context, can have the general meaning that includes all Jewish teaching.

The sages taught "There are 70 dimensions to Tōra." Every time a person studies Tōra, greater and deeper insights into the meaning and implications of the verses are discovered. There are different overall approaches to dealing with the verses: plain meaning, alternate interpretation, conceptual meaning, and foundational concepts. Tōra Study Bible is a starting point, concentrating on the plain meaning of the text. Therefore, it is a mere starting point in Bible study.

Essay 2. G-d

Tōra Study Bible, for the sake of readability, renders all the various holy names of the Creator that occur in the original Hebrew Tōra verses, as G-d. A hyphen is used in the middle of this word instead of using the letter "o" in order to avoid spelling out the Almighty's name, which is reserved for holy books.

Tōra verses use both proper noun names of G-d as well as pronouns to refer to G-d. These pronouns are in the masculine gender because Hebrew does not have a neuter gender in its grammar. Even though a pronoun referring to G-d is often translated as the English word "He," nonetheless, G-d is not masculine. Some names of G-d connote masculinity, while other names of G-d connote femininity (e.g., Shiĥēna).

G-d's ultimate oneness, includes, but is not limited to, the following attributes:
a) G-d is one;
b) G-d is the only deity;
c) G-d transcends time: G-d exists simultaneously in past, present, and future;
d) G-d is infinite: our universe resides within G-d;
e) G-d is not physical. G-d is purely spiritual;
f) G-d has no parts; and
g) The attributes of divine righteousness, kindness, and justness are all one trait. They can be understood as such only in a dimension that transcends the limitations of our physical world.

Certain names of G-d emphasize G–d's attributes of mercy and kindness. Other divine names indicate G-d's attribute of strict judgement, while other names focus on G-d's many facets of power.

King David enumerated the seven aspects in which G-d makes Himself perceived by people (I Chronicles 29:11):
1. Great
2. Powerful
3. Glorious
4. Victorious
5. Majestic
6. Master
7. Regal.

Essay 2. G-d - continued

The 13 articles of Jewish faith provide the cornerstone of belief in G-d:
1. G-d is the creator and is perfect in every manner of existence. G-d is the primal cause of existence.
2. The unity of G-d is absolute.
3. G-d is not corporeal. G-d is not affected by physical occurrences.
4. G-d is eternal.
5. People must worship G-d and only G-d.
6. G-d communicates with people through prophecy.
7. Mōshe is the primary prophet.
8. Tōra comes directly from G-d.
9. Tōra is immutable. Tōra cannot be changed or altered.
10. G-d knows everything.
11. G-d rewards and punishes.
12. G-d will send the true messiah.
13. G-d will bring back to life people who have passed away.

G-d communicated His 13 attributes of mercy to Mōshe (Moses), stated in Shimōt 34:6-7, after some people erred by fashioning a statue.

1 G-d is merciful to people when they plan to sin,
2 G-d is merciful to people who sin,
3 G-d is wisely powerful,
4 G-d mercifully prevents people from sinning,
5 G-d is gracious,
6 G-d is slow to punish,
7 G-d is good to people,
8 G-d faithfully carries out His solemn promises,
9 G-d transfers merits to later generations,
10 G-d forgives premeditated sin,
11 G-d forgives rebellious behavior,
12 G-d forgives accidental sin, and
13 G-d punishes guilty people little by little. However, if descendants continue to sin, G-d punishes them."

Essay 2. G-d - continued

G-d later communicated His Supreme Attributes of Divine Mercy to the prophet Mēka (Micah) 7:18-20. Righteous people try to emulate these attributes.

1. G-d is incomparable.
2. G-d pardons sin.
3. G-d overlooks rebellious sins.
4. G-d especially loves the people who serve Him.
5. G-d does not hold a grudge.
6. G-d cherishes people's acts of kindness.
7. G-d is especially merciful to people who repent.
8. G-d does not let sin override good deeds.
9. G-d sees to it that after a person repents, previous sins are erased.
10. G-d is compassionat to law-abiding people.
11. G-d is kind to ethical people.
12. G-s is gracious, even to imperfect people.
13. G-d is merciful to people who attempt to be righteous.

Essay 3. The Chosen People

The following are the 13 verses in which G-d proclaims that the Jewish people are His chosen people:

3:7	4:23
5:1	6:7
7:4	7:16
7:26	8:16
8:18	8:19
9:1	9:13

and 10:3.

Mōshe (Moses) realizes he is Jewish in verse 2:11.
Mōshe calls the Jewish people "my people" in verse 4:18.
When confronting G-d about Pharaoh's eveil decree, he calls the Jewish people "Your people" in verses 5:22 and 5:23.

After some people erred by declaring a gold statue as being special, G-d tells Mōshe to tend to "your people" in verse 32:7 (portion Kē Tēsa).
Mōshe again refers to the Jewish people when speaking to G-d as "Your people" in verses 32:11 and 32:12.
In verse 32:32 Mōshe shows his love for the Jewish people because he is willing to take upon himself their sins. However, G-d communicates to him that each person must be responsible for his or her own sins.

The ancestors of the Jewish people,
Avraham (Abraham),
Yiźĥak (Isaac), and
Yaakōv (Jacob)
Are mentioned in verses:

2:4	3:6
3:15	3:16
6:3	6:8
32:13	and 33:1.

Note that in verse 32:13 Yaakōv is referred to by his alternate name, Yisrael (Israel).

Essay 4. Serving G-d

G-d dictated Tōra to Mōshe (Moses). As fundamental as belief and trust in G-d is, the practice of Judaism is based on the integrity of the Jewish sages who have faithfully transmitted Tōra philosophy and laws throughout the ages. The 13 articles of Jewish faith provide the foundation of this belief:

1. G-d is the creator. G-d is perfect. G-d is the primal cause of existence.
2. The unity of G-d is absolute.
3. G-d is not corporeal. G-d is not affected by physical occurrences.
4. G-d is eternal.
5. People must worship G-d, and only G-d.
6. G-d communicates with people through prophecy.
7. Mōshe (Moses) is the primary prophet.
8. Tōra comes directly from G-d.
9. Tōra is immutable. Tōra cannot be changed or altered.
10. G-d knows everything.
11. G-d rewards and punishes.
12. The messiah will come.
13. People who have passed away eventually will be resurrected.

Note: The concept of a messiah warrants special attention. In Talmud Tractate Sanhedrin (courts), page 99a, Rav Hilel (a descendant of the great Hilel the Elder), states that there is no messiah. Sefer HaĒkarim (Book of Fundamentals) derives from his statement that belief in messiah is not a fundamental Jewish belief. Therefore, anyone who does not believe in a messiah is not a heretic (See ArtScroll Talmud Tractate Sanhedrin page 99a notes 13-16).

Rambam, in his comprehensive compendium of Jewish law, Mishne Tōra (also know as Yad HaĤazaka (Strong Hand), does not include belief in messiah.

Some rabbis of his time criticized Rambam for that omission, even though leaving it out is based on solid sources. Later on, when Rambam formulated the Principles of Jewish Faith as listed above, Rambam included the concept of messiah as a response to the pressure of other rabbinical leaders.

Divarim 30:3 and Yêrmēa 30:3 assure that G-d will end the exile and bring the Jewish people back to the land of Israel.

Essay 4. Serving G-d - continued

Tōra encourages each person to develop a relationship with G-d. Tōra provides the framework for developing this relationship through fulfilling commandments. Commandments that deal with belief in one G-d are:
Commandment 25: Know there is a G-d – Shimōt 20:2.
Commandment 30: Do not speak G-d's name in vain – Shimōt 20:7.
Commandment 68: Do not curse G-d – Shimōt 22:27.
Commandment 295: Do not profane the name of G-d – Vayikra 22:32.
Commandment 296: Sanctify the name of G-d – Vayikra 22:32.
Commandment 416: Know that G-d is One – Divarim 6:4.
Commandment 417: Love G-d – Divarim 6:5.
Commandment 431: Fear G-d – Divarim 10:20.
Commandment 610: Emulate the traits of G-d – Divarim 28:9.

Tōra Study Bible includes each of the 613 Biblical commandments as enumerated by Maimonidies (Rambam). Tōra Study Bible lists each commandment at the verse in which it is derived. Tōra Study Bible numbers commandments sequentially based on their order in the text.

It is just as important to avoid belief in idols and false deities, as it is to believe in one G-d. G-d reigns alone. Commandments that deal with avoiding idolatry include:
Commandment 27: Do not fashion an idol for yourself - Shimōt 20:4.
Commandment 28: Do not worship idols the way they are worshipped
 - Shimōt 20:5.
Commandment 29: Do not worship idols in the way G-d is worshipped
 - Shimōt 20:5.
Commandment 38: Do not fashion human forms - Shimōt 20:20.
Commandment 85: Do not swear in the name of an idol - Shimōt 23:13.
Commandment 214: Do not study idolatry - Vayikra 19:4.
Commandment 215: Do not fashion an idol for other people
 - Vayikra 19:4.
Commandment 454: Do not listen to a false prophet – Divarim 13:4.
Commandment 460: Do not convince other people to believe in idols
 – Divarim 13:12.

Essay 4. Serving G-d - continued

In addition to commandments directly against idolatry there are other ways to express beliefs that contradict monotheism. Commandments that help people avoid false beliefs include:

Commandment 250: Do not be superstitious – Vayikra 19:26,
Commandment 251: Do not engage in astrology – Vayikra 19:26,
Commandment 256: Do not try to be a medium – Vayikra 19:31,
Commandment 257: Do not try to see the future – Vayikra 19:31,
Commandment 381: Do not follow your lustful feelings
 – Bamidbar 15:39.
Commandment 427: Do not benefit from idols – Divarim 7:25.
Commandment 428: Do not benefit from accessories of idols
 – Divarim 7:26.
Commandment 434: Destroy idols – Divarim 12:2.
Commandment 461: Do not prophesize in the name of an idol
 – Divarim 13:14.
Commandment 463: Demolish the buildings of a city located in Israel that has turned to idol worship – Divarim 13:17.
Commandment 508: Do not try to predict the future – Divarim 18:10,
Commandment 509: Do not trick people into thinking that you can perform magic – Divarim 18:10,
Commandment 510: Do not pronounce magic spells – Divarim 18:11,
Commandment 511: Do not try to contact dead people – Divarim 18:11,
Commandment 512: Do not consult an astrologer – Divarim 18:11, and
Commandment 513: Do not consult a medium – Divarim 18:11.
Commandment 535: A court must punish Jewish people who practiced idolatry – Divarim 21:22.
Commandment 613: Do not drink wine that was used to worship idols
 – Divarim 32:38.

Essay 4. Serving G-d - continued

After the great flood, Tōra specifies seven laws for all people to follow (Brāshēt 9:4-7). All people who observe these laws are assured of a place in heaven in the afterlife and they inherit a place in the World To Come. These laws are enumerated and discussed in Talmud Tractate Sanhedrin p. 56a. These are known as the Nōaĥide laws.

The Nōaĥide laws are:
1. Do not curse G-d.
2. Do not worship idols.
3. Establish courts of law.
4. Do not murder.
5. Do not commit adultery.
6. Do not eat an animal while it is still alive.
7. Do not commit suicide.

Note that these laws do not include a directive to believe in G-d. A person is righteous as long as he or she does not believe in idols, does not worship idols, does not curse G-d, and does obey the 5 other laws listed. Each such person merits a place in heaven and the world to come. Therefore, Judaism discourages a gentile from becoming Jewish because there are hundreds of other commandments that a Jewish person must follow. Unless someone is absolutely sure that he or she is willing and able to take upon oneself the many restrictions that must be obeyed, it is better not to become Jewish.

Essay 5. Jewish Identity

Rambam, in his Mishne Tōra, Laws Against Idolatry, chapter 1, law 3 states that Avraham had thousands of followers, servants, and workers. Tōra emphasizes that all male followers, workers, and servants were circumcised (Brāshēt 17:12-14, 26, 27), although some of them may have followed descendants of Avraham, other than Yiźĥak and Yaakōv.

Jewish Perople Are Descended From A Multiplicity Of Peoples Who Followed The Jewish Ancestors

There were many gentiles who became part of Yaakōv's clan (34:29). Yihūda (Judah), son of Yaakōv married a Canaanite woman (38:2). The son of Yihūda married a local Canaanite girl (38:6). Yaakōv's son Yōsef married an Egyptian woman (Brāshēt 41:45). Ibn Ezra states that children and grandchildren of Yaakōv married Arameans, Midyanites, Edomites, and Egyptians (see Cohen, 1983, p. 285). However, the sons of Yaakōv were careful to marry proper women. (Contrast this with Yiźĥak's other son Āsav (Esau) who married Canaanite girls who did not behave properly (Brāshēt 26:35, 27:46, and 28:9)). (See note on verse 24:3 concerning the wives of the early patriarchs.)

When Yaakōv and his descendants travel to Egypt, the text states that there were 70 people, mostly sons and grandsons, who entered (Brāshēt 46:27). Some commentators state that those 70 people represent groups of people. These groups include wives and children, as well as servants and followers. The descendants of these servants and followers plus other non-descendants (Brāshēt 34:29 and 35:4) took the oath at Mount Sēnī (Sinai). Shimōt 12:44 deals with servants who are circumcised.

Note also that Mōshe married a Midianite woman (Shimōt 2:21).

When the Jewish people left Egypt, Shimōt 12:38 states that other people left with them. Medrash Shimōt Raba 18:10 and Ramban on Bamidbar (Numbers) 9:14 state that sympathetic Egyptians, such as Pharaoh's daughter, left with them. Other commentators state that fellow slaves who were from other nationalities also joined the exodus. During divine revelation at Mount Sinai, all these diverse people took the oath to obey the commandments, and they all became part of the Jewish nation.

After the establishment of the Jewish people, Tōra allows soldiers to marry women they take as captives of war (Divarim 21:10-14).

Essay 5. Jewish Identity – continued

King David Was Descendanded From A Devoted Convert To Judaism
An interesting special case is that of Ruth. As the Jewish people were approaching the land of Mōav (Moab) on their way to Israel, the king of Mōav hired a prophet to try to curse the Jewish people in an effort to weaken them (Bamidbar chapters 22-24). They did cause the Jewish people to sin through immorality (Bamidbar chapter 25). Therefore, commandment 561 in Divarim 23:4 forbids a Jewish woman from marrying a man from the nations of Mōav or Amōn. Significantly, a Jewish man is permitted to marry a woman of those nations. Bōaz, a prominent Jewish man in the land of Israel, married Rút (Ruth) who was descended from Mōav. Their descendants include King David (See the last verse in the Book of Ruth).

King David, his son King Solomon (Shlōmō) and their descendants such as King Hezekiah (Ĥizkēa) ruled from their thrones in Jerusalem (Yerūshalayim) – the City of King David. Yerūshalayim is the capital of Israel, as anyone who reads and believes in the Bible can plainly see.

Formal Process of Converting to Judaism
Throughout the generations, many people of different backgrounds became part of the Jewish people. For instance, in ancient times, when a Jewish person acquired a gentile indentured servant, such a gentile accepted certain commandments, especially negative commandments, such that he or she observed shabat and laws of kosher food, among other laws. (See the last paragraph in this note for a special note about servants.) Men indentured servants underwent circumcision. When, after many years of living a Tōra-based life, such an indentured servant was given his or her freedom, he or she became a full member of the Jewish people (see, for example, Artscroll Talmud Tractate Kiddushin, notes 2-10 on page 6b).

From about 200 BCE, for a few hundred years, there were many Romans who searched for spirituality and monotheism. As a result, thousands of Romans converted to Judaism. There were so many converts to Judaism that the Roman emperor declared the death penalty for anyone who converts. When the emperor's own nephew, Onkelos converted, it caused an uproar and a great embarrassment to the emperor. Onkelos went on to write a Tōra translation that was imminently readable to the people of that time period, and that translation has been studied throughout the ages.

Essay 5. Jewish Identity – continued

Hilel Brought Righteous Gentiles Closer To G-d

Talmud Tractate Shabat 31a tells the stories of three of these converts during this Roman period in history. One person came to the great Rabbi Hilel. He asked Hilel "How many Tōras do the Jewish people have?" This is an amazing question for a gentile to ask. It seems that he must have read the Bible and was wondering why Jewish people have customs and behavior that do not seem to relate to the written Bible. Hilel calmly explained that there is an oral Tōra, handed down from G-d to Mōshe, that explains the practice of Jewish law. Even though the gentile asked to be converted on the condition that he would only follow the written Tōra, Hilel did not refuse. He taught him the basics. The next day, Hilel taught a very different approach to the same material. The gentile complained. Hilel explained that the essence of understanding Tōra lies in trusting the rabbinical teachers. That is the oral Tōra and it is bedrock of authentic Judaism. The gentile kept studying and became a true convert to Judaism.

In another instance, a gentile asked Hilel to teach him the entire Tōra while he balanced on one leg. Hilel famously stated: "Do not do to other people, things that are hateful to you. The rest of Judaism flows from this principle." Hilel agreed to accept the gentile as a student, and he became a true convert to Judaism.

In a third instance, there was a gentile who had overheard a scribe state the description of the beautiful clothes of the high priest in Shimōt chapter 25. He asked Hilel to convert him on the condition that he, once he becomes Jewish, can wear the clothes of the high priest. Hilel calmly agreed, but he told the gentile that he first must study the Bible from the beginning. When they reached the portion that describes the laws of the clothes of priests, the gentile read that it is a sin for any stranger to wear priestly clothing items. The gentile asked Hilel: "To whom does this prohibition apply?" Hilel wanted the convert to understand that any Jewish person, including a convert, can reach the height of spirituality and accomplishment. Therefore, Hilel responded: "Even the great King David." And of course, King David was descended from a convert. Thus, the person continued to study and became a true convert to Judaism.

Essay 5. Jewish Identity – continued

Jewish Indentity Is Not Defined By Genealogy Alone

Talmud Tractate Kidūshin 70b states that there have been many times in history when the Jewish people were subjugated, resulting in gentile men siring Jewish children. This was true in times of the later prophets and during Talmudic times. Therefore, Talmud states that no one can be haughty about his or her genealogical purity (Tractate Kidushin, p.70b). In the 1200s, Rabbi Moshe of Coucy, author of Sefer Hilĥōt Gadōl (Smag: Great Book of Commandments), traveled around Spain and France and found rampant intermarriage among Jewish people in various towns.

Converting To Judaism Is A Formal And Demanding Process

Thus, Jewishness and Jewish identity is not solely defined by genetics or genealogy. But it is also important to understand that the process of converting to Judaism – coming closer to G-d - is a formal process. A person who converts must abide by the Tōra's commandments. It is a solemn oath similar to that which the people promised at the revelation at Mount Sēnī. The conversion process takes years of study and must be presided by a panel of rabbis. Shimōt 12:49 states that converts (Jews by choice) are equal in every way to Jewish-born people. In addition, there are 36 verses that warn not to mistreat or wrong converts.

Tōra Prefers For Gentiles To Be Ethical

It is imperative to understand that Tōra discourages a gentile from becoming Jewish. After the great flood, Tōra specifies seven laws for all people to follow (verses 9:4-7). All people who observe these laws are assured of a place in heaven in the afterlife and they inherit a place in the World To Come. These laws are enumerated and discussed in Talmud Tractate Sanhedrin p. 56a. These are known as the Nōaĥide laws (see note on verse 9:4). Note that these laws do not include a directive to believe in G-d. A person is righteous as long as he or she does not believe in idols, does not worship idols, does not curse G-d, and does obey the 5 other laws listed. Therefore, Judaism discourages a gentile from becoming Jewish because there are hundreds of other commandments that a Jewish person must follow. Unless someone is absolutely sure that he or she is willing and able to take upon oneself the many restrictions that must be obeyed, it is better not to become Jewish.

Essay 5. Jewish Identity – continued

An earlier paragraph mentioned laws about gentile servants, therefore, the following special note is appropriate:

The Hebrew Word for Slave Has Multiple Meanings
Special note: The Hebrew word "*eved*" can mean: slave, servant, indentured servant, worker, or advisor. It is incorrect to translate it as "slave" when dealing with servants of Jewish people. The unfortunate practice of English Bibles to translate it as slave caused Americans in the 1800s to use their "Bible" as proof that a slave trade is permissible. The Tōra law is that a person who is so poor that he or she needs to sell himself or herself as an indentured servant must be treated fairly by the master. The master actually provides such a person with experience and skill-building to enable him or her to eventually be independent. Tōra teaches that it is in fact forbidden for a person to own another person (see, for example, Artscroll Talmud Tractate Kiddushin note 11 on page 6b). Thus, Abraham Lincoln fulfilled a Tōra concept when he signed the Emancipation Proclamation.

Essay 6. The Land of Israel

The Land of Israel For the People of Israel

G-d promised Yaakōv (Jacob = Israel) that he and his descendants, the Jewish people, are given the land of Israel, as stated in Brāshēt (Genesis) 28:13. Brāshēt 35:12 re-states this promise to Yaakōv and adds that this is the promise that G-d had made earlier to Avraham (Abraham) and Yiźĥak (Isaac).

G-d had made the solemn promise of the land of Israel to Yiźĥak in Brāshēt 26:3.

G-d solemnly promised the land of Israel to Avraham, as stated in Brāshēt 13:15, 15:7, 15:18, 17:8, and 18:19. Then G-d specifies that this solemn promise of the land is directed specifically to his son Yiźĥak in Brāshēt 17:19 and 21. Yiźĥak confers this promise solely and specifically to Yaakōv

G-d remembers his promise to the Jewish ancestors in Shimōt 2:24. In Shimōt 3:8, G-d clarifies to Mōshe (Moses) that the promise is that the Jewish people will inherit the land of Israel. G-d reiterates that promise in Shimōt 3:17, 6:4, 6:8, 13:5, 13:11, 23:10, 23:20, 32:13, and in Bamidbar 13:2, 15:2, 15:8, 26:53, and 33:52. The Jewish people acknowledge G-d's promise in Shimōt 15:13 and 15:16. Mōshe states it again in Bamidbar 10:29.

A Land Flowing with Milk And Honey

Shimōt 3:8 is the first time that the land of Israel is described as a land flowing with milk and honey.

Siforno explains this phrase to mean that Israel supports milk-producing cattle, while the term honey means food.

Ramban explains that this term means that the land of Israel is good for growing produce (milk) that has sweet juices and drink (honey).

There are a few other places in the Shimōt where the land of Israel is described as a land flowing with milk and honey. G-d states it again in verse 3:17. When the initial laws of Passover are given, G-d also mentions that Israel is a land flowing with milk and honey (13:5). The final mention of it in the Book of Exodus is when Mōshe asks G-d for atonement after the sin of the gold calf statue (33:3).

Essay 6. The Land of Israel - continued

In Divarim 8:7-8, the land of Israel is described as a land of rivers, springs, valleys and mountains. And that Israel is especially known for seven types of produce: wheat, barley, grapes, figs, pomegranates, olives, and dates.

The land of Israel had been promised by G-d to the Jewish people (Brāshēt: 13:15; 15:7 & 18; 17:8; 18:19, and 26:3). Yet G-d never mentions to the patriarchs that the land is flowing with milk and honey. The reason is that Avraham had experienced a severe famine in the land of Israel (Brāshēt: 12:10), as did Yiźhak (26:1), and as did Yaakōv (42:5).

The fact that G-d promised the land to the patriarchs would seem to be the only reason needed to lead the Jewish people to the promised land. According to Ramban's understanding of Divarim 6:3, Mōshe explains to the Jewish people that G-d selected the land of Israel <u>because</u> it is flowing with milk and honey and it will support their many descendants. This is amplified when Mōshe states in Divarim 11:9 that the Jewish people will endure in the land that is flowing with milk and honey.

The most dramatic use of describing a land as flowing with milk and honey is when, during the mutinous rebellion by Kōraĥ, Datan and Avēran audaciously replied to Mōshe: "you brought us out of Egypt which is a land flowing with milk and honey" (Bamidbar (Numbers) 16:13)!

Other verses in which Israel is described as a land flowing with milk and honey include: Vayikra (Leviticus) 20:24, and Bamidbar 13:27 and 14:8. The declaration made when someone offers first fruits (Divarim 26:9 & 15) includes stating that the land of Israel is flowing with milk and honey. Mōshe reiterates that the land is flowing with milk and honey in Divarim 27:3. Mōshe in Divarim 31:20 warns that because the land is flowing with milk and honey, the Jewish people will forget G-d. Yihōshūa (Joshua) mentions that the land is flowing with milk and honey in the Book of Joshua 5:6. Prophets state this fact in Yêrmēya (Jeremiah) 11:5, Yiĥezkel (Ezēkēel) 20:6 and 15, and Yōel (Joel) 3:18.

Essay 6. The Land of Israel - continued

Early Residents of the Land of Israel

Shimōt verse 3:8 identifies the following tribal peoples as residing in the land of Israe when Avraham was there:
1. Kinaan (Canaan),
2. Emôr (Amorites),
3. Ĥet (Hittites),
4. Ĥiv (Hivites),
5. Pirēz (Perizites), and
6. Yivūs (Jebusites).
In addition, other tribal nations that lived in the land of Israel were:
7. Gêrgash (Brāshēt 15:19),
8. Kadmōn (Brāshēt 15:19),
9. Ken (stated in Brāshēt 15:19),
10. Kinēz (Brāshēt 15:19),
11. Rifaim (Brāshēt 15:19), and
12. Plishtim (Philistines) (Brāshēt 26:1).

Jewish Immigration to the Land of Israel

When the Jewish people, led by Yihōshūa (Joshua), entered into the land of Israel, they did not automatically battle against the inhabitants. Commandment 525 in Divarim (Deuteronomy) 20:10 states that the Jewish people must offer peace terms to a city. Yihōshūa sent a messenger to each town with the following statement: "This land is holy to G-d. You may continue to live here in peace as long as you stop worshipping idols and you destroy your idols. If you do not want to give up idol worship, then you must leave this holy land. If you choose not to do either, then we must enter into battle against you."

Essay 7. Prayer

Prayer is the process by which people address their requests to G-d, thus acknowledging that G-d is all-powerful and rules the universe.

People can
    a) acknowledge G-d,
    b) praise G-d and
and c) thank G-d.
But d) prayer is a request addressed to G-d.

When a person prays, he or she fulfills commandment 91, as stated in verse 23:25. Also, see Holzer, 2011, p.4.

Liturgy is organized so that first people praise G-d and then pray for their needs. This is based on Talmud Tractate Braĥōt (Blessings) page 32b. G-d's greatness and glory is beyond human comprehension. Attempting to declare praise of G-d can only fall woefully short of the reality of G-d's awesomeness. In Divarim (Deuteronomy) 10:17, Mōshe introduces his request from G-d with praise. He uses 3 terms to priase G-d:
  great,
  mighty,
and awesome.

Therefore, the sages follow Mōshe's example in the formal liturgy found in the prayer book. Talmud Tractate Megēla page 18a concludes that trying to add more words that praise G-d's many divine attributes is an act of arrogance, and should be avoided (see Lustiger, 2014, p.125).

The central prayer in Judaism, the Amēda, is organized as 3 main section:
  a) praise G-d,
  b) ask G-d for your needs,
and c) thank G-d for all G-d has done for us.

In the middle section, the sages teach what a person should want, ask for, and request from G-d. Namely, health and peace. As people go through life, they often lose sight of the truly important things. Prayer declares our belief in G-d, and reminds us who we are, what is really important, how we should live our lives, and what we should strive for.

Essay 7. Prayer - continued

The sages instituted morning prayer based on Avraham (Abraham) in Brāshēt (Genesis) verse 18:23 when he prayed for the welfare of neighboring cities. The sages instituted the afternoon prayer based on Yiẑhak (Isaac) in Brāshēt 24:63. The evening prayer is based on Yaakōv (Jacob = Israel) in Brāshēt 32:10.

Avraham prayed to be able to have children (Brāshēt 15:3).

Hagar, Avraham's secondary wife, prays (Brāshēt 16:13).

When Jewish people request (i.e., pray for) help from G-d, they show themselves worthy of redemption.

Verses in Shimōt that deal with prayer of Jewish people are:

Verse 3:9 - G-d accepts the prayers of the Jewish people.

Verse 4:31 - Jewish people heard how Aharōn performed the wonders to the Jewish leaders, and they bowed & prayed.

Verse 12:27 – Jewish people bowed and prayed.

Verse 22:22 - If a widow or orphan prays to G-d because they have been mistreated, G-d will listen to their prayer.

Verse 22:26 - If a poor person is mistreated, G-d will listen to his or her prayer.

Verse 23:25 - Commandment 91: Pray daily.

Verse 23:26 – Pray for various important things.

Verse 25:8 - G-d will accept prayers of Jewish people through the sanctuary.

Verse 33:10 - When people saw the cloud at the door of Mōshe's tent, they stood and prayed.

Verse 38:8 – Women prayed at the Tabernacle.

See note on verse 8:8 for verses where Mōshe prayed.
See note on verse 8:24 where Pharaoh asked Mōshe to pray for him.

Essay 8. Commandmens

Throughout Tōra Study Bible, each Tōra commandment is inserted before the verse from which it is derived.

Rabbi Simlī both in Talmud Tractates Makōt 23b and Yivamōt 47b states that there are (only) 613 commandments in Tōra.

However, Psalm 119:96 states that there are innumerable commandments. Therefore, Ibn Ezra does not accept the limitation of the number 613 (Wax, 2008, p. 17). The Vilna Gaon (Rabbi Elēyahū (Elijah) Kramer (1720-1797)) wrote in his book <u>Sefer Maalōt Hatōra</u> that the 613 commandments are categories within which other similar commandments are subsumed. Thus, there are many more than 613 Biblical commandments. The many verses that define actions to perform or prohibitions to adhere to, even though they are not identified as part of the 613, are also Biblical commandments.

Rambam (1135-1204) listed clearly what he believes are the 613 commandments in his <u>Book of Commandments</u>. There are at least 3 other opinions as to what the exact list is. Raavad (Rabbi Abraham son of David, 1125 – 1198) comments on Rambam and he removes some commandments and adds others. Ramban (1194 – 1270) also removes and adds commandments based on his understanding. For exmaple, Ramban states that Bamidbar (Numbers) 33:53 states one of the Biblical commandments to live in the land of Israel, whereas Rambam does not include in the 613. In addition, a sage who wrote the <u>Book of Education</u> (Sefer HaĤēnuĥ) in which explains each commandment uses a list mostly based on Rambam, but makes his own removals and additions.

(There are earlier lists of commandments as explained in Wax, 2008, pp. 16-21).

If all distinct commandments selected by Rambam, Ramban, Raavad, and <u>Book of Education</u> are combined, there are many more than 613 commandments. Throughout the Tōra text there are many verses that give rise to laws that are explained in the oral law, as written in the Talmud. Therefore, it is more likely that that there are about 1,000 Biblical commandmnets, 613 of which are recognized as the "613."

Tōra Study Bible includes commandments as defined by Rambam, and numbers them in the order they occur in the text.

Shimōt[1] - Section 1   - 17 verse (Total: 124 verses)

SONS OF YAAKŌV

1534 [2] 1:1 These are the names of the sons of Yisrael (Israel = Jacob) who had come[3] to the land of Egypt[4] with Yaakōv (Jacob).

Each son[5] came with his family:
1535 1:2 (1) Riūvān (Reuben),
    (2) Shimōn (Simeon),
    (3) Lāvē (Levi),
    (4) Yihūda (Judah),
1536 1:3 (5) Yēsaĥar,
    (6) Zivūlūn (Zebulon),
    (7) Binyamin (Benjamin),
1537 1:4 (8) Dan,
    (9) Naftalē,
    (10) Gad,
    and (11) Asher.
1538 1:5 When they had traveled to Egypt, there were seventy[6] heads of households[7] who had descended from Yaakōv.

Yōsef (Joseph) was already in Egypt.

THAT GENERATION ENDS

1539 1:6 Yōsef [8] and his brothers[9] and the Jewish people of that generation passed away.[10]

POPULATION EXPANDS

1540 1:7 The Jewish people were fertile: they had many children.
    Their population increased and they became very strong.
    The land was filled with them.

PHARAOH IS FEARFUL

1541 1:8 A new king who had not known Yōsef [11] ruled over Egypt.
1542 1:9 The king said to his people:
    "The Jewish people are too numerous and they are stronger than we are.[12]

Shimōt - Section 1 - continued

1543 1:10 "Come, let us act wisely with regard to them so that their population does not continue to increase.
"In case we will be engaged in a war, our action toward them will avoid their siding with our enemies,[13] fighting against us, and leaving[14] our country."

TASKMASTERS

1544 1:11 Therefore, Egyptians set taskmasters[15] over them to force them to perform exhausting work.[16]
The Jewish workers built for Pharaoh the store cities of Pēsōm and Ramsās.

JEWISH POPULATION CONTINUES TO INCREASE DESPITE PHARAOH'S EVIL EFFORTS

1545 1:12 But the more that Egyptian taskmasters punished the Jewish people, the more the Jewish people multiplied and spread.
Egyptians became very fearful of the Jewish people.

THE WORK INCREASES

1546 1:13 In response, Egyptian taskmasters forced the Jewish people to work even harder.
1547 1:14 Egyptian taskmasters made the lives of the Jewish people miserably bitter[17] by forcing them to build with mortar and mud bricks.[18]
They also made them work in the fields.
All of the work was intended to exhaust them.[19]

MIDWIVES DISOBEY PHARAOH

1548 1:15 The king of Egypt spoke to the supervisor midwives, Shifra and Pūa,[20] who were in charge of the Jewish women.
1549 1:16 The king said to them:
"When you deliver a baby of a Jewish woman, look carefully as the baby starts to emerge.
If the infant is a boy, you should kill him.
If the infant is a girl, you should allow her to live."
1550 1:17 The midwives feared G-d [21] and did not obey the king.
Instead, they allowed the infant Jewish boys to live.

Shimōt - Section 1 - Study Notes

---

[1] The Hebrew word *shimōt* means "names."

[2] "1534" – There are 1,533 verses in the Book of Brāshēt (Genesis). Shimōt starts with verse 1,534.

[3] 1:1 "had come" – Yaakōv came to Egypt in Tōra year 2238. See Table 2, notes on rows 1-13 for the calculation of the year.

[4] 1:1 "These are the names of the sons of Yisrael (Israel = Jacob) who had come[4] to the land of Egypt" - This is the same exact wording as Brāshēt 46:8.

[5] 1:1 "sons" – The births of the first 11 sons are stated in Brāshēt 29:32-30:24. The birth of his youngest son, Binyamin, is stated in Brāshēt 35:16-18.

[6] 1:5 "seventy" – These seventy people are listed in Brāshēt 46:8-27. The fact that there were 70 is also stated in Divarim 10:22.

[7] 1:5 "heads of households" – Brāshēt 46:26 states that the list does not include their wives and children. Yaakōv and his large family came to Egypt with their herdsmen, workers, and followers. Commentators state that these 70 people represent the leaders of the Jewish nation at that time.

[8] 1:6 "Yōsef . . . passed away" – Yōsef passed away in Tōra year 2309, which is 1452 BCE. See Tabe 2, notes on rows 13-15 for the calculation.

[9] 1:6 "all his brothers . . . passed away" - Rashē states that Lāvē was the last of Yaakōv's children to pass away, and slavery started soon after he passed away. Verse 6:16 states that Lāvē lived to be 137, which is Tōra year 2332. See Table 2, note on row 16 for the calculation.

[10] 1:6 "that generation passed away" – Siforno: This is the generation that included Yaakōv's grandchildren, as listed in Brāshēt chapter 46 (portion Vayēgash).

[11] 1:8 "new king who had not known Yōsef" – Amenhotep II probably instituted the slavery of the Jewish people, as shown in Table 2. Yōsef had passed away 27 years before Amenhotep II had taken the throne, while the last of Yōsef's siblings passed away a few years after Amenhotep II started ruling. However, according to Siforno, who states that slavery did not start until all of Yaakōv's grandchildren had passed away, it is possible that Amenhotep III enacted the slavery at the start of his reign.

[12] 1:9 "they are stronger than we are" – It would be in Egypt's interest to let the Jewish people leave, thus eliminating this threat. But the king didn't want surrounding nations to think that Egypt was weak and vulnerable.

[13] 1:10 "siding with our enemies" –The fact that the Jewish people are stronger than the native Egyptians should have been enough of a reason to convince the Egyptian population to accept laws of discrimination against the Jewish people. But the Egyptian people were well disposed towards their Jewish neighbors who had always been model citizens. Therefore, the king had to use this scare tactic to convince his people to agree to his evil decree.

There are other indications that many Egyptians liked the Jewish people as seen in verses:

1:15 -Medrash Yalkūt Shimōnē: Shifra and Pūa were Egyptian women who joined the Jewish people

2:8 - The king's daughter saved a Jewish baby,

8:15 – The king's magicians recognized the G-d's power,

9:20 - There were Egyptians who feared G-d,

10:7 – The king's advisors told the king to let the Jewish people go, and

12:38 - Other peoples, besides the Jewish people, left Egypt during the Exodus. Many of them were Egyptians who sympathized with the Jewish people.

[14] 1:10 "leaving" – A more natural fear is that conquerors would take over the country and expel or enslave the current residents (i.e., the Egyptians). But the king is too frightened to say this possibility out loud. Therefore, he

substitutes the reverse idea that the Jewish people will conquer and then leave.

15 1:11 "taskmasters" – Although many Egyptians liked Jewish people, there was no shortage of Egyptians who were fearful and jealous of them.

Originally, only Egyptians were appointed as taskmasters. Later, Jewish men were forced to be overseers over other Jewish workers, as appears in verse 5:6.

16 1:11 "exhausting work" – Ibn Ezra: Pharaoh wanted Jewish men to be so exhausted they would no longer be interested in, nor have the time, energy, or inclination for having more children.

The king declared that a certain day was set aside for men to show their loyalty to Pharaoh. Every man must make as many bricks as possible. The Egyptian people were told not to participate. The Jewish men of the Levite tribe did not participate. They were recognized as teachers and spiritual leaders. The day after "Loyalty Day" Pharaoh declared that from now on, every family is required to produce that same number of bricks each day. This is how Jewish people were tricked into servitude.

A midrash explains that the wives of the Jewish workers would use mirrors for the purpose of putting on their makeup in order to cause their husbands to want to be intimate with them. This explains why the population continued to grow (1:20). This fact aligns with verse 38:8 in which Mōshe (Moses) accepted the copper mirrors from women for use in the Tabernacle, because the mirrors had been used for the higher purpose of preserving the Jewish population.

17 1:14 "miserably bitter" – This verse is quoted in the Passover Hagada to explain why Jewish people eat bitter vegetables at the Passover Seder.

18 1:14 "mortar and mud bricks" – These materials do not result in lasting structures. Cement and baked clay bricks are used for permanent buildings.

19 1:14 "intended to exhaust them" – Talmud Tractate Sōta 11b: The Egyptians overloaded the Jewish people with busy work and demeaning tasks because accomplishment was not the goal. In fact, quite the opposite, the more menial and meaningless the work, the better.

Ibn Ezra: The purpose of the labor was to slow the Jewish birth rate.

[20] 1:15 "Shifra and Pūa" – There are numerous opinions as to who these two women were.

a. Talmud Tractate Sōta 11b: They were famous Jewish women. One was Yōĥeved and the other was either Miryam or Elēsheva.

b. Rashbam: They were Jewish midwives.

c. Malbim: They were Egyptian women midwives assigned to the Jewish people.

d. Midrash Yalkut Shimōnē: They were gentile (Egyptian) women who joined the Jewish people. (See note on 1:10 about how this fits in with Egyptian attitude toward the Jewish people.)

[21] 1:17 "G-d" - Tōra Study Bible, for the sake of readability, renders all the various holy names of the Creator that occur in the original Hebrew Tōra text, as G-d. A hyphen is used in the middle of this word instead of the letter "o" in order to avoid spelling out the Almighty's name, which is reserved for holy books. See Essays on G-d and on Serving G-d.

Shimōt - Section 2   - 13 verses

MIDWIVES FEAR G-D

1551 1:18 The king of Egypt summoned the midwives and asked:
"Why have you done this?
"You let the baby boys live."
1552 1:19 The midwives answered Pharaoh:
"Jewish women are not like women of Egypt in that they know how to deliver babies.
"They give birth before the midwife even gets there." [22]
1553 1:20 G-d rewarded the midwives.
The population increased [23] and the people continued to be very strong.
1554 1:21 G-d enabled the midwives to have distinguished families[24] because they feared G-d.

PHARAOH DECREES AGAINST JEWISH BOY BABIES

1555 1:22 Pharaoh promulgated his next command to all the people:
"Every boy born must be drowned in the river, but every girl is permitted to live."

THE SAVIOR IS BORN

1556 23 2:1 A man[25] of the tribe of Lāvē (Levi) had marital relations with a woman of the tribe of Lāvē.[26]
1557 24 2:2 The woman became pregnant and gave birth to a son.[27]
She realized how special the son was and she hid him for three months. [28]

THE BABY'S MOTHER PLACES HIM IN A BASKET ON THE RIVER

1558 25 2:3 When she could no longer hide him, she took a box and water-proofed it
She placed her son in it and put it on the river Nile among the water plants along the edge of the river.
1559 26 2:4 The baby's sister watched from a distance to see what would happen to the baby boy.

Shimōt - Section 2 - continued

DAUGHTER OF PHARAOH RETRIEVES THE BABY

1560 27 2:5 The daughter of Pharaoh was bathing in the Nile.

Her servant girls walked along the edge of the river.

Pharaoh's daughter saw the box floating in the water and sent her servant girl to get it.

MIRYAM ARRANGES FOR THE BABY'S MOTHER TO NURSE THE BABY

1561 28 2:6 She opened the box and saw the baby boy.

The baby began to cry and she had pity on him.

She said:

"He is a Jewish boy." [29]

The baby's sister asked her:

"Should I get a Jewish woman who will nurse the baby for you?"

1563 30 2:8 The daughter of Pharaoh replied:

"Go." [30]

The sister brought back the baby's mother.

1564 31 2:9 The daughter of Pharaoh said to the wet-nurse:

"Nurse this child.

"I will pay you to do this."

The woman took the child and nursed him.

PHARAOH'S DAUGHTER NAMES THE BABY: MŌSHE

1565 32 2:10 When the child was weaned off the milk, his mother brought him back to the daughter of Pharaoh.

The daughter of Pharaoh adopted him as her own son and named him Mōshe[31] (Moses) because, as she explained:

"I saved him[32] when I drew him from the water."

Shimōt - Section 2 – Study Notes

---

[22] 1:19 "They give birth before the midwife even gets there" – Because the midwives feared G-d, they had warned the Jewish women about the edict. That is <u>why</u> Jewish women were able to give birth before anyone else came. G-d rewarded those midwives by protecting them from the king such that the king did not punish them, and they were able to have families of their own.

[23] 1:20 "population increased" – Interpreting this as part of the reward to the midwives strengthens those opinions that state they were Jewish or were sympathetic to the Jewish people.

[24] 1:21 "distinguished families" - Yōĥeved is the matriarch of the Levites and priests (kōhanim). Miryam's granddaughter married one of the ancestors of King David (see Scherman, 1993, p.295).
   Rashbam: The verse is translated more literally, and means that Pharaoh placed the disobedient midwives under house arrest.

[25] 2:1 "man . . . woman" – By the fact that their child is Mōshe, it is apparent that these are Amram and Yōĥeved. Their marriage is stated explicitly in verse 6:20. They were already married and had a son (Aharōn = Aaron) and daughter (Miryam = Miriam) before this third child. After the royal decree, this husband and wife decided not to have relations, but as stated in this verse, they changed their mind. A medrash states that it was their daughter Miryam who convinced them to re-marry. See note on verse 6:20 as to the familial reltionship between Amram and Yōĥeved.

[26] 2:1 "woman of the tribe of Lāvē" - The literal words of the verse imply that she was the daughter of Lāvē. However, when these words are taken as their idiomatic expression as used throughout the Hebrew language, the words can be translated as relative, or more directly, granddaughter, Rashē notes that if Yōĥeved was a daughter of Lāvē, she would have been 130 years old when she gave birth to Mōshe.

[27] 2:2 "son" – Mōshe.

[28] 2:2 "she hid him for three months" – Egyptian authorities would come to confiscate each Jewish baby boy when they estimated that a pregnant woman would give birth. She gave birth 3 months early and was able to hide the baby for 3 months.

[29] 2:6 "Jewish boy" – Rashbam: He was circumcised.

She realized that he is Jewish and yet did not turn him over to the authorities because she admired the Jewish people and was sympathetic to them, as were many Egyptians.

Note that once Abraham was commanded that all his descendants and followers must be circumcised, the Jewish people observed this. We see this is true when the sons of Jacob stated that only a circumcised man is permitted to marry into their clan (Brāshēt (Genesis) 34:17). Also, the knowledge of the requirement of circumcision is evident in verse 4:25 in which the circumcision of Mōshe's son is stated.

Rambam identifies Vayikra (Leviticus) 12:3 (portion Tazrēa) as commandment 166 to circumcise Jewish babies on the eighth day. Other commentators identify Brāshēt 17:12 (portion Leĥ liĥa) as the source for the commandmnet of circumcision.

[30] 2:8 "Go" – The king's daughter was fully aware of the plight of the Jewish people and sided with them, as did many Egyptians. Verse 12:38 states that when the Jewish people left Egypt, many other peoples, including Egyptians, went with them. Support for this opinion is verse 9:20 that states many Egyptians feared G-d, and thus, were well-disposed toward the Jewish people. This reinforces the concept stated by the sages that the definition of a Jewish person is not based solely on genetics or genealogy. Rather, it is the formal acceptance of G-d's commandments to the Jewish people, regardless of a person's race or ethnic origin, as explained in Essay 5 on Jewish identity.

[31] 2:10 "Mōshe" – In Egyptian, "mōshe" means "son" (see Kaplan, 1981, p.263). There were certain names taken on by Pharaohs such as Ahmosis and Thutmose, which are variants of the term mōshe.

Ibn Ezra: Pharaoh's daughter named him the Egyptian name Monios which means he was draen from the water. The name Mōshe is the Hebrew form of Monios (see Scherman, 1993, p. 297).

[32] 2:10 "I saved him" - She felt that although she did not give birth to the baby, nonetheless, by saving him, she could claim him as her son.

Shimōt - Section 3   - 15 verses

MŌSHE GROWS UP AND REALIZES THAT HE IS JEWISH

1566 33 2:11 When Mōshe (Moses) was an adult,[33] he started visiting his own people[34] and saw their difficult life.

One day he saw an Egyptian murder a Jewish person.

1567 34 2:12 Mōshe looked around and it seemed that no one was there to see him.

Therefore, Mōshe killed the murderer and hid his body in the sand.

MŌSHE IDENTIFIES WITH HIS PEOPLE

1568 35 2:13 Mōshe ventured out the next day and saw two Jewish men fighting.

Mōshe asked the man who was hitting the other man:

"Why are you hitting your brother?"

1569 36 2:14 The man asked:

"Who made you our ruler and judge?

"Are you going to kill me the way you killed the Egyptian?"

Mōshe was afraid because he thought:

"People know what I did yesterday."

MŌSHE LEAVES HIS BIRTHPLACE

1570 37 2:15 When Pharaoh heard what Mōshe had done, he issued an order for his execution.[35]

Mōshe ran away to the land of Midyan (Midian).[36]

Mōshe was sitting near a well.

1571 38 2:16 The priest of Midyan had seven daughters.

They came to the well to draw water.

When they started to fill their water troughs to water their sheep,

1572 39 2:17 other shepherds[37] came to chase them away.

Mōshe got up to help the women, and he watered their sheep.

Shimōt - Section 3 - continued

1573 40 2:18 The women came home to their father Riūâl.[38]
   Riūâl asked them:
   "How did you manage to come home so early today?"
1574 41 2:19 They answered him:
   "A stranger from Egypt rescued us from shepherds.
   "He drew water for us and watered our sheep."
1575 42 2:20 He asked them:
   "Where is he now?
   "Why did you abandon him?
   "Call him and let him eat with us." [39]

MŌSHE MARRIES ŹĒPŌRA, DAUGHTER OF YITRŌ

1576 43 2:21 Mōshe made a decision to live with Riūâl.
   Riūâl gave his daughter Źēpōra's hand in marriage to Mōshe.

Gârshōm, Mōshe's Firstborn Son

1577 44 2:22 When Źēpōra gave birth to their son, Mōshe named him Gârshōm[40] because he said:
   "I have been a stranger in a strange land."
1578 45 2:23 After much time, the king of Egypt passed away.[41]
   The Jewish people groaned due to their difficult burdens.
   G-d responded when they cried due to the harshness of their enslavement.
1579 46 2:24 G-d heard their cries and remembered his solemn promise to Avraham[42] (Abraham), Yiźĥak[43] (Isaac), and Yaakōv[44] (Jacob).
1580 47 2:25 G-d saw the Jewish people, and was ready to display His concern.

Shimōt - Section 3 – Study Notes

---

[33] 2:11 "adult" – There are numerous opinions as what age Mōshe was when he realized that he is Jewish, including:
   a. Shimōt Raba Chapter 5: he was 12 years old.
   b. Sefer HaYashar: he was 18.
   c. Shimōt Raba Chapter 1: he was 20.
   d. Bamidbar Raba Chapter 14: he was 32.

[34] 2:11 "his own people" – There came a time when Mōshe realized that other men are not circumcised. This caused him to inquire about it and found out that Jewish men are circumcised.

G-d commanded Avraham (Abraham) to be circumcised (Brāshēt 17:10), and to circumcise all descendants and followers (Brāshēt 17:12). The sons of Yaakōv (Jacob = Israel) epress this fact in Brāshēt 34:14.

There is a beautiful alternate interpretation that describes the transformation of Mōshe, based on the openess of the wording of these Tōra verses. When Mōshe realized he is Jewish, he fought an internal struggle: should he remain a royal Egyptian or should he openly declare himself a Jew? He "looked this way and that" – namely, he considered the pros and cons of each. Ultimately, he "murdered" the Egyptian by renouncing his Egyptian position. Many Jews disliked this foreigner entering their community ("Are you coming here to rule us?"). Pharaoh ordered that Mōshe must be executed because he was a defector. G-d chose Mōshe to lead the Jewish people because of his royal upbringing, and more importantly, because he had the honesty, integrity and courage to make difficult decisions.

Although Mōshe identified himself with his people initially, once he becomes their leader, he always refers to them as in the third person. When Mōshe spoke to G-d, he refers to them as "Your people." In verse 32:7, G-d tells Mōshe that the Jewish people are his (i.e., "your") people. Eventually, Mōshe himself speaks of himself as being part of the Jewish people in verse 34:9.

[35] 2:15 "execution" – Normally, capital punishment is justified in a murder case. But the king's immediate insistence on the death penalty for Mōshe without a trial and without hearing Mōshe's side of the story reveals that

there is something more at work here. The king now realized that the boy that he had been told is his grandson is really Jewish. The king felt betrayed, and Mōshe should have been eliminated based on the previous royal decree against Jewish male babies (verse 1:22).

[36] 2:15 "Midyan" – Midyan is southeast of the land of Israel.

Midyan was one of the sons of Avraham and his secondary wife Kitūra (Brāshēt 25:2). It was Midyan merchants who were involved in the sale of Yōsef (Joseph) (Brāshēt 37:28), as were their cousins, the people of Midan (Brāshēt 37:36). Midan was a brother of Midyan (Brāshēt 25:2).

Later, when the Jewish people were in the wilderness, the people of Midyan ensnared the Jewish people into idol worship. Therefore, G-d commands the Jewish people to punish the people of Midyan (see Bamidbar 25:16 and 31:1). Riūâl and his family were kind and generous, in contrast to the general population around them.

[37] 2:17 "other shepherds" – In general, the people of Midyan were mean and took pleasure in bullying. This was not unusual in the ancient world. Protecting oneself, one's family, and one's group often meant being apprehensive of, and belligerent to, other people.

[38] 2:18 "Riūâl" – There are two opinions about who he is. One opinion is that Riūâl is the father of Yitrō (Jethro). According to this opinion, the sisters are Riūâl's granddaughters. The Talmud states that grandchildren are thought of as children to their grandparents. Similarly, grandparents are thought of as parents by their grandchildren.

The other opinion is that Riūâl is one of many alternate names for Yitrō. In verse 6:25, there is an opinion that Pūtēâl is another name for Yitrō (Talmud Tractate Bava Batra).

Hōvav is another possible alternate name for Yitrō. There are two opinions about the name Hōvav. Ibn Ezra states that it is another name for Yitrō. In support of this opinion, Book of Judges verse 4:11 states that Hōvav was the father-in-law of Mōshe (although the Hebrew word could be also translated as brother-in-law).

The opinion of Rasbam and Ramban is that Hōvav is the son of Yitrō, making him the brother-in-law of Mōshe. In Bamidbar 10:29-32, Hōvav travels back home, whereas, earlier in Exodus, verse 18:27, Yitrō travels back to his home, thus supporting this opinion.

Another name for Yitrō is Kān (or Kānē), because he is the ancestor of the Kenites, as stated in the Book of Judges 1:16. The Druze people of today trace their ancestry to Yitrō.

[39] 2:20 "let him eat with us" – Yitrō and his family were kind and generous, which stood in stark contrast to the nature of the typical resident of Midyan. Mōshe and Yitrō had similar ethics and dispositions.

[40] 2:22 "Gârshōm" – Gârshōm is a composite of two Hebrew words:
gâr is the Hebrew word for stranger.
shōm is the Hebrew word for there.
Literally, *gârshōm* can be taken to mean: I am a stranger there.
This name is differnt than that of Gârshōn, who was one of the sons of Lāvē (Levi) (see verse 6:16).

[41] 2:23 "king of Egypt passed away" – Tōra does not provide date information for most of the years that the Jewish people were enslaved. As shown in Table 2, there were a succession of many Pharaohs from the time Mōshe escaped Egypt until he returns. Assuming the latest of the successions, Ramesses I passed away in 1290 BCE, which is 135 years after slavery had started. Seti I took the throne, and about 7 years later, Mōshe returns and confronts Pharaoh. Interestingly, Pharaoh lives for only about another 3 years after the Exodus. Then Ramesses II, the great builder of Egypt (Make Egypt Great Again) becomes king and goes about restoring Egypt to its former glory before the Ten Plagues reeked havoc on Egyptian society.

[42] 2:24 "Avraham" - G-d had communicated a special prophecy about slavery and release from slavery during the Covenant of the Pieces (Brāshēt 15:14). In Brāshēt 17:8 G-d solemnly promises Avraham that his descendants will inherit the land of Israel forever. In Brāshēt 22:17, G-d tells Avraham that his descendants will be as numerous as the stars.

[43] 2:24 "Yiẑĥak" – In Brāshēt 26:3-4, G-d solemnly promises Yiẑĥak that his descendants will be a numerous as the stars and the Jewish people will

inherit the land of Israel.

[44] 2:24 "Yaakōv" – Brāshēt verses 28:13 and 35:12 state that all the solemn promises that G-d made to Avraham and Yiẑhak were transferred to Yaakōv, the ancestor specifically of the Jewish people. G-d specifies to Yaakōv that the land of Israel belongs to the Jewish people

Shimōt - Section 4   - 15 verses

THE BURNING BUSH

1581 48 3:1 Mōshe (Moses) was shepherding the flock of Yitrō (Jethro).[45]

He led the flock to a far end of the wilderness and came to the mountain of G-d,[46] namely, Ĥōrev.[47]

1582 49 3:2 A divine agent[48] appeared to him in a flame in a bush.

Mōshe saw that the bush was on fire but the bush did not burn up.[49]

1583 50 3:3 Mōshe said:

"I will go over to this wondrous sight and see how it is possible for this bush not to burn up." [50]

G-D REVEALS HIMSELF TO MŌSHE

1584 51 3:4 G-d communicated[51] to Mōshe from the bush as follows:

"Mōshe, Mōshe."

Mōshe responded:

"Here I am." [52]

1585 52 3:5 G-d communicated:

"Do not come closer.

"Take off your sandals because the ground upon which you stand is holy.

1586 53 3:6 "I am the G-d of your ancestors -

of Avraham (Abraham),

of Yiźĥak (Isaac), and

of Yaakōv (Jacob = Israel)." [53]

Mōshe hid his face because he was afraid to look at G-d's glory.

1587 54 3:7 G-d communicated:

"I have acknowledged the suffering of My people – the Jewish people - who are in Egypt.

"I have heard their cry that is due to the cruelty of their taskmasters, and I understand their pain.

Shimōt - Section 4 - continued

Land of Milk and Honey
1588 55 3:8 "I have revealed Myself.
"And will now begin to save them from slavery in Egypt, and I will bring them to a land[54] that is flowing with milk and honey.[55]
"This is the land of the peoples[56] of
Kinaan (Canaanites),
Ĥāt (Hittites),
Emôr (Amorites),
Pirēz,
Ĥēv (Hivites),
and Yivūs."
1589 56 3:9 "I accept the prayer[57] and the repentance[58] of the Jewish people.

G-D APPOINTS MŌSHE TO CONFRONT PHARAOH AND LEAD THE JEWISH PEOPLE
1590 57 3:10 "I will send you[59] to Pharaoh so you can lead the Jewish people out of Egypt."

Mōshe's Negative Response 1: Do I Have the Ability To Succeed?

Mōshe's Negative Response 2: Are the Jewish People Worthy?
1591 58 3:11 Mōshe said to G-d:
"Who am I to appear to Pharaoh?
"And who am I to lead the Jewish people out of Egypt."

G-D'S ANSWER 1: I WILL BE WITH YOU

G-D'S ANSWER 2: JEWISH PEOPLE WILL BECOME WORTHY
1592 59 3:12 G-d responded:
"I will be with you.
"Once you have led the Jewish people out of Egypt, they will prove themselves worthy of redemption,[60] and you will serve G-d on this mountain." [61]

Shimōt - Section 4 - continued

Mōshe's Negative Response 3: Why Should The Jewish People Believe Me?

1593 60 3:13 Mōshe said to G-d:
"When I come to the Jewish people and inform them:
'The G-d of your fathers has sent me to you.'
"They will interrogate me as to my validity by asking me:
'What is G-d's name?'
"How should I reply?"

G-d's Answer 3: The Password

1594 61 3:14 G-d responded:
"I Am Who I Am"
G-d communicated:
"You should tell the Jewish people:
'I Am has appointed me to lead you.' "

G-d's Concealed Name

1595 62 3:15 G-d communicated to Mōshe:
"Say to the Jewish people:
'G-d,[62] the G-d of your ancestors – of Avraham, of Yiźĥak, and of Yaakōv has sent me to you.
'This is My concealed name.' [63]

Shimōt - Section 4 – Study Notes

---

[45] 3:1 "Yitrō" - He is Mōshe's father-in-law (see 2:21 and the note on 2:18).

[46] 3:1 "mountain of G-d" – At first, Mōshe did not know that this mountain is special. But once he experienced divine revelation here, he knew that it is the mountain of G-d. G-d drew Aharōn toward this mountain to meet Mōshe (verse 4:27), where Mōshe told Aharōn that this is the mountain of G-d (4:28). After the Jewish people left Egypt and traveled, Mōshe and Aharōn knew it as the mountain of G-d, as it is so described in verses 18:5 and 24:13.

An interesting fact is that there was a river that flowed from that mountain, as stated in Bamidbar (Numbers) 9:21. See note on verse 32:20.

[47] 3:1 "Ĥōrev" – There are numerous opinions as to this name, including:
    a. Ibn Ezra: Ĥōrev is another name for Mount Sēnī (Sinai),
    or b. Ĥōrev is a sister mountain to Mount Sēnī,
    or c. Ramban: Ĥōrev is the large region within which Mount Sēnī is located.

Bamidbar verses 33:5-15 list the stops that the Jewish people made when traveling from Egypt to Israel. Mount Sēnī is the eleventh stop. The arrival of the Jewish people at Sēnī is recorded in Shimōt 18:3, where it is called the mountain of G-d. Shimōt 19:1 explicitly calls it Mount Sēnī. Mōshe calls it Ĥōrev when reviewing their history in Divarim (Deuteronomy) 5:2.

Mount Sēnī is located toward the south of the Sinai Peninsula, midway east-west between the Gulf of Suez and the Gulf of Aqaba (see map of Israel. Also see map in Kaplan, 1981, p. 333).

[48] 3:2 "divine agent" – Usually translated as an angel. At first Mōshe experiences an agent of G-d because G-d did not want to reveal His Glory immediately, in order not to frighten Mōshe. After Mōshe approaches the bush, G-d communicates with him directly. Thus, Mōshe experienced the full divine glory of G-d, and saw how qualitatively greater it is compared to a "mere" divine agent. This has a bearing on later events and Mōshe's

reaction to them.

Verse 13:21 states that G-d created a cloud pillar and a column of fire when the Jewish people travelled from Egypt. Verse 14:19 states that G-d appointed a divine agent to relocate the cloud pillar to be a separation between the Jewish people and the oncoming Egyptian army.
Later, this experience motivated Mōshe to lobby against settling for a divine agent to lead the Jewish people. When the Jewish people are in the wilderness, G-d informs Mōshe that, instead of G-d leading them directly, an agent will lead them (23:20-23). G-d informs Mōshe that having an agent is a good thing because now, the agent to be appointed will not destroy people the way G-d Himself would if the people sin (32:34 and 33:2-3). But Mōshe expresses dissatisfaction with having a mere agent (33:12) and G-d agrees to imbue the agent with some of His divine glory (33:14). Yet Mōshe states that such an agent will not possess enough divine glory to make it clear to the world that the Jewish people are not merely conventionally conquering the land of Israel, and that he, Mōshe, is not just an ordinary leader (33:15). Finally, Mōshe asks again (34:9) and G-d agrees to lead the Jewish people Himself (34:10).

[49] 3:2 "the bush was on fire but did not burn up" – The burning bush symbolizes the Jewish people who will suffer terrible pain and injustice throughout history, but will survive.

[50] 3:3 "how it is possible for this bush not to burn up." – Mōshe wanted to know how the Jewish people survive. G-d revealed Himself through a burning bush to communicate that the Jewish people survive because
a) He is with them
and b) each Jewish person has a fierce (firey) dedication to G-d.

[51] 3:4 "communicated" - G-d is in no way corporeal. Tōra expresses actions of G-d in terms that people can understand. But even the verb "communicated" instead of "spoke" is more physical than the actual spirituality of G-d.

[52] 3:4 "Here I am" – Mōshe is thus declaring that he is ready for whatever G-d asks of him. Great people answer the call of G-d. So too, Avraham responded to G-d with "Here I am" in Brāshēt (Genesis) 22:1. Also, Yōsef (Joseph) responded to his father with "Here I am" (Brāshēt 37:13).

[53] 3:6 "G-d of your ancestors: of Avraham, of Yiẑhak, and of Yaakōv" - G-d mentioned them again in verse 6:3 (portion Vaāra, section 1) after Mōshe experiences a major setback in his mission.

[54] 3:8 "land" - G-d specifically promised Yaakōv that he and his descendants, the Jewish people, are given the land of Israel, as stated in Brāshēt 28:13. See Essay 6 for details about the promise of the land of Israel to the Jewish people. (Also see note on verse 3:17 for a list of all 12 tribal peoples who had resided in the land of Israel.)

[55] 3:8 "flowing with milk and honey" –
Siforno: milk - The land supports milk-producing cattle. Honey means food.
Ramban: The land is good for growing produce that has sweet juices and drink.
See Essay 6 concerning how the land of Israel flows with milk and honey.

[56] 3:8 "peoples" – See also verses 23:23 and 33:2 where these six nations are listed. To see where, geographically, these various original peoples lived in relation to the land of Israel, see Kaplan, 1981, p.181. There are 10 peoples mentioned to Avraham in Brāshēt 15:19. There are 12 tribal nations mentioned in various verses, as listed in the note on verse 3:17.

[57] 3:9 "prayer" – This is the meaning according to Ibn Ezra. Prayer is the manner in which people address their requests to G-d, thus acknowledging that G-d is all-powerful and rules the universe. See Essay 7 for details about the nature of prayer.

[58] 3:9 "repentance" – This is the meaning according to Siforno. Commentators explain that at this point in time people started to hear the cries and prayers of their fellow slaves. This demonstrated repentance and now the Jewish people deserved to be saved.

[59] 3:10 "send you" – G-d doesn't give Mōshe the command to actually go to Egypt until verse 4:19. Mōshe and his brother confront Pharaoh for the first time in verse 5:1. According to chronology as shown in Table 2, this is King Seti I.

[60] 3:12 "worthy of redemption" – This is the understanding of Siforno.

[61] 3:12 "you will serve G-d on this mountain" – This is how Mōshe knew to tell the king that they must have a 3-days journey to serve G-d (verse 5:3).

[62] 3:15 "G-d" – Siforno: Here, the Tetragrammatan name of G-d is used. By invoking this special name of G-d, the Jewish people will know that Mōshe is a true agent of G-d. Today, no one knows the actual pronunciation of the Tetragrammatan. Holy books vocalize the Tetragrammatan with the vowels of G-d's name that means "Master." But this has nothing to do with how the Tetragrammatan is pronounced. Therefore, any attempt to infer the pronunciation of the Tetragrammatan is futile.

[63] 3:15 "concealed name" – Rashē: This name is not pronounced as written. Yōsef (Joseph) had told his brothers the pronunciation of this special name of G-d and that a savior would come (Brāshēt 50:24) and pronounce that name. This information had been handed down to the elders.

Shimōt - Section 5   - 24 verses

G-d Commands Mōshe To Convene the Jewish Leaders To Address Pharaoh

1596 63 3:16 "When you arrive in Egypt, convene the elders[64] of the Jewish people and inform them:

'G-d, the G-d of your ancestors, Avraham (Abraham), Yiźĥak (Isaac), and Yaakōv (Jacob = Israel), had appeared to me and communicated:

"I have remembered you and I have seen what has been perpetrated against you in Egypt.

1597 64 3:17 "I had told the Jewish people:[65]

'I will release you from the pain you will suffer in Egypt and I will lead you to the land of Israel [66] which is flowing with milk and honey.' [67]

1598 65 3:18 "The Jewish people will believe you.

"You and the elders should present yourselves to the king of Egypt and tell him:

'G-d of the Jewish people has revealed Himself to us.

'Please allow us to travel for three days[68] into the wilderness so that we can offer to G-d.'

Pharaoh Will Not Give Permission Unless He Is Pressured

1599 66 3:19 "I know that the king will not give you permission unless he is pressured to do so.[69]

G-d Plans To Pressure Pharaoh

1600 67 3:20 "I plan to punish Egypt with My wonders.[70]

The People of Egypt Will Give Their Valuables To The Jewish People

1601 68 3:21 "I will cause the people of Egypt to like you.[71]

"Therefore, when you do leave Egypt, you will not go out empty-handed.

Shimōt - Section 5 – continued

1602 69 3:22 "Each Jewish woman will ask her neighbors[72] for silver, gold, and clothes.
    "You will clothe your children with those garments.
    "You will be taking[73] with you much of the riches of Egypt."

MŌSHE'S NEGATIVE RESPONSE 4: JEWISH PEOPLE WILL DOUBT ME AS PROPHET

1603 70 4:1 Mōshe (Moses) responded:
    "But the Jewish people will not listen to me because they will claim:
        'G-d never appeared to you.' "[74]

G-D'S ANSWER 4: WONDROUS ACTS

G-d Transforms Mōshe's Staff Into A Snake

1604 71 4:2 G-d responded to him:
    "What is in your hand?"
    Mōshe answered:
    "A shepherd's staff."[75]
1605 72 4:3 G-d communicated to him:
    "Throw it to the ground."
    Mōshe threw it onto the ground and the staff turned into a snake.
    Mōshe ran away in fear.

G-d Transforms The Snake Back To A Staff

1606 73 4:4 G-d communicated to Mōshe:
    "Extend your arm and grab the snake by its tail."
    Mōshe did so, and it turned back into his staff.
1607 74 4:5 G-d communicated:
    "This shows that the Jewish people will believe[76] that you[77] are a true agent of G-d."

Shimōt - Section 5 – continued

G-d Turns The Skin Of Mōshe's Hand White

1608 75 4:6 G-d communicated further:
"Place your hand on your chest."
Mōshe did so.
When he moved his hand off his chest, his hand was white.[78]

G-d Turns The Skin Of Mōshe's Hand Back To Normal

1609 76 4:7 G-d communicated:
"Place your hand back on your chest."
Mōshe did so.
When he moved it off, his hand was back to its normal color.

G-d Communicates About Turning Water To Blood

1610 77 4:8 G-d communicated:
"If the Jewish people don't respond to the snake, they will respond[79] to the white skin.
1611 78 4:9 "If they do not respond to either of these, then pour river water onto land and that water will turn to blood."

Mōshe's Negative Response 5: I Am Not A Fluent Eloquent Speaker

1612 79 4:10 Mōshe protested:
"But I am not an orator.
"I am not able to speak fluently and clearly.[80]
"And I am not able to think up appropriate sentences when confronted with difficult and demanding circumstances."

Shimōt - Section 5 – continued

G-D'S ANSWER 5: G-D PROMISES TO GUIDE MŌSHE

1613 80 4:11 G-d responded:

"Who gives people the power of eloquent speech?"

"Who causes a person to be unable to speak, or unable to hear, or unable to see?"

"Doesn't G-d have these powers?"

1614 81 4:12 "I will guide you[81] as to what to say."

MŌSHE'S NEGATIVE RESPONSE 6: APPOINT SOMEONE ELSE

1615 82 4:13 Mōshe said:

"Please appoint someone else[82] who is truly worthy."

G-D BECOMES ANGRY WITH MŌSHE; AHARŌN WILL DO THE SPEAKING

1616 83 4:14 G-d became angry with Mōshe:

"Your brother Aharōn is a good speaker.[83]

"He will come to meet you.

"He will be happy to see you.

1617 84 4:15 "You will tell him what to say.

"I will guide both of you in speech and in action.

1618 85 4:16 "Aharōn will be your spokesman to the people and you will be G-d's agent[84] to him.

1619 86 4:17 "Use your staff whenever you perform wonders."

Shimōt - Section 5 – Study Notes

---

[64] 3:16 "convene the elders" – Mōshe and Aharōn do this in verse 4:29.

[65] 3:17 "I had told the Jewish people" – In Brāshēt (Genesis) 48:21, Yaakōv (Jacob = Israel) tells his son Yōsef (Joseph) that G-d will bring the Jewish people out of Egypt. In Brāshēt 50:24, Yōsef informs his brothers of this. Throughout the years in exile, the Jewish elders transmitted this information to the next generation.

[66] 3:17 "land of Israel" – Verse 3:8 identifies it as the land of the peoples of
1. Kinaan (Canaan),
2. Emôr (Amorites),
3. Ĥet (Hittites),
4. Ĥiv (Hivites),
5. Pirēz (Perizites), and
6. Yivūs (Jebusites).
In addition, other tribal nations that lived in the land of Israel were:
7. Gêrgash (Brāshēt 15:19),
8. Kadmōn (Brāshēt 15:19),
9. Ken (stated in Brāshēt 15:19),
10. Kinēz (Brāshēt 15:19),
11. Rifaim (Brāshēt 15:19), and
12. Plishtim (Philistines) (Brāshēt 26:1).

[67] 3:17 "milk and honey" – See note on verse 3:8 and Essay 6.

[68] 3:18 "three days" – Although Mōshe, Aharōn and the Jewish elders know that the ultimate plan is for the Jewish people to emigrate to the land of Israel, throughout the negotiations with Pharaoh, Mōshe asks only for a 3-day journey. A 3-day journey, plus a day to worship G-d, and a 3-day journey back means that the Jewish people will be away for a week. Initially, Pharaoh is concerned about the lost productivity. But the fact is, once the plagues start, the Jewish people were no longer forced to perform slave labor. Pharaoh eventually states that he will allow some of the Jewish people to leave. This shows that Pharaoh realizes that once the entire Jewish people would leave, they probably would never come back.

The verses that deal with the negotiations between Mōshe and Pharaoh regading the Jewish people leaving Egypt are:
Verse 5:1 & 3 Mōshe asks that Pharaoh allow the Jewish people to travel for 3 days and have a holy day to G-d.
Verse 7:16 Mōshe asks Pharaoh to allow the Jewish people to worship G-d.
Verse 7:26 Mōshe asks Pharaoh to allow the Jewish people to worship G-d.
Verse 8:4 Pharaoh promises to allow the Jewish people to offer offerings.
Verse 8:16 Mōshe asks Pharaoh to allow the Jewish people to worship G-d.
Verse 8:21 Pharaoh wants the Jewish people to worship while in Egypt.
Verse 9:13 Mōshe asks Pharaoh to allow the Jewish people to worship G-d.
Verse 9:17 Mōshe asks Pharaoh: Will you not allow the Jewish people to leave?
Verse 10:3 Mōshe and Aharōn tell Pharaoh to allow the people to leave and worship.
Verse 10:8 Pharaoh will allow the Jewish men to leave and worship G-d.
Verse 10:24 Pharaoh will allow them to leave and worship but not with their livestock.

[69] 3:19 "unless he is pressured" – Mōshe is told this again in 4:21. We see that this is true in verse 5:2. Yet, in verses 5:22-23, Mōshe is astonished due to the extraordinary harshness of the punishment toward the Jewish people by Pharaoh. Later, in verse 7:3, G-d communicates that He will make the heart of Pharaoh stubborn. See the note on verse 7:3 for a list of all instances where Pharaoh's heart is stubborn.

[70] 3:20 "I plan to punish Egypt with My wonders." – G-d states this also in verse 6:1, as an answer to Mōshe; and states it again in verse 7:4.

[71] 3:21 "to like you" – This occurs in verses 11:3 and 12:36.

[72] 3:22 "ask neighbors" – The people are told to ask this in verse 11:2, although that verse does not mention clothes. During the exodus, they did ask, as is stated in verse 12:35.

[73] 3:22 "you will be taking" – The Jewish people are told to ask for silver, gold, and jewels in verse 11:2. This occurred, and is stated in verse 12:36 in the active tense, i.e., "the people of Egypt gave them." G-d had told this

to Avraham in Brāshēt (Genesis) 15:14.

[74] 4:1 "G-d never appeared to you" – Even if Mōshe knows G-d's special name, he still must prove that he is a prophet. In fact, the elders did require the wonders to be performed for them (verse 4:30).

[75] 4:2 "staff" – His ordinary shepherd's staff becomes an object of special interest. G-d wants Mōshe to understand that He can perform miracles and wonders without any special props, and make it seem as if it being done through an object. So too, G-d is utilizing Mōshe, an ethical quiet person, to be the greatest leader.

The following are verses that reference Mōshe' staff (and those that conspicuously do not mention the staff):

Verse 4:3 the staff turns into a snake.

Verse 4:4 staff/snake turns back into a staff.

Verse 4:17 G-d directs him to use the staff to perform wonders.

Verse 4:20 Mōshe held the staff as he walked.

Verse 7:9 G-d tells Mōshe to tell Aharōn to throw down the staff.

Verse 7:10 Aharōn throws down the staff and it becomes a snake.

Verse 7:15 G-d tells Mōshe to have his staff with him when he goes to the Nile to meet the king.

Verse 7:17 G-d tells Mōshe to tell the king that the water will turn to blood when he hits the water with his staff.

Verse 7:19 G-d tells Mōshe to tell Aharōn to motion the staff over the Nile.

Verse 7:20 Aharōn hits the Nile with the staff to effect the first plague, blood.

Verse 8:1 G-d tells Mōshe to tell Aharōn to motion the staff over the rivers to cause plague 2, frogs.

Verse 8:12 G-d tells Mōshe to tell Aharōn to hit the ground with the staff to cause plague 3, lice.

For plagues 4 & 5, swarms & fatal animal disease, G-d caused them to happen after Mōshe had warned the king. The staff is not utilized.

For plague 6, Mōshe tossed soot into the air (verses 9:8 & 10). The staff is not utilized.

Verse 9:23 Mōshe raised his staff toward the sky and caused plague 7, hail. Note that in verse 9:22, G-d had instructed Mōshe to raise his hand (not the staff).

Note that for plague 8, G-d told Mōshe to raise his hands (10:12), which he did (10:13).

Note that for plague 9, G-d told Mōshe to raise his hands (10:21), which he did (10:22).

Note that the staff plays no part in the last plague.

Verse 14:16 G-d told Mōshe to raise his staff over the Reed Sea. Note that verse 14:21 states that Mōshe raised his hands over the sea.

Verse 14:26 G-d told Mōshe to raise his hand so the sea would return and drown the attacking Egyptian army.

Verse 17:5 G-d tells Mōshe to hit the rock with his staff and water will flow out.

Verse 17:9 Mōshe held his staff as Joshua battled Amalāk.

In Bamidbar (Numbers) 17:16, G-d instructs each tribe to take a staff. A leader of each tribe wrote the name of his tribe on the staff (see Kaplan, 1981, p. 749). The staff that Aharōn writes on is not Mōshe's special staff.

Bamidbar 20:7-11 – After the passing of Miryam (Miriam) there was no water to drink. G-d instructs Mōshe to hold his staff and speak to the rock. Instead, Mōshe hits the rock with his staff.

[76] 4:5 "the Jewish people will believe" – Ramban: G-d showed Mōshe that his refusal to believe that the Jewish people will believe, is groundless slander. Slander is symbolized by a snake.

[77] 4:5 "you" – Mōshe told everything to Aharōn and gave him the knowledge to perform the wonders. Verse 4:30 states that it was Aharōn who told the information to the elders and performed the wonders for the elders. (See verses 4:10, 4:16 and 6:9.)

[78] 4:6 "his hand was white" – Ramban: G-d punished Mōshe with this condition, which Tōra, and especially the traditional commentaries, connect with slanderous statements, telling lies, and/or prideful speech. See Bamidbar 12:1-15, where Miryam, Mōshe's sister, is punished with white skin for 7 days because she spoke disparagingly about Mōshe. Laws of this spiritual malady are specified in Vayikra (Leviticus) chapters 13 and 14.

[79] 4:8 "they will respond" – In verse 4:30, Aharōn told the elders the

information and performed some or all of the wonders. This fact indicates that they in fact did not believe until they saw wonders.

[80] 4:10 "speak fluently and clearly" – At first, the verses indicate that Aharōn did the public speaking, although, eventually, Mōshe gained confidence and fluency. Verse 6:9 is the first time that Mōshe spoke directly to an audience, namely, the Jewish leaders. However, even by verses 6:12 and 6:30, Mōshe still tells G-d that he is not a fluent speaker.

[81] 4:12 "I will guide you" – G-d intends to improve Mōshe's speaking ability - and this is what happens - eventually. Once the interactions between Mōshe and Pharaoh get underway, along with the interactions between Mōshe and the Jewish people (after verse 4:30), the Tōra text states that Mōshe did most of the speaking. But at first Mōshe had difficulties expressing himself, as stated in verse 6:30 where Mōshe states that he cannot speak well, and G-d states in 7:1 that Aharōn will do the speaking. One possibility is that Mōshe was overwhelmed by the enormity of transmitting the word of G-d.

[82] 4:13 "please appoint someone else" – When Mōshe experiences a major setback at the start of his interactions with the king, this deep-seated reluctance to be a leader re-emerges, as he asks in verse 5:22 "why did You appoint me?"

[83] 4:14 "Aharōn is a good speaker" – G-d's anger results in the fact that G-d does not initially improve Mōshe's speaking ability, and instead appoints Aharōn as the speaker. Once Mōshe became acclimated to his role and to his relationship to G-d, G-d improved his speaking ability as He had originally promised.

[84] 4:16 "Aharōn . . . spokesman . . . you . . . agent" – This does occur as stated in verses 4:30 and 7:2. But throughout the rest of Tōra, it appears that Mōshe did in fact overcome his speech problems and did his own speaking

Shimōt - Section 6   - 14 verses

MŌSHE ASKS FOR, AND RECEIVES, PERMISSION FROM YITRŌ TO RETURN TO EGYPT

1620 87 4:18 Mōshe (Moses) returned to Yitrō (Jethro) and told him:
"Please allow me[85] to return to my people who are in Egypt."
Yitrō answered:
"Go in peace."

1621 88 4:19 G-d communicated to Mōshe while he was still in the land of Midyan:
"Return to Egypt[86] because all the people who wanted to execute you are no longer alive." [87]

1622 89 4:20 Mōshe prepared his pregnant wife and their son[88] for travel and they set out toward Egypt.
Mōshe held his staff[89] as he walked.

1623 90 4:21 G-d communicated to Mōshe:
"When you confront Pharaoh, you are permitted to perform[90] the wonders that I have shown you.
"I plan for Pharaoh to refuse[91] to allow the Jewish people to leave.

1624 91 4:22 "Tell Pharaoh:
'G-d proclaims to you:
"The Jewish people are My favorite people.
"They are like My firstborn child.

1625 92 4:23 "Allow My people to travel and offer offerings to Me.
"If you refuse, I will execute your first born[92] children." ' "

ŻĒPŌRA CIRCUMCISES THEIR NEWBORN SON

1626 93 4:24 When Mōshe and his family had stopped at an inn, G-d caused Mōshe to be ill.[93]

1627 94 4:25 Żēpōra used a flint knife to perform the circumcision.[94]
She showed her husband the foreskin and said:
"Now we have complied with the law of circumcision." [95]

1628 95 4:26 Żēpōra said:
"We have fulfilled the commandment of circumcision."

Shimōt - Section 6 - continued

AHARŌN MEETS MŌSHE AT THE MOUNTAIN OF G-D

1629 96 4:27 G-d communicated to Aharōn (Aaron): "Travel into the wilderness so you can meet your brother Mōshe." Aharōn met Mōshe at the mountain of G-d,[96] and he kissed him

MŌSHE RELATES G-D'S COMMANDS TO AHARŌN

1630 97 4:28 Mōshe told Aharōn everything that G-d had communicated to him and had shown to him.[97]

MŌSHE AND AHARŌN CONVENE THE JEWISH LEADERS

1631 98 4:29 Mōshe and Aharōn convened the Jewish leaders.

AHARŌN PERFORMS THE WONDERS FOR THE JEWISH LEADERS

1632 99 4:30 Aharōn told them all the instructions of G-d, and he performed [98] the wonders for them.

1633 100 4:31 The Jewish people heard about this and they believed [99] that G-d acknowledged their suffering.

The Jewish people bowed and prayed.[100]

Shimōt - Section 6 – Study Notes

[85] 4:18 "please allow me" – Mōshe felt that he must act in a grateful way and be respectful to his father-in-law who helped him in time of need. Even a direct divine command does not release a person from courtesy to others.

The next time Yitrō is mentioned is verse 18:1 (Portion Yitrō), when Tōra states that Yitrō heard qbout G-d and Mōshe leading the Jewish people out of Egypt.

Avraham also displayed a similar respectful behavior when he interrupted his conversation with G-d in order to attend to travelers (Brāshēt (Genesis) 18:2).

[86] 4:19 "return to Egypt" – This is the actual directive to travel. The previous lengthy conversation between Mōshe and G-d (verses 3:10-22), established the objectives and expectations.

[87] "are no longer alive" – Table 2 shows that by this time, the eighteenth dynasty of Egypt had ended and the nineteenth dynasty had recently started. All the edicts and decrees of the past dynasty were null and void. There was no longer an order for Mōshe's arrest and execution.

[88] 4:20 "wife and son" – Taking a young family on an arduous journey is not a good idea, and G-d had not mentioned doing so. Verse 18:5 states that Źēpōra and their two sons traveled back to Mōshe with Yitrō from Midyan to Mt. Sēnī (Sinai) where the Jewish people were encamped. There is a midrash that explains that when Mōshe met Aharōn (4:27), Aharōn convinced him that it is not a good idea to bring a family into a slavery situation. At that point Źēpōra and their two sons (see note on verse 4:24) traveled back to her father.

[89] 4:20 "held his staff" – G-d had directed Mōshe to utilize his staff when performing miracles and wonders (verse 4:17). When Aharōn performed the wonders, Mōshe gave the staff to him. However, as becomes apparent, the staff had no special power in and of itself. See note on 4:2 for the many times the staff is utilized.

[90] 4:21 "you are permitted to perform . . ." – Based on Rashē: G-d had told Mōshe to perform these wonders to the Jewish elders so they will believe

he is the agent of G-d. Now G-d communicates to Mōshe that if he feels the need, he can perform them in order to convince Pharaoh. Note that in this same statement, G-d informs Mōshe that performing these wonders will not make a difference in the king's attitude.

[91] 4:21 "I plan to have Pharaoh refuse" – G-d mentioned this to Mōshe earlier in verse 3:19. See note on verse 7:3 for a list of all instances where Pharaoh is stubborn.

[92] 4:23 "execute your first born" – This becomes the final plague (12:29).

[93] 4:24 "caused Mōshe to be ill" – Żēpōra had given birth during the journey. The baby was now 8 days old.
   Ibn Ezra: Mōshe knew that if a baby is not well 8 days after he is born, the circumcision must be delayed until the child is well. He thought that allowing a delay applies also when a child is traveling, so he continued to travel on the 8th day. But his assumption is wrong. G-d appeared, thus causing them to stop traveling and stay at an inn.
   The name of this baby is not mentioned until verse 18:4, when Yitrō brings them to Mōshe at Mount Sinai. He was named Elēezer.

[94] 4:25 "circumcision" – Circumcision was first commanded to Avraham in Brāshēt (Genesis) verse 17:10. His first son, Yishmael was circumcised at that time. Avraham circumcised Yiẑhak (Isaac) when he was 8 days old (Brāshēt 21:4). Brāshēt 17:27 states that all men in Avraham's household underwent circumcision. This includes his followers, workers, and the rest of Avraham's sons. In Brāshēt 34:17, the sons of Yaakōv explain that an uncircumcised man cannot marry into their family.
   As sons of Avraham, Midyan, the ancestort of Yitrō, and the other sons of Kitūra (Brāshēt 25:2) were circumcised. This explains why Żēpōra knew how to perform circumcision.

[95] 4:25 "complied with the law of circumcision" – This is the interpretation of Ibn Ezra.

[96] 4:27 "mountain of G-d" – It is first called Mountain of G-d in verse 3:1, where G-d reveals Himself in a burning bush. G-d drew Aharōn toward this

mountain. It is also called Mountain of G-d in verse 18:5 when the Jewish people encamp for the divine revelation.

[97] 4:28 "shown to him" – Mōshe told his brother about the burning bush, which established the fact that Mount Sinai is the mountain of G-d.

[98] 4:30 "told . . . performed" – As had been stated in 3:16.

[99] 4:31 "believed" – As G-d had stated in 4:8.

[100] 4:31 "bowed and prayed" – See note on verse 3:9.

Shimōt - Section 7   - 21 + 3 verses

Mōshe and Aharōn State Their Request To Pharaoh

1634 101 5:1 Mōshe (Moses) and Aharōn (Aaron) appeared before Pharaoh[101] and said to him:

"G-d commands:

'Let My people travel into the wilderness[102] and celebrate a holy day for Me.'"

Pharaoh Refuses

1635 102 5:2 Pharaoh responded:

"Who is this G-d that I should listen to Him and allow the Jewish people to go?

"I do not know of any such deity and I will not allow Jewish people to leave." [103]

1636 103 5:3 Mōshe and Aharōn said:

"The G-d of the Jewish people has instructed us.

"We must take a 3-day journey[104] into the wilderness and offer to G-d.

"If we do not, G-d will cause us to become sick[105] or worse."

1637 104 5:4 The king of Egypt said:

"How dare you, Mōshe and Aharōn, cause the people to reduce their labor output.

"You should mind your own business."

1638 105 5:5 Pharaoh said:

"There are many Jewish laborers who work for me.

"Will you cause me such a great loss by freeing them from their work?"

Pharaoh Increases The Burdens Of The Jewish People

1639 106 5:6 On that day, Pharaoh commanded the taskmasters and Jewish overseers: [106]

1640 107 5:7 "You will no longer give workers straw for making bricks.

"Jewish workers must find their own straw.

Shimōt - Section 7 - continued

1641 108 5:8 "The required number of bricks each day must still be made by each worker.

"The reason why the Jewish people request:

'Let us offer to our G-d'

"is that they are not working hard enough.

1642 109 5:9 "They must work harder so they will not ask for time off."

1643 110 5:10 The taskmasters and Jewish overseers announced to the people:

"Pharaoh has decreed:

'I will no longer give you straw.

1644 111 5:11 'You must find your own straw.

'But you must still make the required daily number of bricks.'"

1645 112 5:12 Therefore, the Jewish people were forced to spend much time searching all over Egypt for straw.

1646 113 5:13 The taskmasters continually hounded the Jewish people:

"You must produce the same daily number of bricks as before, back when we had provided you with straw."

1647 114 5:14 The overseers, who were Jewish men who had been appointed by the taskmasters, were beaten daily because the Jewish workers were not able to meet their required quota of bricks.

JEWISH OVERSEERS BRING THEIR COMPLAINT TO PHARAOH

1648 115 5:15 The Jewish overseers complained to Pharaoh:

"Why are you being mean to us, your faithful servants?

1649 116 5:16 "We are not given straw, and yet the taskmasters scream at us:

'Make bricks.'

"And we are beaten because the Jewish workers are not able to make enough bricks.

"But the fault is that the taskmasters did not give straw to the Jewish workers." [107]

Shimōt - Section 7 - continued

PHARAOH CONFIRMS HIS EVIL EDICT

1650 117 5:17 Pharaoh responded:
"You have too much time to spare.
"That is why you ask me to have time off to worship G-d.
1651 118 5:18 "Go and do your work.
"You will not be given straw, and yet you must make the full number of bricks every day."
1652 119 5:19 The Jewish overseers now realized that the demand:
"You must produce the same number of bricks every day"
is legally in effect even though they were not provided with straw.

THE OVERSEERS BLAME MŌSHE AND AHARŌN FOR THE TROUBLES OF THE JEWISH PEOPLE

1653 120 5:20 When the Jewish overseers left Pharaoh, they saw Mōshe and Aharōn, who had been standing near the palace.
1654 121 5:21 The overseers said to Mōshe and Aharōn:
"Let G-d evaluate you and judge you because you have caused us to be hated by Pharaoh and his officers[108] such that they are determined to work us to death."

Shimōt – Last Section

MŌSHE ASKS G-D: WHY?

1655 122 5:22 Mōshe spoke to G-d:

"G-d, why have You allowed this evil [109] to happen to Your people? [110]

"Why did You appoint me[111] to free the people?

1656 123 5:23 "Ever since I told Pharaoh Your message, Pharaoh has made things unbearable for the Jewish people.

"You certainly have not saved Your people." [112]

G-D REPLIES: NOW YOU WILL SEE

1657 124 6:1 G-d communicated to Mōshe:

"Now you will see what I will do to Pharaoh.

"He will eventually allow the Jewish people to leave because of severe punishments.[113]

"Eventually he will chase the Jewish people out[114] of his country."

Shimōt - Section 7 – Study Notes

---

[101] 5:1 "appeared to Pharaoh" – G-d had instructed Mōshe to confront Pharaoh in verse 3:10. Verse 7:7 states that at this point in time, Mōshe was 80 and Aharōn was 83 years old.

[102] 5:1 "G-d commands: Let My people travel into the wilderness" – G-d told this to Mōshe in verse 3:18.

[103] 5:2 "I will not allow the Jewish people to leave" – This initial reaction of Pharaoh is expected (see verse 3:19). Only later did G-d cause Pharaoh to continue to refuse even in the face of severe punishments.

[104] 5:3 "3-day journey" – In verse 3:18, this is what G-d instructs Mōshe to request. See note on verse 3:18 for a list of all verses with Mōshe's requests.

[105] 5:3 "cause us to become sick" – Rashē: Actually they meant that Pharaoh will become sick if he does not listen to G-d, but Mōshe and Aharōn decided not to speak disrespectfully to the king.

[106] 5:6 "Jewish overseers" – Previously, in verse 1:11, only gentile taskmasters were set over the Jewish workers. Over time, they forced Jewish men to be the direct masters over their Jewish brothers. This demeaning cruelty was also perpetrated in the Jewish ghettos in Europe during World War II, when the oppressors appointed a Jewish committee, which would have to carry out the cruel orders. And this was even more so in the concentration camps during World War II by having Jewish capos oversee the camp inmates.

[107] 5:16 "taskmasters did not give straw to the Jewish workers" – This is the plain meaning of the verse, as explained by Siforno.

However, Rashē had a version of the Tōra in which one Hebrew word in the text was slightly different such that the translation of this phrase becomes: "the people of Egypt have committed a sin against the Jewish people."

[108] 5:21 "you have caused us to be hated by Pharaoh and his officers" – Much later, when the Jewish people are threatened by Pharaoh's approaching army, some people complain to Mōshe by remembering this incident (verse 14:12).

[109] 5:22 "why have You caused this evil" – Even though in verse 3:19, G-d told Mōshe that Pharaoh will agree only if pressured, this hardship went beyond anyone's imagination.

[110] "5:22 "Jewish people . . . Your people" – Here Mōshe emphasizes that G-d has a responsibility to the Jewish people, and yet the feeling that Mōshe has not warmed to his people persists.

[111] 5:22 "Why did You appoint me" – Mōshe is still uncomfortable with his role, as he had stated before in verses 3:11, 4:10, and 4:13.

[112] 5:23 "You certainly have not saved Your people" – Mōshe still has a distant feeling about his people.
 Note that this is the last verse in chapter 5, but the section as read as part of the shabat services ends on the next verse, the first verse of the next chapter, because Jewish tradition ends the section on the positive hopeful note of the salvation stated by G-d in the next verse. Unfortuneately, there are gentiles who feel that the chosenness of the Jewish people is a thing of the past. In reality, throughout history Jewish people have maintained their connection to G-d. Even during the darkest periods of history, Jewish people have kept faith and their steadfast relationship with G-d has resulted in success. The sages communicate this in the way they interpret and teach Bible and Tōra.

[113] 6:1 "punishments" – As G-d had stated in verse 3:20.

[114] 6:1 "he will chase the Jewish people out" – This occurs in verse 12:31.

Vaāra[115] - Section 1 - 12 verses (Total: 121 verses)

G-D EXPLAINS HIS STRATEGY

1658 125 6:2 G-d communicated[116] to Mōshe (Moses):
"I am G-d.
1659 126 6:3 "I had appeared to Avraham (Abraham), Yiźĥak (Isaac), and Yaakōv (Jacob = Israel)[117] as G-d, but I did not reveal My sacred name to them.
1660 127 6:4 "I made a solemn promise to them that their descendants will own the land on which they were living.
1661 128 6:5 "I have acknowledged the groans of the Jewish people due to their enslavement by the leaders of Egypt.
"And I have remembered my solemn promise.
1662 129 6:6 "Therefore, you should tell the Jewish people:
    a) 'I am G-d and
    b) 'I will [1] free you from the slavery in Egypt,
    c) 'I will [2] save you from the Egyptians,
    d) 'I will [3] redeem you by performing wonders, and
1663 130 6:7   e) 'I will [4] form you into My people
    f) 'and I will be your G-d.
    g) 'And you will know that I am your G-d who freed you from the slavery of Egypt.
1664 131 6:8 h) 'I will [5] bring[118] you to the land that I had promised to Avraham, Yiźĥak, and Yaakōv, and that land will be your inheritance' "

Vaāra - Section 1 - continued

MŌSHE RELATES G-D'S MESSAGE TO THE JEWISH PEOPLE, BUT THEY DO NOT BELIEVE

1665 132 6:9 Mōshe told this to the Jewish people but they did not believe him because they were so upset and because their enslavement was so harsh.

1666 133 6:10 G-d communicated to Mōshe as follows:

1667 134 6:11 "Come and tell Pharaoh, king of Egypt, that he must allow the Jewish people to leave his country."

1668 135 6:12 Mōshe replied to G-d:

"If the Jewish people don't believe, why should Pharaoh listen to me?

"After all, I am not a fluent speaker." [119]

1669 136 6:13 G-d communicated to Mōshe and Aharōn and instructed them as follows:

a. Do not be impatient with the Jewish people, [120]

b. act respectfully to the king, [121]

and c. continue the efforts to free the Jewish people from Egypt.

Vaāra - Section 1 - Study Notes

---

[115] "Vaāra" – The Hebrew word *vaāra* means "I had appeared."

[116] 6:2 "communicated" – G-d is not physical and does not speak the way physical beings do, as explained in the note on verse 3:4.

[117] 6:3 "Avraham, Yiẑhak, and Yaakōv" - G-d had mentioned them previously in verse 3:6.

[118] 6:6-8 "free . . . save . . . redeem . . . form . . . bring" – The sages used these 5 verbs as the basis for the cups of wine at the Pesaĥ (Passover) sāder. Four cups of wine are part of the ceremony, one for each of the first 4 words. The fifth word is the basis for the custom of the cup of Elēyahū (Elijah) the prophet.

[119] 6:12 "not a fluent speaker" – This was Mōshe's negative response 5 during his original encounter with G-d (verse 4:10). And he will state this again in 6:30.

[120] 6:13 "do not be impatient with the Jewish people" – This is the understanding of Ibn Ezra.

[121] 6:13 "act respectfully to the king" – This is the understanding of Midrash Shimōt Raba 7:2 and quoted by Rashē.

Vaāra - Section 2 — 15 verses

Partial Genealogy

Riūvān

1670 137 6:14 The following are family heads of the three oldest sons of Yaakōv (Jacob = Israel):
Sons of Riūvān (Reuben):
Ĥanōĥ,
Palū,
Ĥeźrōn, and
Karmē.

Shimōn

1671 138 6:15 Sons of Shimōn (Simeon):
Yimūâl,
Yamin,
Ōhad,[122]
Yaĥin,
Źōhar,[123] and
Shaūl, whose mother was of the people of Kinaan (Canaan).[124]

Lāvē – Lived To Be 137

1672 139 6:16 Sons of Lāvē (Levi):
Gârshōn,[125]
Kihat,[126] and
Mirarē.[127]
Lāvē lived to be 137 years old.[128]

Gârshōn

1673 140 6:17 Sons of Gârshōn:
Livnē and
Shimē.

Vaāra - Section 2 - continued

Kihat

1674 141 6:18 Sons of Kihat:
    Amram,
    Yiźhar,
    Ĥevrōn,[129] and
    Ūzēâl.
Kihat lived to be 133 years old.

Mirarē

1675 142 6:19 Sons of Mirarē:
    Maĥlē and
    Mūshē.

Amram - lived to be 137

1676 143 6:20 Amram married Yōĥeved, who was his father's relative.[130] Their children were Mōshe[131] (Moses) and Aharōn (Aaron).
Amram lived to be 137 years old.

Yiźhar

1677 144 6:21 Sons of Yiźhar:
    Kōraĥ,[132]
    Nefeg, and
    Ziĥrē.

Ūzēâl

1678 145 6:22 Sons of Ūzēâl:
    Mēshaâl,
    Elźafōn,[133] and
    Sisrē.

Vaāra - Section 2 - continued

Aharōn

1679 146 6:23 Aharōn married Elēsheva.[134]
   Her father is Amēnadav.
   Her brother is Naȟshōn.[135]
   Their sons are:
      Nadav,
      Avēhū,[136]
      Elazar,[137] and
      Ētamar.[138]

Kōraȟ

1680 147 6:24 Sons of Kōraȟ:[139]
   Asêr,
   Elkana, and
   Avēasaf.

Elazar

1681 148 6:25 Elazar married one of the daughters of Pūtēâl.[140]
   Their son is Pinȟas (Phineas).[141]

RECAP: G-D REVEALS HIMSELF

1682 149 6:26 The above mentioed Aharōn and Mōshe are the persons with whom G-d communicated as follows:
   "Lead the Jewish people out of Egypt."
1683 150 6:27 They confronted Pharaoh in order to convince him to allow the Jewish people to leave.
1684 151 6:28 On the day that G-d revealed Himself to Mōshe in
   Egypt[142] . . .

Vaãra - Section 2 - Study Notes

[122] 6:15 "Ōhad" – He is not mentioned later in Bamidbar (Numbers) 26:12, when the Jewish people are in the wilderness.

[123] 6:15 "Źōhar" – Also known as Zerah (Bamidbar 26:13).

[124] 6:15 "Shaūl, whose mother was of the people of Kinaan" – Some commentators feel that this verse indicates that the other sons and grandsons of Yaakōv did not marry women of Kinaan. However, Brāshēt 38:2 states that Yihūda married a woman of Kinaan. Ibn Ezra states that the other brothers married woman from Aramea, Egypt, Edōm, and Midyan.

There were 12 tribal nations that lived in the land of Kinaan, (see Shimōt 3:8 above, and Brāshēt 15:19-21). They are:
1. Kinaan
2. Ken,
3. Kinēz,
4. Kadmōn,
5. Ĥet (Hittites),
6. Prēz,
7. Rifaim,
8. Emôr,
9. Gêrgash, and
10. Yivūsê.
11. Plishtim (Philistines) (Brāshēt 21:32), and
12. Ĥiv (as stated in Shimōt 13:5).

[125] 6:16 "Gârshōn" – His descendants would be tasked to transport tapestries, roof, and entrance curtain of the Tabernacle (Bamidbar 4:22).

A similar name, Gârshōm was the name of one of Mōshe's sons.

[126] 6:16 "Kihat" – His descendants would be tasked to transport the holy box of testimony and the curtain of the holiest area of the Tabernacle (Bamidbar 4:4).

[127] 6:16 – "Mirarē" – His descendants would be tasked to transport the beams, bars, pillars, and bases, etc. of the Tabernacle (Bamidbar 4:29).

[128] 6:16 "Lāvē lived to be 137 years old." - Rashē: He was the last of the brother to pass away.

Pharaoh did not institute their slavery until after he had passed away. Siforno states that slavery did not start until all of Yaakōv's grandchildren passed away (see note on verse 1:8).

[129] 6:18 "Ĥevrōn" – His descendants are not mentioned here. The fact that he had descendants is mentioned in Bamidbar 26:58. Ĥevrōn is also the name of the place were the patriarchs and matriarchs are buried (see Brāshēt 23:2)

[130] 6:20 "father's relative" – The literal words in this verse states that Yōĥeved is Amram's father's sister. Once Tōra was given, it is forbidden for a man to marry his aunt (Vayikra 18:12 and 20:19).

In a similar example, Yaakōv (Jacob) had married sisters, which Tōra forbids (Vayikra 18:18).

Note that the marriage of Yōĥeved to Amram was recorded earlier in verse 2:1, where they are each described merely as being from the tribe of Lāvē.

Rashē notes that if Yōĥeved was Lāvē's daughter, she would have been 130 years old when she gave birth to Mōshe.

[131] 6:20 "Mōshe" – Although Mōshe is listed first, Aharōn was 3 years older than Mōshe (verse 7:7). Also, the verse does not mention that Amram had a daughter Miryam (Miriam).

Although Aharōn's wife and descendants are listed below, Mōshe's are not. We already read that he married Źepōra (4:21). Their firstborn is Gârshōm (4:22). Although the birth of their second child occurs in verse 4:25, his name, Elēezer, is not mentioned until 18:4. Similarly, in Bamidbar chapter 3, it states that it will list the descendants of Aharōn and Mōshe, but goes on to list only the sons of Aharōn. Therefore, it is somewhat interesting when G-d, in verse 32:10, offers to start the Jewish nation over with Mōshe's children.

A possible reason for the omission of Mōshe's descendants is that once he became the greatest prophet, he no longer was a family man on a personal level. The entire nation became his family instead of his own family. This becomes evident in Bamidbar 12:1 where Miryam (Miriam) found out that Mōshe had stopped being intimate with his wife because he was in such close communication with G-d.

Another possible reason why Mōshe's descendants are not mentioned is that at least one of them did not observe the commandments. The Book of Judges (Shōftim) 18:30 states that the grandson of Mōshe, and the children of that grandson, all served as idolatrous priests. Tōra is so pained by this fact that when stating the lineage, the verse states that their ancestor was a man named Menashe. However, everyone knew that the ancestor referred to is Mōshe.

[132] 6:21 "Kōraĥ" – He is the central character in the insurrection (Bamidbar chapter 16).

[133] 6:22 "Mēshaâl, Elźafōn" – They were directed to remove the remains of Nadav and Avēhū from the Tabernacle (see note on Nadav and Avēhū in the next verse).

[134] 6:23 "Elēsheva" – In the Septuagint, the Jewish sages translated her name into Greek as Elizabeth (see Kaplan, 1981, p.285).

[135] 6:23 "Naĥshōn" – He became the leader of his tribe, Yihūda (Bamidbar 1:7). He is an ancestor of King David (Book of Ruth 4:20).

[136] 6:23 "Nadav, Avēhū" – They were fatally punished during the dedication ceremony of the Tabernacle (Vayikra (Book of Leviticus) 10:1-2).

[137] 6:23 "Elazar" – He trained to be the High Priest and took office after his father passed away (Bamidbar 3:32, 4:16, 17:2, and 19:3, 20:26, 26:1, and Divarim (Deuteronomy) 10:2).

[138] 6:23 "Ētamar" – He was put in charge of keeping accounts of the Tabernacle (verse 38:21) and was in charge of managing the transport of the Tabernacle (Bamidbar 4:28, 33, and 7:8).

[139] 6:24 "Sons of Kōraĥ" – His sons did not join their father's insurrection against Mōshe (Bamidbar 26:11). They authored Psalms 42, 44-48, 84, and

87.

[140] 6:25 "Pūtēâl" – There are five main opinions as to who Pūtēâl is:
  1. Ibn Ezra: Pūtēâl is a Jewish man.
  Talmud Tractate Bava Batra 109b:
  or 2. Pūtēâl is another name of Yitrō (Jethro).
      See note on verse 2:18 for other names of Yitrō.
  or 3. Pūtēâl is another name for Yōsef.
  or 4. Pūtēâl is a descendant of Yōsef. Even though Tōra only mentions two children of Yōsef, namely his two sons Menashe and Efrayim (see Brāshēt (Genesis) 41:50-52, 46:20, and 48:1), Yaakōv in Brāshēs 48:6 alludes to the fact that Yōsef had at least one other child born after them.
  or 5. The statement in Bava Basra 109b can mean that the wife of Elazar was descended from both Yitrō and Yōsef.

[141] 6:25 "Pinĥas" – He distinguished himself by stopping idol worship (Bamidbar 25:7). Although he is the son of a priest (a grandson of Aharōn), Pinĥas was born before the priesthood was established and he had not been selected for the priesthood. However, because of his zealous act, G-d elevated him to the priesthood.

[142] 6:28 "On the day that G-d revealed Himself to Mōshe in Egypt" – The revelation described here took place after verse 4:28, once Mōshe was in Egypt. Commentators have diverse opinions as to how this instruction of G-d relates to previous ones. This may have taken place
  a. before their first appearance to Pharaoh,
  or b. after their initial disappointing reaction from Pharaoh,
  or c. at this point in time when their spirits were very low.

Vaāra - Section 3   - 9 verses

1685 152 6:29 . . . G-d communicated to Mōshe (Moses) as follows:
"I am G-d.
"Tell Pharaoh, king of Egypt everything I command you to tell him."
1686 153 6:30 Mōshe responded:
"I am not a fluent speaker.[143]
"Why would Pharaoh listen to me?"

1687 154 7:1 G-d communicated to Mōshe:
"I am appointing you as G-d's agent to Pharaoh.
"Your brother Aharōn (Aaron) will act as the prophet.
1688 155 7:2 "You will speak everything that I command you, and Aharōn will tell it to Pharaoh[144] in the hope that Pharaoh will allow the Jewish people to leave.
1689 156 7:3 "But I will cause Pharaoh to be stubborn[145] and he will refuse[146] so that I can produce many wonders[147] in this country.
1690 157 7:4 "Pharaoh will not listen to you.
"Therefore, I will intervene with great judgments and I will lead My people, the Jewish people, out of Egypt.
1691 158 7:5 "The people of Egypt will acknowledge G-d[148] when I stricken them with wonders, and when I lead the Jewish people out."
1692 159 7:6 Mōshe and Aharōn did exactly as G-d had commanded.

MŌSHE IS 80, AND AHARŌN IS 83 YEARS OLD

1693 160 7:7 Mōshe was 80 years old and Aharōn was 83 years old, when they first confronted Pharaoh.[149]

Vaāra – Section 3 - Study Notes

---

[143] 6:30 "I am not a fluent speaker" – This difficulty had already been addressed when G-d appointed Mōshe at the burning bush (verse 6:30). At this point, Mōshe's concern is that he is not authoritative enough for a king to take him seriously.

[144] 7:2 "You will speak . . . and Aharōn will tell it to Pharaoh" – as G-d had communicated in verse 4:14. Commentators point out that the elders of the tribe of Lāvē (Levi) had been the religious leaders. The king and the people of Egypt respected this and exempted them from labor. Aharōn, a descendant of Lāvē thus had stature even to the king.

[145] 7:3 "I will cause Pharaoh to be stubborn" – G-d has stated this previously in verses 3:19 and 4:21. The word for stubborn can be alternatively translated as obstinate. Tōra text uses the phrase "stubborn heart." The following are the relevant verses:
    7:13 – Pharaoh became stubborn (after seeing the snake)
    7:14 – Pharaoh is stubborn (snake)
    7:22 - Pharaoh was stubborn. (plague 1, blood))
    7:23 - Pharaoh did not change his stubborn approach (plague 1)
    8:11 – Pharaoh made himelf stubborn (plague 2, frogs)
    8:15 – Pharaoh became stubborn. (plague 3, lice)
    8:28 – Pharaoh made himself stubborn yet again. (plague 4, mosquitoes)
    9:7 – The heart of Pharaoh was stubborn.
                   (plague 5, fatal animal disease)
    9:12 – G-d caused Pharaoh to be stubborn. (plague 6, blisters)
    9:34 – Pharaoh made himself stubborn. (plague 7, hail)
    9:35 – Pharaoh was stubborn. (plague 7)
    10:1 – G-d caused Pharaoh and his servants to be stubborn (before plague 8)
    10:20 – G-d caused Pharaoh to be stubborn (plague 8, locusts)
    10:27 – G-d caused Pharaoh to be stubborn (plague 9, darkness)
    11:10 – G-d caused Pharaoh to be stubborn (plague 10, death of firstborn)
    14:4 – G-d states that he will impart boldness in the king so he would chase after the Jewish people.
    14:8 –The king was stubborn, such that he will chase after the Jewish people after he had chased them out.
    14:17 – G-d caused the Egyptian soldiers to be stubborn.

[146] 7:3 "cause Pharaoh to refuse" – In contrast, in verse 3:19 G-d communicates only that Pharaoh <u>will</u> refuse, which will seem to other people as Pharaoh's own choice of action. In verse 5:2 Pharaoh does refuse. At that point Mōshe is astonished (verses 5:22-23) even though G-d had already informed him that he would refuse.

[147] 7:3 "many wonders" – G-d had informed about this in verse 3:20, where it is described as punishment on Egypt.

[148] 7:5 "Egypt will acknowledge G-d" – This is the first time this idea is presented. However, more importantly, it is the Jewish people who make these divine wonders part of their heritage, and recount them to this day.

[149] 7:7 "first confronted Pharaoh" – As was narrated previously, starting with verse 5:1.

Table 2 correlates Tōra years of events with archeological dates of the Egyptian Pharaohs. An interesting fact is that Mōshe returns to Egypt a little after the beginning of Dynasty 19, as verse 4:19 states: "The people who wanted to execute you are no longer alive."

Vaāra - Section 4   - 28 verses

G-D INSTRUCTS: BE PREPARED TO TRANSFORM YOUR STAFF INTO A SNAKE

1694 161 7:8 G-d communicated to Mōshe (Moses) and Aharōn (Aaron) as follows:

1695 162 7:9 "When Pharaoh demands that you show your power, you should tell Aharōn:[150]

'Throw your staff [151] down in front of Pharaoh.'

"It will turn into a snake."

MŌSHE AND AHARŌN CONFRONT PHARAOH

1696 163 7:10 Mōshe and Aharōn came to Pharaoh and followed G-d's instructions.

Aharōn threw down the staff in front of Pharaoh, his advisors and servants.

The staff turned into a snake.

1697 164 7:11 In response, Pharaoh commanded his magicians to do the same, which they did.

AHARŌN'S STAFF SWALLOWS THE OTHER SNAKES

1698 165 7:12 The magicians each threw down their staffs, each of which turned into a snake.[152]

But Aharōn's staff swallowed all the other snakes.[153]

PHARAOH'S HEART IS STUBBORN

1699 166 7:13 Pharaoh became stubborn[154] such that he would not give in to Mōshe and Aharōn.

This is just as G-d had previously communicated.[155]

1700 167 7:14 G-d communicated to Mōshe:

"Pharaoh's heart is stubborn such that he refuses to allow the people to leave.

VAĀRA - SECTION 4 - Continued

PLAGUE 1: BLOOD: G-D INSTRUCTS TO TELL PHARAOH WHY HE IS BEING PUNISHED

1701 168 7:15 "Go to Pharaoh[156] early tomorrow morning[157] when he goes to the river.

"Get to the river bank first.

"Have your staff with you.

1702 169 7:16 "Tell him:

'G-d has appointed me as His agent to tell you:

"Allow My people, the Jewish people, to leave[158] so they can worship Me in the wilderness.

"So far, you have refused to do so."

1703 170 7:17 'G-d communicates:

"You are going to acknowledge G-d because when I hit the river water with this staff, the water will transform into blood.

1704 171 7:18 "The fish in the river will die, the river will stink, and the people of Egypt will wear themselves out trying to dig for pure water." ' "

1705 172 7:19 G-d communicated to Mōshe:

"Tell Aharōn:

'Take the staff and wave the staff across the rivers, streams, pools, and ponds of Egyptians[159] such that they will all transform into blood.

'Even water in buckets will transform into blood.' "

PLAGUE 1: AHARŌN PERFORMS

1706 173 7:20 Mōshe and Aharōn did as G-d commanded.

Aharōn lifted the staff and hit the river water where Pharaoh and his servants[160] could see.

All the waters transformed into blood.

1707 174 7:21 The fish in the river died,

the water stank,

the people of Egypt could not drink the river water,

and there was blood throughout the land.

Vaāra - Section 4 - Continued

Plague 1: Pharaoh Refuses

1708 175 7:22 The magicians of Egypt were able to transform bowls of water into blood.[161]
Pharaoh became stubborn[162] and he did not agree to the request of Mōshe and Aharōn, just as G-d had previously informed Mōshe.

1709 176 7:23 Pharaoh went back to his palace and did not have a change of heart.[163]

1710 177 7:24 All people of Egypt dug wells[164] for water because they could not drink river water.

1711 178 7:25 Seven days after[165] the water had been transformed into blood . . .

Plague 2: Frogs: Mōshe Gives Pharaoh Opportunity

1712 179 7:26 G-d communicated to Mōshe:
"Come to Pharaoh and tell him:
'G-d demands:
"Allow My people to leave[166] so they can worship Me.

1713 180 7:27 "If you refuse, I will fill your land with frogs.

1714 181 7:28 "The rivers will swarm with frogs, which will invade your homes, bedrooms, beds, ovens, and pans.

1715 182 7:29 "The frogs will be on you and on all your people." ' "

Plague 2: Aharōn Performs

1716 183 8:1 G-d communicated to Mōshe:
"Tell Aharōn:
'Wave the staff over the rivers, canals, and pools, and cause frogs to come out of the water and fill the land of Egypt' "

1717 184 8:2 Aharōn did so, such that frogs covered the land.

1718 185 8:3 The magicians reproduced this wonder.[167]

Vaāra - Section 4 - Continued

Plague 2: Pharaoh Promises

1719 186 8:4 Pharaoh sent messengers to bring Mōshe and Aharōn to the palace.
Pharaoh said to them:
"Ask G-d to remove the frogs from me and my people.
"Then I will allow[168] Jewish people to offer offerings to G-d." [169]

1720 187 8:5 Mōshe said to Pharaoh:
"I want you to realize that G-d has absolute power and control.
"When exactly do you want the frogs to die and only be found in the river?"

1721 188 8:6 Pharaoh answered:
"Tomorrow."
Mōshe said:
"It will happen at the time you have specified so you will realize that G-d is unique . . . .

Vaāra - Section 4 - Study Notes

---

[150] 7:9 "tell Aharōn" – The literal verse states that this was communicated to both Mōshe and Aharōn. This supports the opinion that throughout Tōra, even when both men are addressed by G-d, only Mōshe heard G-d. This approach is also consistent with what G-d has already communicated in verses 4:15-16, 4:28, and 7:1-2.

[151] 7:9 "your staff" – The verse seems to indicate that Aharōn had his own staff. However, Ibn Ezra understands the verse to mean that Mōshe gave his staff to Aharōn.

Each time a staff is used, it is to confuse onlookers into thinking that the staff has power. G-d needs no instrument to perform wonders. Even the utilization of Mōshe and Aharōn as instruments of G-d is superficial. G-d wants the Jewish people to realize truth, even though other people may believe in magical powers of certain people and objects.

[152] 7:12 "magicians . . . staffs, each of which turned into a snake"

Siforno: Their staffs simply moved like snakes, but were not alive.

Others: When Pharaoh ordered his magicians to simulate the divine wonder performed by Aharōn, the magicians went to the back room, took harmless snakes out of the baskets that they are kept in, charmed the snakes into a trance so they looked like tree branches, brought them out, and then snapped the snakes out of their trance.

[153] 7:12 "Aharōn's staff swallowed all the other snakes" – Rashē states that all this happened after Aharōn's snake turned back into a staff.

Siforno translates the word "staff" in the verse as "snake" to emphasize that fact the G-d has the power to transform an inanimate object into a true living creature.

[154] 7:13 & 14 "stubborn" – see note on 7:3.

[155] 7:13 "just as G-d had previously communicated" – in verse 7:3.

[156] 7:15 "go to Pharaoh" - This is the start of the ten plagues, which occurred over a period of about one year. Once the plagues started, the Jewish people no longer had to perform slave labor.

[157] 7:15 "early tomorrow morning" – Pharaoh pretended to be super-human by going to the river each early morning before anyone else was awake, to relieve himself so that no one would ever see him go to the bathroom. By waiting for him before Pharaoh got there, Mōshe and Aharōn showed that they knew of his deception. The king might as well drop the pretense and deal with them openly and honestly. There is nothing that a person does that is not known by G-d.

[158] 7:16 "leave" - In verse 5:3, Mōshe asked for a 3-day journey. That is the standing request here and throughout the further negotiations. See note on verse 3:18 for a list of all verses of Mōshe's requests.

[159] 7:19 "of Egyptians" – This plague and all others did not affect the Jewish people. Tradition states that as soon as Pharaoh realized that only his people were affected by the plagues, he no longer made the Jewish people perform slave labor.

[160] 7:20 "servants" – These may be his personal servants or his close trusted advisors, or both. There are two approaches to this verse. One approach is that these servants and advisors came with Pharaoh every morning and were sworn to secrecy about how Pharaoh was indeed not a deity.
    Another approach is that the previous verses took place in the early morning while still dark, and Pharaoh was alone. This verse, however, took place later in the day when Pharaoh's court was with him, to perform a daily blessing of the Nile.

[161] 7:22 "magicians . . . transform . . . water into blood" – Based on the literal words of the verse, the magicians wanted to show that this was

nothing more than a trick that they also knew how to perform. But they could not do so with flowing water.

An alternative understanding is that the magicians intended to turn the blood back into fresh water, which makes more sense from their point of view. Unlike the staff/snake trick, where duplicating the trick would show their power, and doing so was to their advantage, here, turning more water into blood makes things worse for the Egyptians. They wanted water, not blood. But try as they might, the only effect their efforts had was to make things worse. This understandably embarrassed and angered Pharaoh.

[162] 7:22 "stubborn" – See note on 7:3.

[163] 7:23 "change of heart" – See note on 7:3.

Whereever a verse states that Pharaoh is stubborn, the literal meaning is that is heat was stubborn. Tōra Study Bible treats the Hebrew phrase as idiomatic. However, the verses teach that Pharaoh's decisions were not based on his logical assessment, but rather on his feelings.

[164] 7:24 "dug wells" – Only Egyptians were forced to dig for water because the plague did not affect the Jewish people in Gōshen. All of the plagues differentiated between Jewish people and gentiles, as explicitly stated in verse 8:19. Specific indications in the text include:

7:28 – plague 2, frogs, was only "on you and your"

8:15 – plague 3, lice, was called the finger of G-d by the king's advisors. This indicates that there was more to it than just the plague itself, namely, the plague was directed only at Egyptians.

8:18 – plague 4, mosquitoes, did not invade the Jewish neighborhood of Gōshen.

9:7 – plague 5, fatal animal disease, did not affect Jewish-owned animals.

9:26 – plague 7, hail, did not occur in Gōshen.

10:23 – plague 9, darkness: Jewish people could see.

11:7 – plague 10, death of firstborn: Jewish houses with lamb's blood on doorpost were not affected.

[165] 7:25 "seven days after" – Tōra never mentions how long the Nile remained blood. However, the way this verse is worded indicates that it remained as blood for seven days.

[166] 7:26 "leave" - In verse 5:3, Mōshe asks for a 3-day journey. That is the standing request here and throughout the further negotiations. See note on verse 3:18 for a list of all verses of Mōshe's requests.

[167] 8:3 "magicians reproduced this wonder" – Again, it was self-detrimental for them to bring more hardship upon themselves. The reality is that the magicians tried in vain to make the frogs go back into the river. But their efforts only made things worse, which embarrassed and angered Pharaoh further.

[168] 8:4 "Then I will allow" – The next time the king gives initial permission for them to leave is in verse 8:24, in response to plague 4.

[169] 8:4 "offer offerings to G-d" – Pharaoh has, until this point, refused to allow even this basic request because giving in would show that he is a weak leader. He also felt that granting this request could cause widespread instability in the country, causing other slaves to revolt.

Vaāra - Section 5   - 12 verses

1722 189 8:7 . . . "The frogs[170] will leave you, your homes, your servants, and all your people.
"Living frogs will be only in the river."
1723 190 8:8 Mōshe (Moses) and Aharōn (Aaron) left Pharaoh.
Mōshe prayed[171] to G-d concerning the frogs.

PLAGUE 2: FROGS ARE REMOVED

1724 191 8:9 G-d honored the prayer request of Mōshe.
The frogs jumped out of the houses, yards and fields.
1725 192 8:10 The dead frogs were piled up[172] making the air stink.

PLAGUE 2: PHARAOH REFUSES

1726 193 8:11 When Pharaoh saw that the difficulty was gone, he made his heart stubborn,[173] just as G-d had informed.

PLAGUE 3: LICE: G-D INSTRUCTS MŌSHE AND AHARŌN

1727 194 8:12 G-d communicated to Mōshe:
"Tell Aharōn:
'Hit the ground with the staff and the sand will transform into lice[174] throughout the land of Egypt.' "

PLAGUE 3: MŌSHE AND AHARŌN PERFORM

1728 195 8:13 Mōshe and Aharōn did as G-d instructed.
1729 196 8:14 The magicians tried to do the same,[175] but were not successful.
There were lice on people and animals.

PLAGUE 3: PHARAOH REFUSES

1730 197 8:15 The magicians reported to Pharaoh:
"This wonder is the finger of G-d."
But the heart of Pharaoh was made stubborn and he did not follow the instructions of Mōshe and Aharōn, just as G-d had previously informed.

VAĀRA - SECTION 5 - CONTINUED

PLAGUE 4: MOSQUITOES: MŌSHE GIVES PHARAOH OPPORTUNITY

1731 198 8:16 G-d communicated to Mōshe:
> Wake early tomorrow morning and meet Pharaoh at the river and tell him:
> "G-d instructs:
> 'Allow My people, the Jewish people, to leave[176] so they can worship Me.

1732 199 8:17 'If you do not, I will send swarms of mosquitoes[177] on you and on your people, and into your homes.
> 'They will cover the ground.

1733 200 8:18 'The mosquitoes will not affect the land of Gōshen[178] where My people live.
> 'You will realize that I control the universe.

Vaāra – Section 5 - Study Notes

---

[170] 8:7 "The frogs" - This statement is a continuation of Mōshe's speech. The plagues continue. They occurred over a period of about one year. Once the plagues started, the Jewish people no longer had to perform slave labor.

[171] 8:8 "Mōshe prayed" – Prayer is the vehicle by which people make requests from G-d. Prayer demonstrates a person's belief in G-d and acknowledgement that G-d rules the universe as all-powerful. Other verses in Shimōt which Mōshe prayed are:
  Verse 8:26 – Mōshe prayed to have plague 4 stop.
  Verse 10:18 – Mōshe and Aharōn prayed to stop plague 8, locusts
  Verse 15:25 – Mōshe prayed at Mara when all that was available was bitter water.
  Verse 17:4 – Mōshe prayed when there was no water at Refēdim.
  Verse 32:11 – After the sin of the gold calf statue, Mōshe prayed for G-d not to destroy the nation.
  Verse 34:8 – After hearing the divine attributes, Mōshe prayed for G-d to accompany the Jewish people throughout their journey to the land of Israel.
  For a list of Jewish people praying, see note on verse 3:9. For a list of when Pharaoh asks Mōshe to pray for him, see note on verse 8:24.

[172] 8:10 "the dead frogs were piled up" – Mōshe had promised that the frogs will only be in the river (verse 8:7). This was true about live frogs, but having dead frogs stink up the streets made it seem that perhaps G-d was not all-powerful. This may have emboldened Pharaoh to not give in to Mōshe. Combine this with the fact that the blood of the Nile of the previous plague simply washed itself out rather than be changed back by G-d's power, the king felt he could outlast Mōshe.

[173] 8:11 & 15 "stubborn" – see note on 7:3.

[174] 8:12 "lice" – Some commentators translate this word as gnats.

[175] 8:14 "magicians tried to do the same" – They tried to eliminate the lice, but could not.

[176] 8:16 "leave" - In verse 5:3, Mōshe asks for a 3-day journey. That is the standing request here and throughout the further negotiations. See note on

verse 3:18 for a list of all verses in which Mōshe requests agreement from Pharaoh.

[177] 8:17 "mosquitoes" – There is a wide variety of opinions as to what the animals of this plague were (see Kaplan, 1981, p.293):
    Rabbi Neĥemya (in Shimōt Raba 11:4): flies
    Rabbi Yihūda (in Shimōt Raba 11:4): mix of wild animals
    Septuagint: fleas
    Sefer HaYashar: snakes and insects
    Rashbam: wolves
    Midrash Tehilim (Homiletics on Pslams): jaguars
    Philo (De Vita Mosis): mosquitoes

[178] 8:18 "will not affect the land of Gōshen" – The other plagues also did not affect the Jewish people (see note on 7:24).

Vaāra - Section 6 — 26 verses

PLAGUE 4: MŌSHE CONTINUES TO WARN PHARAOH

1734 201 8:19 'I am differentiating[179] My people, the Jewish people, so that you will realize that I am G-d.' "

PLAGUE 4: G-D PERFORMS

1735 202 8:20 G-d did so.
   The land was ruined because of the swarms of mosquitoes.[180]

PLAGUE 4: PHARAOH PLEADS AND PROMISES

1736 203 8:21 Pharaoh summoned Mōshe (Moses) and Aharōn (Aaron), and said to them:
   "Go and offer to G-d here in this place."
1737 204 8:22 Mōshe responded:
   "If we perform offerings here, your people will threaten us.[181]
1738 205 8:23 "We must travel for 3 days into the wilderness and offer to G-d, as He commanded us."
1739 206 8:24 Pharaoh responded:
   "I will allow you to leave, but do not go too far away.[182]
      "And please pray for me." [183]
1740 207 8:25 Mōshe said:
   "I will leave here and pray for you so that the mosquitoes leave you, your people, and your land.
   But please do not behave deceitfully by not allowing the Jewish people to offer offerings to G-d."

PLAGUE 4: MŌSHE PRAYS AND THE PLAGUE STOPS

1741 208 8:26 Mōshe left, and prayed[184] to G-d.
1742 209 8:27 G-d listened to Mōshe and removed all the mosquitoes.

PLAGUE 4: PHARAOH REFUSES

1743 210 8:28 Pharaoh caused his heart to be stubborn[185] and did not allow the Jewish people to leave.

VAĀRA - SECTION 6 - CONTINUED

PLAGUE 5: FATAL ANIMAL DISEASE: MŌSHE GIVES PHARAOH OPPORTUNITY

1744 211 9:1 G-d communicated to Mōshe:
   "Tell Pharaoh that G-d commands as follows:
   'Allow My people, the Jewish people, to leave and worship Me.'
1745 212 9:2 "If you refuse . . .
1746 213 9:3 ". . . the hand of G-d will strike your cows, horses, donkeys, camels, sheep and goats with a fatal disease.
1747 214 9:4 "G-d will differentiate between Jewish-owned animals and your animals.
   None of the Jewish-owned animals will die.
1748 215 9:5 "G-d has set a specific time, communicating:
   'Tomorrow G-d will perform this plague.' "

PLAGUE 5: G-D PERFORMS

1749 216 9:6 G-d enacted the plague as He had warned so that most[186] of their animals died, although none of the Jewish-owned animals died.

PLAGUE 5: PHARAOH REFUSES

1750 217 9:7 Pharaoh sent agents to see whether any Jewish-owned animals had died.
   They reported back to him that none had died.
   Nonetheless, Pharaoh was stubborn and he did not allow the Jewish people to leave.

PLAGUE 6: BLISTERS: G-D INSTRUCTS MŌSHE AND AHARŌN

1751 218 9:8 G-d communicated to Mōshe and Aharōn:
   "Go to Pharaoh, and toss a handful of soot into the air.
1752 219 9:9 "It will cause blisters on the skin of people and animals throughout the land of Egypt."

VAĀRA - SECTION 6 - CONTINUED

PLAGUE 6: MŌSHE AND AHARŌN PERFORM

1753 220 9:10 Mōshe and Aharōn took soot from a furnace, stood in front of Pharaoh, and threw the soot into the air and it caused blisters on people and animals.

1754 221 9:11 The magicians were covered in blisters and were too ashamed[187] to be seen by Pharaoh.

PLAGUE 6: PHARAOH REFUSES

1755 222 9:12 G-d caused Pharaoh to be stubborn[188] such that he refused to obey, just as G-d had previously informed.

PLAGUE 7: HAIL: MŌSHE GIVES PHARAOH OPPORTUNITY

1756 223 9:13 G-d communicated to Mōshe:
"Wake up early and tell Pharaoh:
'G-d commands:
"Allow My people, the Jewish people, to leave[189] so they can worship Me.

1757 224 9:14 "Otherwise, I will bring plagues upon you, your advisors, your servants, and your people, so that you will realize that I am G-d.

1758 225 9:15 "So far, I have performed terrible plagues and I could easily have killed you.

1759 226 9:16 "But I specifically want you to live so that you can see My power . . . ."

Vaāra - Section 6 - Study Notes

---

[179] 8:19 "differentiating" – See note on verse 7:24 for the many indications that this was true throughout the plagues.

In this section, the plagues continue. They occurred over a period of about one year. Once the plagues started, the Jewish people no longer had to perform slave labor.

[180] 8:20 "mosquitoes" – See note on 8:17 about the various opinions as to what this plague consisted of.

[181] 8:22 "they will threaten us" – This is evident from an incident that occurred in a previous generation. Yōsef (Joseph) had told his brothers to tell Pharaoh that they are shepherds (Brāshēt (Genesis) 46:33). Yōsef informs them that shepherds are not welcome in Egypt. That will make it likely that Pharaoh will let them settle in Gōshen, which is on the east side of the Nile delta, rather than having them live in the capital, which is on the west side of the delta. Egyptians did not allow the slaughter of livestock. That is why Mōshe states here that if they offer offerings in the more central areas of Egypt, people will threaten them.

However, in Brāshēt 47:6, Pharaoh mentions to Yōsef that some of his brothers could be chief shepherds over Pharaoh's livestock (perhaps in private Pharaoh cheated on his vegan diet). Thus, shepherds were a part of the workforce in Egypt, but they would not be welcome in the main populated areas in Egypt.

[182] 8:24 "but do not go too far away" – Previously, in verse 8:4, during the plague of frogs, the king said he would allow the Jewish people to leave. Here, the king places a condition on his permission. There are 3 other plagues where he initially gives permission:

9:28 – During the plague of hail Pharaoh says that the Jewish people can leave unconditionally, but changes his mind once the hail stops.

10:11 – During the locust infestation the king states that the men can go, but of course this is unacceptable.

10:24 – After the 3 days of darkness, the king states that all the people can go, but they must leave the livestock here, which of course is unacceptable.

[183] 8:24 "pray for me" – Other verses where Pharaoh asks Mōshe to pray for him:
   Verse 9:28 - Pray for the hail to stop.
   Verse 10:17 – Pray to G-d for the locusts to go away.
   Verse 12:32 – After that last plague, Pharaoh said to Mōshe: "bless me and pray for me."

[184] 8:26 "prayed" – See note on verse 8:8.

[185] 8:28 "stubborn" – See note on 7:3.

[186] 9:6 "most" – This is the interpretation of Ibn Ezra based on verses 10 and 19, where the Egyptians still had animals.

[187] 9:11 "too ashamed" – This is the interpretation of Ramban.

[188] 9:12 "stubborn" – See note on 7:3.

[189] 9:13 "leave" - In verse 5:3, Mōshe asks for a 3-day journey. That is the standing request here and throughout the further negotiations. See note on verse 3:18 for a list of all verses that state Mōshe's requests.

Vaāra - Section 7 - 15 + 3 verses

1760 227 9:17 ". . . Are you so conceited that you will not allow the Jewish people to leave? [190]

1761 228 9:18 "Tomorrow at about this time I will cause a hail storm that is greater than any ever experienced here.

1762 229 9:19 "Get every animal out from open areas.

And all people should stay indoors, because great and terrible hail stones will kill any living thing outdoors." ' "

1763 230 9:20 All advisors and servants of Pharaoh who feared G-d,[191] stayed indoors and kept their family, servants, and animals indoors.

1764 231 9:21 Those men who did not fear G-d, did not.

1765 232 9:22 G-d communicated to Mōshe (Moses):

"Raise your hand toward the sky so that hail will rain down throughout Egypt."

PLAGUE 7: MŌSHE PERFORMS

1766 233 9:23 Mōshe raised his staff toward the sky, and G-d sent thunder, hail, and fire to come down throughout Egypt.

1767 234 9:24 There was a hail and fire storm that was greater than any ever experienced in Egypt.

1768 235 9:25 The hail killed people and animals that were outside.

The hail destroyed plants and broke trees.

1769 236 9:26 But in the land of Gōshen there was no hail.

1770 237 9:27 Pharaoh summoned Mōshe and Aharōn (Aaron) and told them:

"I have sinned.

"G-d is right, whereas I and my people are evil.[192]

1771 238 9:28 "Pray[193] to G-d to stop the thunder and hail.

"Then I will allow you to leave,

and you no longer have to live here." [194]

1772 239 9:29 Mōshe said to him:

"As soon as I am outside the city I will spread out my hands to G-d and the thunder and hail will stop, and you will realize that all the world belongs to G-d.

1773 240 9:30 "But I know you and your advisors and servants.[195]

"I know you do not and will not fear G-d."

Vaāra - Section 7 - continued

1774 241 9:31 The flax and barley plants had been destroyed by the hail because they had been in bloom.
1775 242 9:32 But the wheat crops had not been destroyed because they ripen later in the year.

Vaāra – Last Section
1776 243 9:33 Mōshe left the city and raised his hands to G-d and the thunder and hail stopped, and there was no rain.

PLAGUE 7: PHARAOH REFUSES
1777 244 9:34 When Pharaoh saw that the hail and thunder stopped, he, his advisors, and his servants continued to sin and Pharaoh became stubborn.[196]
1778 245 9:35 Pharaoh was stubborn and he refused to allow the Jewish people to leave, just as G-d had informed Mōshe.

Vaāra - Section 7 - Study Notes

───────────────

[190] 9:17 "leave" - In verse 5:3, Mōshe asks for a 3-day journey. That is the standing request here and throughout the further negotiations. See note on verse 3:18 for a list of all verses that state Mōshe's requests.

Until now, Tōra has described the drama of the first 6 plagues. This section describes the seventh plague, while the next portion describes the last 3 plagues. The plagues occurred over a period of about one year. Once the plagues started, the Jewish people no longer had to perform slave labor.

[191] 9:20 "who feared G-d" – See notes on verses 1:10 and 2:8.

[192] 9:27 "I and my people are evil" – The king is trying to shift the blame away from himself and onto the Egyptian people. There were many Egyptians who were favorable toward the Jewish people, as mentioned in the note on verse 1:10.

In terms of the king's advisors and servants, who were closer to the king, there were some who sided with Mōshe and the Jewish people. This is evident in verse 8:15 (finger of G-d, in relation to the third plague, lice) and 9:20 (they feared G-d, in relation to the seventh plague, hail). But there were some who were loyal to the king even though it was obvious that the king was wrong. This was a clear case of groupthink. In verse 10:7, the advisors and servants tell the king to stop his destrctive policy and instead, let the Jewish people go.

During the interim, Mōshe, adhering to the instruction from G-d to be respectful to the king, in verse 9:30, includes the king's advisors and servants in his statement. Note that in verse 9:34, Tōra states that the advisors and servants continued to sin. In keeping with the current interpretation, their sin was falling into the error of groupthink.

[193] 9:28 "pray" – See note on verse 8:24.

[194] 9:28 "you no longer have to live here" – All along, the king feared that if the Jewish people take a 3-days journey, they would leave forever. See note on verse 8:24.

[195] 9:30 "your advisors and servants" – Verse 9:20 states that there were

advisors and servants who did fear G-d. The people referred to in this verse had survived the hail by staying indoors not because they feared G-d, but rather to stay and protect their king.

[196] 9:34 & 35 "stubborn" – See note on 7:3.

Bō[197] - Section 1   - 11 verses   (Total 106 verses)

[There are 21 commandments[198] in this portion: 9 positive; 12 negative.]

Tell Your Children About The Miracles

1779 246 10:1 G-d communicated[199] to Mōshe (Moses):
  "Come[200] to Pharaoh because I have caused him and his advisors to be stubborn[201] in order to give Me the opportunity to demonstrate miraculous events to them.[202]
1780 247 10:2 "Therefore, you will be able to tell your descendants how I was harsh with the people of Egypt and how I performed miracles.[203]
  "Through this, you will fully realize that I am G-d." [204]

PLAGUE 8: LOCUSTS: PHARAOH CAN CHOOSE TO AVOID DISASTER

1781 248 10:3 Mōshe and Aharōn (Aaron) came to Pharaoh and said to him:
  "G-d has communicated:
    'How long will you refuse to submit to Me?
    'Allow My people, the Jewish people, to leave[205] and worship Me.
1782 249 10:4 'If you refuse, then tomorrow I will bring so many locusts
1783 250 10:5 'that no one will be able to see the ground.
    'The locusts will devour all plants that were not destroyed by the hail.
784 251 10:6 'Your homes will be filled with locusts.
    'This will be the worst infestation of locusts that anyone has ever experienced in the entire existence of Egypt.' "
1785 252 10:7 Pharaoh's advisors said to him:
  "How long will this man trouble us?
  "Let the Jewish men leave and worship G-d.[206]
  "After all, our country has suffered greatly."

Bō – Section 1 - continued

Plague 8: Pharaoh Reconsiders

1786 253 10:8 Mōshe and Aharōn were summoned to appear before Pharaoh.

Pharaoh said to them:

"You can leave and worship G-d.

"But who will go?"

1787 254 10:9 Mōshe said:

"We must leave with our children, elders, men, women, flocks and cattle, because we must have a celebration to G-d."

Plague 8: Pharaoh Refuses

1788 255 10:10 Pharaoh said to them:

"If G-d allows you to leave, then I will allow your children to go with you.

"Obviously you are up to no good.[207]

1789 256 10:11 "Your men can leave[208] and worship G-d.

"That is enough to accomplish your worship."

Mōshe and Aharōn were chased out.

Bō - Section 1 - Study Notes

[197] The Hebrew word *bō* means "come." The last 3 of the 10 plagues are described in this portion.

[198] The commandments as defined in Tōra Study Bible are those that are selected by Rambam. Other commentators, such as Ramban and Raavad, have certain diffrneces in terms of the commandments as they identify them.

[199] 10:1 "communicated" – See note on verse 3:4.

[200] 10:1 "Come" - In reference to going to Pharaoh, this word "come" occurs in 6:11, 7:26, and 9:1.
  Other words used in a similar way include:
    Verse 5:1 - they went to Pharaoh, and
    Verse 9:10 – they stood in front of Pharaoh (there is no command mentioned).
  Other commands to interact with Pharaoh include:
    6:29 (speak), 7:14 (go), 8:16 and 9:13 (confront).
    Pharaoh summons them: 8:4, 8:21, 9:27, and 10:8.

[201] 10:1 "stubborn" – See note on verse 7:3.

[202] 10:1 "demonstrate miraculous events to them" – However, G-d's more important reason for performing the Ten Plagues is stated in the next verse: "so that you, the Jewish people, will fully realize that I am G-d." Every year, Jewish people at the Passover Seder recount the Ten Plagues and all the other miracles G-d performed for the Jewish people. It has created an identity on a personal and national level that has lasted for generations.

[203] 10:2 "harsh . . . miracles" - G-d was harsh on the Egyptians by bringing the plagues upon the, G-d performed miracles by having the plagues avoid the Jewish people.

[204] 10:2 "Through this, you will fully realize that I am G-d" - Throughout the wonders that G-d performs, including the revelation at Mount Sinai,

there are verses that state that now the Jewish people will believe. But, time and again, the Jewish people lapse and backslide. The true message that Tōra communjcates to us is that even if we would live in an age of overt divine miracles, we would still be faced with tests of faith.

[205] 10:3 "leave" - In verse 5:3, Mōshe asks for leave for a 3-day journey. A 3-day journey means 3 days travelling, a day to worship, and 3 days to return. That is the standing request here and throughout further negotiations. See note on verse 3:18 for a list of all verses that state Mōshe's requests.

[206] 10:7 "Let the Jewish men leave and worship G-d . . ." – Those of his advisors who, until now, decided to support Pharaoh have had enough of his obviously bad decision making. See note on verse 9:27.

[207] 10:10 "Obviously you are up to no good" - This phrase can be translated in many ways. The rendition here is loosely based on Ibn Ezra's understanding.

[208] 10:11 "Your men can leave" – See note on verse 8:24.

Bō – Section 2   12 verses

1790 257 10:12 G-d communicated to Mōshe (Moses):
"Raise your hands over the land so locusts[209] can come and destroy the remaining plants."

PLAGUE 8: MŌSHE PERFORMS

1791 258 10:13 Mōshe raised his hands and G-d caused an east wind for the entire day and night.
By the next morning, the east wind brought locusts.
1792 259 10:14 The locusts spread throughout the land of Egypt.
It was the worst infestation ever experienced.
1793 260 10:15 The locusts covered the ground such that the ground was dark, and the locusts ate the remaining plants.
1794 261 10:16 Pharaoh quickly summoned Mōshe and Aharōn (Aaron) and told them:
"I have sinned against G-d and against you.
1795 262 10:17 "Please forgive me and pray[210] to G-d to remove this death from me."
1796 263 10:18 They[211] left and prayed[212] to G-d.

PLAGUE 8: G-D REMOVES THE LOCUSTS

1797 264 10:19 In response, G-d changed the direction of the wind so that it blew the locusts into the Reed Sea[213] so that all locusts were gone.

PLAGUE 8: G-D CAUSES PHARAOH'S HEART TO BE STUBBORN

1798 265 10:20 But G-d made the heart of Pharaoh stubborn so that he did not allow the Jewish people to leave.

PLAGUE 9: DARKNESS: G-D INSTRUCTS MŌSHE

1799 266 10:21 G-d communicated to Mōshe:
"Raise your hands to the sky and there will be darkness throughout the land of Egypt.
"The darkness will be so thick that it can be felt."

Bō – Section 2 - continued

Plague 9: Mōshe Performs

1800 267 10:22 Mōshe raised his hands upward and a thick darkness set in for three days.

1801 268 10:23 No one could see other people, and everyone stayed still for three days.

However, the Jewish people had light in their homes.

Bō – Section 2 - Study Notes

[209] 10:12 "locusts" – The plagues occurred over a period of about one year. Once the plagues started, the Jewish people no longer had to perform slave labor.

[210] 10:17 "pray" – See note on verse 8:24.

[211] 10:18 "they" – The Tōra uses the singular verb, but it is understood from the context that Mōshe and Aharōn were a team.

[212] 10:18 "prayed" – See note on verse 8:8.

[213] 10:19 "Reed Sea" – This is the literal translation of the Tōra's name for the sea: "Suf." The following opinions as to why it became known as the Red Sea are found in Kaplan, pp. 305 and 321.
  Septuagint: Erythrean (Red) Sea. This translation by the sages gives credence for translating it the Red Sea. Reasons why it is red include:
  a. The reeds along the sea are red.
  b. The corals in the water were red.
  c. The mountains along the sea are red. Significantly, at sundown, the red color of the mountains reflects onto the water.
  d. The people of Erythria painted their faces red.
  Ibn Ezra: The Hebrew name, yam suf, can mean: Sea at the End. This is possibly the area at the area of today's Suez Canal which separates Egypt from Sinai Peninsula.
  Others: In Egyptian, the word "sufi" means swampy Nile delta. Lake Manzaleh, on the eastern Nile Delta, has reeds. This would make Tanis, a city on the lake, the site where the Jewish people became trapped and experienced the miraculous crossing of the sea.
  Others: Lake Sirbonis.

Bō – Section 3   - 8 verses

1802 269 10:24 Pharaoh summoned Mōshe (Moses):
   "You can leave and worship G-d, but leave your sheep and cattle.[214]
   "Your children can leave with you."
1803 270 10:25 Mōshe replied:
   "You must allow us to take our animals so we can offer offerings to G-d.
1804 271 10:26 "This means that all of our animals must come with us."

PLAGUE 9: PHARAOH REFUSES

1805 272 10:27 But G-d made the heart of Pharaoh stubborn so that Pharaoh would not allow the Jewish people to leave.
1806 273 10:28 Pharaoh told him:
   "Leave and do not come back.[215]
   "The day you see me – you will die."
1807 274 10:29 Mōshe retorted:
   "Fine. I will no longer see you." [216]

PLAGUE 10: G-D INFORMS MŌSHE

1808 275 11:1 G-d communicated to Mōshe:
   "I have one more plague to bring upon Pharaoh and Egypt.
   "After that, Pharaoh will allow you to leave.
   "In fact, he will chase you out.[217]
1809 276 11:2 "Tell the Jewish people to ask for gifts from their neighbors.
   "Women should ask for silver and gold items." [218]
1810 277 11:3 G-d caused the people of Egypt to like[219] the Jewish people.
   Pharaoh's advisors and servants, as well as the people of Egypt admired Mōshe.

Bō - Section 3 - Study Notes

---

[214] 10:24 "but leave your sheep and cattle" – See note on verse 8:24 concerning times when Pharaoh is willing to allow the Jewish people to worship G-d – but with conditions which were unacceptable to Mōshe.

[215] 10:28 "do not come back" – But in fact, the king calls them back in verse 12:31, after plague 10. Note however that Mōshe and Aharōn do not respond verbally to him. Rather, they simply leave the country.

[216] 10:29 "I will no longer see you" – This can be interpreted as a promise or vow. Note that when the king summons Mōshe and Aharōn after plague 10, in verse 21:31, they do not respond to the king – they simply leave - thus keeping the vow that Mōshe had made. However, Mōshe does tell the king about the last plague in verses 11:4-8. There are a number of ways that the commentators resolve this difficulty.
   Ramban: Mōshe spoke verses 11:4-8 in the darkness of night such that Mōshe and Pharaoh did not see each other, thus keeping the words of the vow.
   Ibn Ezra: Mōshe here means that he will not come to (rather than taking the word "see" literally) the king anymore, although the king might come to Mōshe.
   Siforno: This statement is Mōshe's way of telling the king that he, the king, is doomed. It was never meant to be literal.
   other commentators: The statements Mōshe made to the king in verse 11:4–8 were stated at this point in the narrative, so in fact after this, they did not see each other. According to this approach, verses 11:1-3 must have been stated just before verse 10:24.

[217] 11:1 "he will chase you out" – Note that Tōra doesn't indicate that G-d told Mōshe the nature of the last plague. But in verse 11:5 we see that Mōshe does know what the plague will be. Therefore, G-d did tell him here even though the Tōra doesn't include that detail. There are many examples of details being left out throughout Tōra. This is especially true as Mōshe reveals many new details in his discourses in Divarim.

[218] 11:2 "silver and gold items" – Mōshe was told that they would be asked to ask, as had been stated in verse 3:22. In the earlier verse, clothing was also specified as items to ask for. They do ask, even for clothing, as stated in verse 12:35.

[219] 11:3 "like" – G-d caused even those Egyptians who were not well-disposed to the Jewish people, to like the Jewish people just as G-d had communicated in verse 3:21.

Bō – Section 4   - 27 verses

1811 278 11:4 Mōshe (Moses) said to Pharaoh:[220]

"G-d has communicated as follows:

'Approximately at midnight[221] I will survey Egypt.

1812 279 11:5 'Every firstborn[222] in Egypt will die.

'This includes the firstborn of the king down to the firstborn of servants, as well as the firstborn of animals.

1813 280 11:6 'There will be screaming all over the country more than ever before, and there will not be screaming like this in the future.

1814 281 11:7 'But no harm will come to the Jewish people.[223]

'Dogs will not even bark[224] at a Jewish person.

'I will do this so you will realize that G-d has differentiated between people of Egypt and the Jewish people.

1815 282 11:8 'All your advisors will come to me, bow to me, and demand:

"You and the people who follow you must leave."

'Once that happens, then I will leave.' "

Mōshe then left Pharaoh.[225]

1816 283 11:9 G-d communicated to Mōshe:

"Pharaoh is not going to consent to your demand because I want to increase the wonders that I will perform in Egypt."

1817 284 11:10 Mōshe and Aharōn (Aaron) had performed all these wonders in front of Pharaoh.

G-d caused the heart of Pharaoh to be stubborn so that he would not permit the Jewish people to leave his country.

1818 285 12:1 G-d communicated to Mōshe and Aharōn:

Bō – Section 4 - continued

Commandment 3:[226] Court Must Calculate the Start of Each New Month

1819 286 12:2 "Today will be the first day of the month.[227]
   "This month will start your new year.[228]
1820 287 12:3 "Tell the Jewish people:
   'Each head of household should select a lamb[229] on day 10 of this month.
   'The lamb will be a meal for the family.
1821 288 12:4 'Small families, for whom a lamb provides more meat than they can eat in one meal, should combine with another small family.
1822 289 12:5 'The lamb selected should look nice.
   'It should be a male lamb that is less than a year old.
   'It can be a lamb or a young goat.

Commandment 4:[230] Slaughter The Pesaĥ Offering On Nēsan 14

1823 290 12:6 'Keep it until day 14 of the month.
   'Everyone should slaughter their lamb or goat in the late afternoon.
1824 291 12:7 'People should brush its blood onto the two doorposts and lintel[231] of their homes in which they will eat their meal.

Commandment 5: Eat The Pesaĥ Offering With Maźa And Bitters

1825 292 12:8 'Roast the meat and eat it that night with maźa, along with bitter vegetables.[232]

Commandment 6: Do Not Boil The Pesaĥ Offering, But It Cannot Be Raw

1826 293 12:9 'Do not eat the meat raw or boiled.

Commandment 7: Do Not Leave Pesaĥ Offering Past Sunrise

1827 294 12:10 'All the meat must be consumed before morning.
   'Any meat that is not eaten must be burned up.

1828 295 12:11 'When you eat that meal you should be fully dressed, wearing your belt and shoes, with all your belongings ready, because you will be leaving in a hurry.
   'This is the Passover of G-d.

Bō – Section 4 - continued

1829 296 12:12 'I will pass over the land of Egypt during that night and I will punish all their firstborn.[233]
  'I will destroy all the idols as well.
  'I am G-d.
1830 297 12:13 'When I see the blood, I will pass over your house.
1831 298 12:14 'This day will be a holy day from now on.

Commandment 8:[234] Destroy Leavened Food On Nēsan 14

1832 299 12:15 'The holy festival will last for 7 days.
  'You must remove all leavened foods and not have any leavened foods during the entire 7-day festival.
1833 300 12:16 'The first and seventh days are holy.
  'Do not perform any forbidden activities on those two days.
  'However, you may perform activities needed for food preparation.
1834 301 12:17 'Observe the holy festival of unleavened bread because today I bring all of you out of Egypt.
  'Observe this holy festival every year.[235]

Commandment 9: Eat Matźa On The First Night Of Pesaĥ

1835 302 12:18 'Eat maźa from day 14 [236] to day 21 of the month.

Commandment 10: Do Not Have Leavened Food On Your Property

1836 303 12:19 'For the 7 days of Pesaĥ, there must not be any leaven food on your property.

Commandment 11: Do Not Eat Foods That Are Partial Leaven

1837 304 12:20 'Do not eat any leaven. Instead, eat unleavened foods.' "

Bō - Section 4 - Study Notes

---

[220] 11:4 "Mōshe said to Pharaoh" – In verse 10:29 Mōshe had agreed not to see Pharaoh again. According to some commentators, Mōshe had told these statements to Pharaoh at their last meeting, at about verse 10:26. See note on 10:29 for various other possible answers.

In this section, before the final plague strikes (as recorded in section 6), the Jewish people are given comandments that orient them as a sovereign nation who are free to serve G-d.

[221] 11:4 "approximately at midnight" – In verse 12:29, Tōra states that it happened exactly at midnight. See note on 12:29 as to why there is a difference in the wording.

[222] 11:5 "firstborn" – G-d had told Mōshe the nature of the last plague even though verse 11:1 does not include this detail (see notes on verses 11:1 and 12:23).

Interestingly, Mōshe does not mention to the Jewish people that the Egyptian firstborn will die. In verses 12:21-25 he gives the Jewish people the instructions they need for the night of Passover. He mentions only (12:23) that "G-d will pass through the land and punish the Egyptians, but will pass over your houses." The Jewish people find out later what had happened when they are told in verse 13:15 that when their children ask them why Passover is special, among other things, they should tell them that G-d had killed the firstborn of Egyptians, while the Jewish people remained safe. Verse 12:29 states that all Egyptian firstborn people and animals died.

Bamidbar 3:13 and 8:17 state that when G-d caused the Egyptian firstborn to die, He acquired the Jewish first born. And Shimōt 34:19 states that because the Jewish firstborn had been spared, Jewish people must sanctify their first born kosher animals. This is the basis of commandments that deal with firstborn people and animals:

Commandment 21 Shimōt 13:12 Set aside the firstborn of kosher animals as a gift to priests. (See also Shimōt 22:28-29.)

Commandment 22 Shimōt 13:13 A firstborn donkey can be redeemed (i.e., exchanged) with a lamb which is given to a priest.

Commandment 23 Shimōt 13:13 If a firstborn donkey is not redeemed, it must be put down. (See also Shimōt 34:20.)

Commandment 386 Bamidbar (Numbers) 18:16 When a son is one month old, redeem him by giving a priest 5 silver shekel coins to a priest. Today, in the United States, a parent gives 5 silver dollars to a priest to redeem a first born son.

Commandment 387 Bamidbar 18:17 Do not exchange firstborn kosher animals (because they must be given to a priest). Note that firstborn animals are mentioned along with firstborn sons in Shimōt 13:2.

Commandment 447 Divarim (Deuteronomy) 12:17 Priests must not eat firstborn animal offerings outside of Yerūshalayim (Jerusalem).

In addition, the concept of first fruits can be thought of as being a tribute to the miracle of the firstborn:

Commandment 89 Shimōt 23:19 Give the first fruits of the 7 types of produce to a priest.

A consequence of the miracle of the firstborn was that initially, firstborn Jewish men were designated as the teachers and religious leaders of the Jewish people as indicated in the following verses:

Shimōt 13:2 Sanctify Jewish firstborn boys and firstborn animals.

Shimōt 19:22 Firstborn men are permitted to come closer to G-d if they sanctify themselves. (Although right afterwards, G-d told them to stay at the base on the mountain.)

But after they had participated in the gold calf statue, their special role was taken away from them and given to the Levite tribe (Shimōt 32:28-29) because the tribe of Lāvē respond to Mōshe's call to action. Mōshe declares them as agents of G-d and spiritual leaders of the Jewish people. Note that Divarim 10:8 makes it clear that Mōshe did not make this decision, but rather, he was communicating G-d's decision.

Bamidbar 8:16 The Levites were now in place of the first born as G-d's special servants.

Bamidbar 8:18 G-d selected the Levites instead of the firstborn.

Divarim 10:8 Mōshe explains that it was G-d who had selected the Tribe of Lāvē as the spiritual leaders

[223] 11:7 "no harm will come to the Jewish people" – The Jewish first born were not affected by the plague.

[224] 11:7 "bark" – According to Ibn Ezra.

[225] 11:8 "left Pharaoh" – As stated in verse 10:29.

[226] Commandment 3 – This is defined and described in Mishne Tōra by Rambam – Book 3: Seasons: Laws of Sanctification of Months. There are 2 commandments of the 613 commandments in Brāshēt (Genesis):
  Commandment 1: Have children (Brāshēt 1:28).,
and Commandment 2: Do not eat the thigh sinew of an animal (Brāshēt 32:33).

[227] 12:2 "first day of the month" – In the Jewish calendar, as soon as the moon is a new crescent, that very day is the first day of the month.

This is in contrast to the Egyptian lunar calendar. The Egyptians, once they saw the new crescent moon, declared the next day as the first day of the month. This is the reason why gentiles believe the number 13 is unlucky. The plague of the firstborn occurred at midnight after the fourteenth day of the Jewish month. But that morning was the thirteenth of the month for the Egyptians.

[228] 12:2 "start your new year" – Today we call this month Nēsan. It occurs in the spring.

[229] 12:3 "select a lamb" – This was commanded only for the first Passover. It does not apply afterward, as opposed to the other laws of Passover which do apply every year as stated in verses 12:17 and 24. That is why this verse does not give rise to one of the 613 commandments

[230] Commandments 4–7 – Book 9: Offerings: Laws of Pascal Offering.

[231] 12:7 "two doorposts and lintel" – The people perform this commandment as stated in 12:22, where lintel is mentioned first. Commentators state that the order of where to brush the animal blood was not important, therefore, the order is switched in the two verses.

There is a connection between this and the ceremony of prolonging the term of a Jewish indentured servant, as noted in verse 21:6.

[232] 12:8 "bitter vegetables" – The Passover offering is eaten with bitter vegetables because, as stated in verse 1:14, the taskmasters made the lives of the Jewish people bitter with hard labor.

[233] 12:12 "punish all their firstborn" - The word in the verse could be taken to mean kill, as many translations do. However, in verse 12:23, when Mōshe relates this to the elders, he states that there will be a plague that night - without specifying that it will be on firstborn, nor specifying the nature of the plague.

[234] Commandments 8-11 – Book 3: Seasons: Laws of Leaven and Matza.

[235] 12:17 "every year" – This is stated again in verse 12:24. G-d informs them in verse 13:5 that this observance will not start until they enter the land of Israel. Further clarification specifies that they did not start observing the Passover offering until after the land of Israel was conquered (which took 7 years) and settled (which took another 7 years) after they crossed the Jordan River and entered Israel.

[236] 12:18 "14" – This verse makes it sound as if Pesach (Passover) lasts for 8 days, starting from day 14 of the month. But this is not true, as the next verse states that Passover lasts for 7 days. The lamb is slaughtered on the afternoon of day 14 and Passover starts on that night, which is day 15 of the month. Day 14 is a special day unto itself as indicated by commandment 483 in verse Divarim16:3 – do not eat leaved food on the afternoon of day 14. On that day, Jewish people do not eat matzo in order to allow the taste of matzo to be fresh and interesting that night.

As an additional note, outside of the land of Israel, today, Jewish people do keep an extra day of Passover as a Rabbinical enactment due to historical circumstances. The last day is not called the eighth day of Passover, but rather, it is referred to as the last day or the trailing day of Pesach.

Bō – Section 5   - 8 verses

Mōshe Instructs The Jewish People

1838 305 12:21 Mōshe (Moses) instructed the Jewish leaders to tell the Jewish people:

"Select a lamb for your family and slaughter it as the Pesaĥ (Passover) offering.

1839 306 12:22 "Take hyssop branches that you will dip into the offering's blood and use it to brush the blood onto your lintel and two doorposts.[237]

"Be sure not to leave your home all night.

1840 307 12:23 "G-d will pass through the land and punish[238] the people of Egypt with a plague.

"When G-d sees the blood around the door, He will pass over your home.

1841 308 12:24 "You and your descendants will observe Pesaĥ
    every year.[239]

1842 309 12:25 "Once you arrive at the country that G-d has promised to you, you will offer the Pesaĥ offering.

Children Ask: Why Observe All These Rules Of Pesaĥ

1843 310 12:26 "When your children ask:[240]

'Why do you observe all the rules and restrictions[241] of the Pesaĥ offering?'

1844 311 12:27 "You should answer:

'This is the offering to G-d's passover because G-d passed over the Jewish homes in Egypt and saved us.' "[242]

The Jewish people bowed and prayed.[243]

1845 312 12:28 The Jewish people followed all the instructions that G-d had commanded Mōshe and Aharōn (Aaron).

Bō - Section 5 - Study Notes

---

[237] 12:22 "lintel and two doorposts" - Originally stated in 12:7 (see study note there).

[238] 12:23 "punish" – Mōshe does not tell the Jewish people the nature of the plague. They do not find out until verse 13:15, well after they left Egypt, that all firstborn of Egypt were killed.

[239] 12:24 "every year" – As stated in 12:17. See note on that verse.

[240] 12:26 "When your children ask" – The rabbinic sages throughout the centuries have added customs to the Passover seder that teach, motivate questions by, and encourage active participation of, children. Verse 13:8 is the commandment to tell the Passover story. Verses 12:26, 13:8, 13:14, and Divarim (Deuteronomy) 6:20 form the basis for the section in the Hagada known as the Four Children (often translated as Four Sons).

Note that in the Hebrew language, there is no neuter pronoun (such as "it"). The word for "son" also means "child" – boy or girl. And the word for "sons" also means "children" – a group of boys, or a group of boys and girls. Overly literal translations can be very misleading.

[241] 12:26 "Why do you observe all the rules and restrictions?" - In the Passover Hagada, this question is attributed to a child who is skeptical or antagonistic or resentful or hostile (often translated as "the wicked son"). There is an overtone of disdain and derision in the way he or she asks this question.

In contrast, a similar verse in Divarim 6:20 phrases the question as "What are all these meaningful laws that G-d has commanded you?" This question in the Hagada is attributed to the wise child because he or she shows respect and belief in G-d by the way the question is worded. Wisdom is more than just knowing facts. Rather, it is an approach to life, people, and society.

[242] 12:27 "G-d passed over the Jewish homes in Egypt and saved us" – This answer, which Jewish people are directed to tell children, is not part of the Four Children section of the Hagada. Instead, it is part of the declaration in

the Hagada as to why there is an offering on Passover.

[243] 12:27 "bowed and prayed" – There are two ways to treat this verse. Either it is a statement not connected to what Jewish people should tell their children, or it is a continuation of what should be told to children. Many translations treat it as a separate statement of fact, not part of the narrative to teach.

However, in the Hagada, this statement is included as part of the reason there is a Passover offering. Because the Jewish people themselves took the initiative to ask G-d to save them, they merited being saved. (Note that prayer is a request from G-d. Praising G-d, thanking G-d, and acknowledging G-d are worthy actions, but prayer is specifically a request.) Essay 7 lists the occurrences of prayer in the verses.

Bō – Section 6 - 23 verses

PLAGUE 10: G-D PERFORMS

1846 313 12:29 At midnight[244] G-d passed through Egypt and caused the firstborn of Pharaoh down to the firstborn of prisoners to die, as well as firstborn animals.

1847 314 12:30 Pharaoh and his advisors woke up at night due to the people's loud wailing.

There was not an Egyptian house[245] in which no one had died.

PHARAOH FORCES THE JEWISH PEOPLE TO LEAVE IMMEDIATELY

1848 315 12:31 Pharaoh summoned[246] Mōshe (Moses) and Aharōn (Aaron) that night and said to them:

"Leave my people and worship G-d, just as you have demanded. [247]

1849 316 12:32 "Take all your sheep and cattle as you had demanded, and leave.

"Bless me and pray[248] for me."

1850 317 12:33 The people of Egypt urged the Jewish people to leave immediately[249] because they said:

"We are all going to die."

THEIR DOUGH IS NOT FERMENTED

1851 318 12:34 The Jewish people packed up their dough, which had not risen yet and which was still on the baking pans.

They tied the pans onto their belongings and carried them like backpacks.

1852 319 12:35 The Jewish people followed Mōshe's instructions, namely, they asked their neighbors[250] for silver, gold, and clothing.

1853 320 12:36 G-d caused the people of Egypt to like[251] the Jewish people such that they gave[252] the Jewish people whatever they asked for.

The Jewish people took much of the personal valuables of Egypt.

Bō - Section 6 - continued

TRAVEL FROM RAMSĀS TO SŪKŌT; ABOUT 600,000 MEN

1854 321 12:37 The Jewish people traveled[253] from Ramsās to Sūkōt.[254]
   There were approximately 600,000 adult men.[255]
   In addition, there were children.

OTHER PEOPLES LEFT WITH THE JEWISH PEOPLE

1855 322 12:38 Also, there were other peoples[256] who left Egypt with them.
   They traveled with their flocks and cattle.
1856 323 12:39 The people baked maźa which they carried with them when they left Egypt.
   Their dough had baked into maźa instead of bread[257] because the people had to leave in a hurry.
   They also did not bring prepared foods[258] with them.
1857 324 12:40 The Jewish people had been in Egypt for 430 years.[259]
1858 325 12:41 All of them left Egypt.

PESAĤ NIGHT IS A NIGHT OF DIVINE PROTECTION

1859 326 12:42 The previous night was a night during which G-d protected the Jewish people and enabled them to leave Egypt.
   This night, day 15 of the month of Nēsan, is a night during which G-d protects the Jewish people from now on.

Commandment 12: [260] Do Not Permit Non-Believers To Eat The Pesaĥ Offering

1860 327 12:43 G-d communicated to Mōshe and Aharōn:
   "This is the law of the Pesaĥ (Passover) offering: only Jewish people may eat it.
1861 328 12:44 But circumcised servants[261] are permitted to partake of the Pesaĥ offering.

Commandment 13: Hired Servants Must Not Partake Of The Pesaĥ Offering

1862 329 12:45 But hired servants[262] are not permitted to partake.

Bō - Section 6 - continued

Commandment 14: Do Not Move The Pesaĥ Offering Out Of The Building

Commandment 15: Do Not Break Bones Of The Pesaĥ Offering

1863 330 12:46 The family unit must eat all of it in their home.
 Do not take some of it to another location.
 And do not break any of the bones of the offering.
1864 331 12:47 All Jewish people must observe the festival offering and unmarried people can join with families.

Commandment 16: If Not Circumcised, Must Not Eat Pesaĥ Offering

Commandment 17:[263] If A Priest Is Not Circumcised, He Must Not Eat Trūma

1865 332 12:48 Converts[264] must also observe the festival offering.
 If a Jewish man is not circumcised for whatever reason, he should not partake of the offering.
1866 333 12:49 Converts and Jewish-born people all have the same laws.
1867 334 12:50 The Jewish people observed everything that Mōshe and Aharōn had taught them.
1868 335 12:51 G-d brought the Jewish people out of Egypt on that very day.

Bō - Section 6 - Study Notes

---

[244] 12:29 "at midnight" – In verse 11:4, Mōshe tells the king that it will occur approximately at midnight. G-d knows exactly when midnight occurs, although people can only approximate it.

[245] 12:30 "there was not a house" – Although not every home necessarily contained a firstborn, there are numerous interpretations to explain this verse:

Rashē: In each home, the head of the household died.

Ibn Ezra: The verse means that the vast majority of households were affected, and the verse should not be taken literally. There are numerous verses that use words that can mean "all" or "every" where Ibn Ezra states that it is not meant literally. This is true for the verses that describe the events concening Noah and the great flood.

Ramban: The firstborn of every mother, as well as every father, died. This greatly increases the likelihood that there was a firstborn in every home.

Others: It includes firstborn women as well as men.

[246] 12:31 "Pharaoh summoned" – The king broke his own vow that he made in verse 10:28. This is yet another humiliating aspect of the erosion of the king's power. Note that Mōshe kept his vow not to interact with the king anymore (verse 10:29) because he does not bother to respond to the king.

[247] 12:31 "as you have demanded" - Pharaoh is only giving permission for a 3-day journey to offer offerings to G-d, which is what Mōshe had asked for all along.

After a few days, Pharaoh decides to chase after the Jewish people, as recorded starting in verse 14:5. It is not entirely clear on what day he decided to chase them, but he reached them 7 days after they ahd left Egypt.

[248] 12:32 "pray" – There is no indication that Mōshe prayed for him. There was no need to. See note on verse 8:24.

[249] 12:33 "leave immediately" – The king and the Egyptian people urged the Jewish people to leave that night. But the Jewish people waited until morning and asked for their rightful compensation for the decades of slave labor that they had provided to Egypt. They left in full daylight in dignity.

[250] 12:35 "they asked their neighbors" – G-d communicated to Mōshe in verse 3:22 that this would occur. The Jewish people had been instructed to ask in verse 11:2, although in the instruction, clothing is not mentioned. Some of this gold was used to make the gold calf statue (32:3). After the sin, the people were ashamed and stopped wearing jewelry (33:4) and G-d directed them to continue to not wear jewelry (33:5), which they followed (33:6). For the needs of the Tabernacle, people brought gold, silver, and jewels (see verse 35:22).

[251] 12:36 "to like" – This is promised in verse 3:21 and is mentioned in verse 11:3. Although some Egyptians liked the Jewish people all along, other Egyptians now also liked them.

[252] 12:36 "gave" – This is first mentioned by G-d in verse 3:22. Mōshe is told by G-d to instruct the Jewish people about this in verse 11:2.

[253] 12:37 "traveled" – Tables 4, 5, and 7 list the major events after the exodus.

[254] 12:37 "Ramsās to Sūkōt" – This is mentioned again in Bamidbar 33:5, where the series of journey interim stops are listed. See Kaplan, 1981, p. 315 for possible location for Sūkōt. One opinion is that it is near today's Cairo. The seat of Egypt's capital back then was Thebes.

[255] 12:37 "600,000 adult men" – In Jewish law, a person at 20 years of age is cnsidered to be an adult citizen. The concept of bar/bat mitzva concerns taking on religious obligations.

In terms of the Jewish population at the time of the exodus, we can assume there were about 600,000 adult women. We can also assume that most adults were married couples with many children, there could easily have been about 5 million people leaving. Later, each man twenty years and older gave a half-shekel coin for a total of 603,550 coins, as stated in verse 38:26. This effectively is the first census of the Jewish population. The study note on 38:26 discusses the various census counts.

[256] 12:38 "other peoples" – Sympathetic Egyptians as well as slaves of other nationalities left Egypt with the Jewish people. Some commentators believe that they went their separate ways once outside of Egypt. Other commentators feel that they stayed with the Jewish people and became fully part of the Jewish people at the divine revelation at Mount Sinai.

[257] 12:39 "Their dough had baked into maźa instead of bread" – This verse is given. in the Hagada. as the reason why there is a commandment to eat matzo on Passover.

[258] 12:39 "did not bring prepared foods" – Verse 13:18 states that they did have provisions, which means they had utensils so they could cook and prepare meals once they had a chance. The Jewish people had been told to pack and prepare for a long journey, and they did so.

[259] 12:40 "430 years" – The actual duration in Egypt was about 200 years. However, adding the years from the birth of Isaac, it tallies to 430. Abraham had been informed that his descendants would not be really free and would not rule their own land for 400 years (Genesis 15:13).

[260] Commandments 12-16 – Rambam: Mishne Tōra: Book 9: Offerings: Laws of Pascal Offering

[261] 12:44 "circumcised servants" – When a gentile was acquired as an indentured servant, he was taught the basic Tōra laws and he underwent circumcision. Therefore, he could partake of the offering. Once his master set him free, the gentile became fully Jewish. Gentile maidservants also observed basic Tōra laws and became fully Jewish once they were free. Freed gentile servants would become part of the Jewish tribe of their master.

[262] 12:45 "hired servants" – Even if a gentile servant (not an indentured servant) lives on the premises and participates in some family activities, he or she is not permitted to partake in the meat of the Pascal offering.

[263] Commandment 17 – Rambam: Book 7: Produce: Laws of Gifts to Priests

[264] 12:48 & 49 "converts" - Being Jewish is not defined solely by genetics or genealogy. A Jewish convert is someone who has studied Jewish philosophy, customs, and law, and has demonstrated an honest commitment to Tōra. A Jewish court presides over the process of elevating such a person to the heights of Tōra. In order to instill a respect for converts there are many statements and commandments throughout Tōra about treating converts as fully Jewish and warning against any negative or unequal treatment against them. There are 36 places in Tōra that state: do not wrong a convert. Throughout Jewish history, there have been many Jewish converts who were distinguished religious and civic leaders. See Essay 5 on Jewish Identity.

The Hebrew word in Tōra is gâr. It can mean:
a. someone from a foreign country
b. a righteous gentile
c. a convert

Bō – Section 7 - 13 + 3 verses

1869 336 13:1 G-d communicated to Mōshe (Moses):
1870 337 13:2 "Sanctify Jewish firstborn boys[265] and firstborn animals owned by Jewish people."

Commandment 18:[266] Do Not Eat Leavened Food On The Pesaĥ Festival

1871 338 13:3 Mōshe told the people:
"Remember this day on which you left Egypt and its slavery.
"The strength of G-d is what brought you out.
"You must not eat any leavened food during the holy festival of Pesaĥ (Passover).
1872 339 13:4 "Today you leave during the spring[267] season.
1873 340 13:5 "Once you enter[268] into the land of Israel,[269] which G-d promised your ancestors that He would give to you, a land flowing with milk and honey,[270] then you must observe the Pesaĥ offering each year.
1874 341 13:6 "Eat only unleavened food for 7 days.
"Observe day 7 as a holy festival to G-d.

Commandment 19:[271] Do Not Have Leavened Food During The Pesaĥ Festival

1875 342 13:7 "Eat only unleavened food for 7 days.
"You must not have any leavened food on your property.

Commandment 20:[272] Tell The Exodus Story On The First Night Of Pesaĥ

1876 343 13:8 "On the first night of Pesaĥ you must tell your children:[273]
'G-d saved us[274] because we observed the Pesaĥ offering.' [275]
1877 344 13:9 "These verses should be inserted into tifilin leather boxes (phylacteries[276]) because G-d took us out with a strong hand.
1878 345 13:10 "Be sure to observe the holy festival of Pesaĥ in
the spring[277] season.
1879 346 13:11 "Once you enter the land of Israel

Commandment 21: Offer Your Firstborn Animals

1880 347 13:12 "you should set aside your firstborn animals that are of kosher species.

Bō - Section 7 - continued

Commandment 22[278]: Redeem Your Firstborn Donkey

Commandment 23:[279] Put Down A Firstborn Donkey If You Decide Not To Redeem

1881 348 13:13 "A firstborn donkey should be redeemed with a lamb.

"Anyone who does not redeem a firstborn donkey must kill the donkey.

"Every firstborn son must be redeemed.[280]

Bō – Last Section

IF YOUR CHILD ASKS: WHAT IS THIS ABOUT?

1882 349 13:14 In the future when your children ask you:

'What is this[281] ceremony all about?'

"You should answer:

'G-d brought us out of the slavery of Egypt with a strong hand.

1883 350 13:15 'When Pharaoh had refused to allow the Jewish people to leave, G-d killed the firstborn[282] in Egypt.

'Therefore, I offer all firstborn animals and I redeem firstborn sons.

1884 351 13:16 'And therefore,[283] these verses are placed in the tifilin leather boxes because G-d brought us out of Egypt' "

Bō - Section 7 - Study Notes

---

²⁶⁵ 13:2 "firstborn boys" – See note on verse 11:5 for its connection to the fact that the Jewish firstborn were saved from the last of the 10 plagues. This directive is stated again in Bamidbar (Numbers) 18:15 as commandment 386.

²⁶⁶ Commandment 18: This commandment is explained by Rambam in his legal work Mishne Tōra: Book 3: Seasons: Laws of Leaven and Matza

²⁶⁷ 13:4 "spring" – Here it is stated as a fact. In verse 13:10, Tōra instructs that the Jewish leaders should make sure that future Pesaĥ holy festival will fall out during the spring season. Verses 23:15 and 34:18 state that Pesaĥ must be observed in the spring time because that is the season when the Jewish people left Egypt. This is restated in Divarim (Deuteronomy) 16:1.

Twelve lunar months add up to about 355 days, which is about 10 days shorter than the solar year. Therefore, if Pesaĥ falls in the late spring on year A, it will fall in mid-spring in the next year, year B, Then it will fall in early spring in year C. If there were no leap month, Pesaĥ would fall in the winter in year D. To prevent this, a leap month is added every 3-4 years. The sages created a 19-year cycle of leap months that keeps Pesaĥ in the spring.

²⁶⁸ 13:5 "once you enter" – Although verses 12:17 and 24 state that the Passover offering must be offered every year, this verse clarifies that this law does not take effect right away. Pesaĥ was not observed during the years of traveling through the wilderness. When the Jewish people entered Israel, they observed Pesaĥ (Book of Yihōshūa (Joshua) 5:1-9). Further clarification specifies that the Passover offering took full effect after the land of Israel was conquered and settled, processes which each took 7 years, for a total of 14 years after they entered Israel.

²⁶⁹ 13:5 "land of Israel" – See note on 3:8 for the promise that G-d made to the Jewish people.

²⁷⁰ 13:5 "milk and honey" – See note on verse 3:8 and Essay 8.

[271] Commandment 19: Book 7: Produce: Laws of First Fruits and Other Gifts to Priests

[272] Commandment 20 & 21 - Book 3: Seasons: Laws of Leaven and Matza

[273] 13:8 "you must tell your children" – Even if they do not ask.

[274] 13:8 "G-d saved us" – In the Passover Hagada, this reply is used for both the child who is skeptical and the child who shows up at the seder but does not ask questions. However, the tone with which this response is made is different toward children with differing temperaments. This verse is also in the Hagada right after the reasons given by Rabbi Gamlēel for each of three main items at the seder: Passover offering, matza, and bitter vegetables.

[275] 13:8 "because we observed the Pesaĥ offering" – This is Ibn Ezra's understanding of this verse.

[276] 13:9 "phylacteries" – This is the Greek word which the Septuagint uses as a translation of tefilin. The word phylactery is derived from the root word which means "to guard." Tefilin on the head and arm act as guards for the mind (thoughts) and actions (how limbs are used).

Tefilin consists of two leather boxes, each with an attached strap. One box has four compartments with its strap fashioned into a headband for securing it onto the head. Each compartment contains a different paragraph from Tōra on parchment. The other box has a single compartment containing the paragraphs on parchment. It is held in place with a strap for the arm.

Commandments 420 and 421, derived from Divarim 6:8, specify the wearing of tefilin of the head and arm respectively. Divarim 11:18 reiterates this commandment. Each box contains parchment with paragraphs of scripture written on them:
    Shimōt 13:1-10,
    Shimōt 13:11-16,
    Divarim 6:4-9 (first paragraph of Shema), and

Divarim 11:13-21 (second paragraph of Shema).
The Shema is a central declaration of belief in one G-d and a declaration of commitment to the commandments. It is recited each morning and night.

[277] 13:10 "spring" – See note on verse 13:4.

[278] Commandment 22 – Book 9: Offerings: Laws of First Born Animals

[279] Commandment 23 – Book 7: Produce: Laws of First Fruits and Gifts to Priests

[280] 13:13 "firstborn son must be redeemed" – On day 30 after birth, a son is redeemed by the parent giving a Jewish priest (kōhān) 5 silver shekel coins. Today, in America, 5 silver dollars are given. See 22:28, and Bamidbar 3:47, 18:15, and Vayikra 8:16. The commandment as identified by the Rambam is in Bamidbar 18:15. See note on 30:13 for the weight and value of a shekel.

[281] 13:14 "What is this . . .?" – In the Passover Hagada, this question is attributed to a child who is timid (This is usually translated as "simple." However, the same Hebrew word is used to describe the overriding character trait of Yaakōv. There, in Brāshēt 25:27, the word is variously translated as whole-hearted, honest or scholarly.) In the Hagada, the answer given to such a child is that G-d freed us from slavery forcefully, with great wonders.

[282] 13:14 "G-d brought us out of the slavery . . . G-d killed the firstborn" – This is the first time that the Jewish people learn the nature of the tenth plague. This comprehensive answer is not made part of the Four Children section although it is part of the Passover Hagada in various other places.

[283] 13:16 "And therefore . . . " – This verse may be part of the answer to the child, or the answer may have ended with verse 13:15

Bishalaĥ[284] - Section 1 - 14 verses (Total: 116 verses)
(There is 1 negative commandment in this portion)

THE JEWISH PEOPLE TRAVEL OUT OF EGYPT

1885 352 13:17 After Pharaoh forced the Jewish people to leave,[285] G-d did not lead the Jewish people along the road that would lead toward the Philistine nation.[286]

G-d holds the Jewish people close to Him.[287]

G-d did this because G-d determined that if the people would have to face battle, they would falter and return[288] to Egypt.

1886 353 13:18 Instead, G-d led the people roundabout through the wilderness toward the Reed Sea.[289]

The Jewish people left Egypt with provisions.[290]

MŌSHE TAKES ALONG THE BONES OF YŌSEF

1887 354 13:19 Mōshe (Moses) carried the bones of Yōsěf (Joseph) because Yōsěf had made the Jewish people promise:[291]

"G-d will remember you.

"Carry my bones with you away from here."

THE PEOPLE REACH ĀTAM, THE EDGE OF THE WILDERNESS

1888 355 13:20 On the second day of travel, they traveled[292] from Sūkōt and camped in Ātam which is on the edge of the wilderness.

G-D LEADS THE PEOPLE VIA CLOUD PILLAR DURING THE DAY AND FIRE PILLAR AT NIGHT

1889 356 13:21 G-d placed a cloud in front of them during the daytime in order to guide them.

G-d[293] placed a pillar of fire in front of them at night in order to give them light so that they could travel during both day and night.

1890 357 13:22 The cloud during the day and the fire at night[294] never left the front of the people.

Bishalaĥ - Section 1 - continued

THE JEWISH PEOPLE CAMP AT FREEDOM VALLEY (PĒ HAĤĒRŌT) ALONG THE REED SEA

1891 358 14:1 G-d communicated[295] to Mōshe:

1892 359 14:2 "Tell the Jewish people to travel back toward Egypt and camp at Pē Haĥērōt (Freedom Valley), which is between Migdōl[296] (Tower) and the sea.

"They will be facing the large statue known as North Lord.[297]

"Camp near the sea.

1893 360 14:3 "Pharaoh will think that the Jewish people are lost and trapped in the wilderness.

1894 361 14:4 "I will impart boldness in the king so he will be brave enough to come after the Jewish people.

"I will triumph over the king and his army and Egypt will know that I am G-d."

THE ENEMY DECIDES TO CHASE AND RECAPTURE THE JEWISH PEOPLE

1895 362 14:5 The king of Egypt received news that the people had no intention of returning.[298]

The king and his cabinet changed their minds about the people and declared:

"What have we done?"

"How could we allow the Jewish people to stop working for us?"

1896 363 14:6 The king ordered that his chariot be harnessed and he summoned his people to go with him.

1897 364 14:7 He amassed 600 chariots with the best drivers as well as the entire chariot corps of Egypt, along with the support of the infantry.[299]

1898 365 14:8 G-d made the heart of the king of Egypt stubborn[300] such that he pursued the Jewish people.

The Jewish people were marching in triumph.

Bishalaĥ - Section 1 - Study Notes

---

[284] The Hebrew word *bishalaĥ* means "when they were sent out"

[285] 13:17 "Jewish people to leave" - The Jewish people left Egypt on Nēsan 15 (verse 12:42), which according to Talmud Tractate Shabat page 86a was a Thursday morning.

[286] 13:17 "along the road toward the Philistine nation" – This route, which they did not take, goes east along the Mediterranean Sea toward the land known today as Gaza, which in Hebrew is Aza.

Gaza is part of the land of Israel as described in Brāshēt (Genesis) 15:18, Bamidbar (Numbers) 34:3-12 and Divarim (Deuteronomy) 1:7. This is evident when G-d instructed Yiźĥak (Isaac) to never leave the land of Israel, G-d but permitted Yiźĥak to stay in the land of the Philistines (Brāshēt 26:2).

On a historical note, Pilash was the ancestor of the Philistines. He was a descendant of Mitzrīyim (Brāshēt 10:13-14). Mitzrīyim and Kinaan (Canaan) were brothers, sons of Ĥam (Brāshēt 10:6), who was a son of Noaĥ.

The reason why G-d did not lead them along the route toward Gaza is that G-d had already informed Mōshe that the Jewish people will travel to the mountain of G-d – Mt. Sēnī (Sinai) (verse 3:12). However, it is a shorter and easier path for them to have traveled east and then south to Sēnī. What is described here is that G-d led the Jewish people in a somewhat more southerly direction, which placed them on the west side of the Gulf of Suez. See the map located after the tables on page 46. Also see the map in Kaplan, 1981, p.333.

The disadvantage, which is evident on the map on page 46 is the strategic mistake of being blocked-in by water on all three sides. See note on verse 14:5 where the king decides to chase and recapture them.

[287] 13:17 "G-d holds the Jewish people close to Him." - This is the understanding of the Daat Zikānim. G-d chose the route that would do the greatest good for the spiritual development of the Jewish people.

[288] 13:17 "return" - G-d wanted to eliminate any temptation to retreat

because the people were still a victim of slave mentality, as would become evident during their travels. The southeast route was not as easy to traverse.

[289] 13:18 "Reed Sea" – See note on verse 10:19 concerning the name of this sea, which today is commonly known as the Red Sea.

[290] 13:18 "with provisions" – This is the meaning according to Ibn Ezra. Note that they left Egypt with no fully prepared foods (see note on verse 12:39). But this verse states that they did have ingredients and utensils.

[291] 13:19 "Yōsěf had made the Jewish people promise" – As stated in Brāshēt 50:25.

[292] 13:20 "traveled" - This is mentioned again in Bamidbar 33:5, where the series of interim stops are listed.

[293] 13:21 "G-d" – Verse 14:19 states that G-d appointed a divine agent (such as an angel) to relocate the cloud pillar as a separation between the Jewish people and the oncoming Egyptian army.

Another example of a divine agent is that Mōshe encountered a divine agent at the burning bush (verse 3:2), but once Mōshe interacted, G-d communicated directly with him (verse 3:4).

Later, Mōshe lobbied against settling for a divine agent to lead the Jewish people. When the Jewish people are in the wilderness, G-d informs Mōshe that, instead of G-d leading them directly, an agent will lead them (23:20-23). G-d informs Mōshe that having an agent is a good thing because now, the agent to be appointed will not destroy people in the way that G-d Himself would do if the people sin (32:34 and 33:2-3). But Mōshe expresses dissatisfaction with having a mere agent (33:12), and therefore, G-d agrees to imbue the agent with some of His divine glory (33:14). Yet Mōshe states that such an agent will not possess enough divine glory to make it clear to the world that the Jewish people are not merely conventionally conquering the land of Israel, and that he, Mōshe, is not just an ordinary leader (33:15). Finally, Mōshe asks again (34:9), and G-d agrees to lead the Jewish people Himself (34:10).

[294] 13:22 "cloud during the day and the fire at night" – The cloud/fire pair is mentioned during the crossing of the sea (14:19-24). It is also mentioned in regard to the Tabernacle and the further travels of the Jewish people in verses 40:34-38. See note on 17:1 which explains that it may have been the signal used by G-d even before the Tabernacle was built.

[295] 14:1 "communicated" – In the poem sung by Mōshe, anthropomorphisms such as "right hand" (verses 15:6 & 12) and "nostrils" (verse 15:8) are examples that describe G-d in terms that people can relate to. In actuality, G-d is not physical and has no parts. See Essay 2 as to the nature of G-d.

[296] 14:2 "Pē Haĥērōt . . . Migdōl" – This is recounted in Bamidbar 33:7.

[297] 14:2 "North Lord" - Cairo Papyrus 31169 mentions the similarly named Megdal Pef Bla Żapnū, which is 8 miles north of Suez. At this place, the ancient Gulf of Suez extended to what is known as the Bitter Lakes. (see Kaplan, 1981 for details.)

[298] 14:5 "no intention of returning" - The king's spies saw that if the Jewish people had intended to hold to their 3-days' journey request, they would have started back by now. The fact that they were blocked in by water further emboldened the king.

[299] 14:7 "chariots . . . infantry" - Flavius Josephus, a Jewish general captured by the Roman army, wrote in his History of the Jews that Pharaoh amassed an army of 250,000 men, along with 50,000 chariots, for this battle (see Kaplan, 1981, p. 322).

[300] 14:8 – "stubborn" – See note on verse 7:3 for the many occurrences of Pharaoh being stubborn, and having G-d cause him to be stubborn.

Bishalaĥ - Section 2   - 6 verses

THE ENEMY CATCHES UP

1899 366 14:9 The army of Egypt reached the Jewish people[301] while they were camped along the sea at Freedom Valley near North End.
   A great army of chariots, cavalry and infantry of Egypt approached.

JEWISH PEOPLE ARE GRIPPED WITH FEAR

1900 367 14:10 As the army came closer, the Jewish people saw them approaching the rear and they became very frightened.
   They called to G-d.

JEWISH PEOPLE COMPLAIN

1901 368 14:11 Some complained[302] to Mōshe (Moses) as follows:
   "Isn't there enough grave sites in Egypt?
   "Why bring us here to die in the wilderness?
   "How could you do this to us – how could you bring us out of Egypt?
1902 369 14:12 "Didn't we ask you[303] when we were in Egypt to leave us alone and let us continue to work for our masters?
   "It is better to be slaves in Egypt than to die here in the wilderness."

MŌSHE REASSURES THE JEWISH PEOPLE

1903 370 14:13 Mōshe replied:
   "Do not be afraid.
   "Stand firm and you will see how G-d will rescue you.
   "You will be seeing the people of Egypt for the last time.
1904 371 14:14 "G-d will fight for you.
   "You must remain silent."

Bishalaȟ - Section 2 - Study Notes

---

[301] 14:9 "reached the Jewish people" – This occurred a week after the exodus, on Wednesday, Nēsan 21. This corresponds to the seventh day of the Passover festival.

[302] 14:11 "complained" – Throughout the years in the wilderness, due to stress, difficulties, and dissatisfaction, there are groups that mutiny or complain. Sometimes the complaints and dissension was due to hunger and thirst. But the way they react – to doubt Mōshe and doubt G-d – is unjustifiable. Some of the dissension is attributed to the slave mentality that the Jewish people developed over many decades of slavery in Egypt. Some of the other verses in which discontent and dissent occur include:

Shimōt 15:24 There is only bitter water. "What will we drink?"

Shimōt 16:2 Mutiny because there is a food shortage

Shimōt 16:20 Some people disobeyed Mōshe and tried to keep some manna for the next day.

Shimōt 16:27 Some people went out looking for manna on shabat (Sabbath) even though they were told not to do so.

Shimōt 17:3 "Why did you lead us out of Egypt?" (Attributed to their slave mentality.)

Shimōt 32:1 Sin of the golden calf statue.

Vayikra 24:10 A man blasphemed G-d.

Bamidbar 11:1 Some people complained bitterly.

Bamidbar 11:4 A group remembered Egypt and wanted something other than manna to eat. (Slave mentality.)

Bamidbar 14:2 Some people said: "We wish we had died in Egypt!" (Slave mentality.)

Bamidbar 14:10 Some people threatened to stone Mōshe & Aharōn (Aaron) to death as a continuation of the complaint in 14:2. (Slave mentality.)

Bamidbar 14:40 A group decides to go to war, against the directive of G-d.

Bamidbar 15:32 A man violated the Sabbath.

Bamidbar 16:1 Rebellion of Kōraȟ against Mōshe's leadership.

Bamidbar 17:6 Some people wrongly accuse Mōshe: "You killed holy people."

Bamidbar 20:5 When there was no water after Miryam's passing, some people complained: "Why did you lead us out of Egypt and bring us to this terrible place?" (Slave mentality.)

Bamidbar 21:4 Some people became discouraged and spoke against G-d and Mōshe. "We are tired of this manna."

[303] 14:12 "Didn't we ask you" – When Mōshe first confronts Pharaoh, Pharaoh reacts by making the life of the Jewish people more unbearable. As a result, some people criticize Mōshe for it (verse 14:12). Even after all the wonders, plagues, and miraculous turn of events that result in their freedom, some people are still fixated on the distant past.

Bishalaĥ - Section 3   - 11 verses

G-D INFORMS MŌSHE OF HIS DIVINE PLAN

1905 372 14:15 G-d communicated to Mōshe (Moses):
"I have responded to your prayer.[304]
"Speak to the Jewish people and let them start walking.
1906 373 14:16 "Raise your staff and extend your hand over the sea so the Jewish people will be able to walk on dry land."
1907 374 14:17 "I will cause the Egyptian soldiers to be stubborn such that they will chase you.
"This is how I will triumph over the king and his army of chariots and cavalry.
1908 375 14:18 "Once I have triumphed over Pharaoh and his army, the Egyptians will realize that I am G-d."

G-D USES THE PILLARS TO HOLD THE ENEMY BEHIND AND AWAY FROM THE JEWISH PEOPLE

1909 376 14:19 A divine agent[305] who had been traveling in front of the Jewish people, now relocated to the back, such that the cloud pillar moved from the front to their backs.

THE JEWISH PEOPLE CROSS THE SEA AT NIGHT BY THE LIGHT OF THE DIVINE FIRE PILLAR

1910 377 14:20 Thus the cloud pillar was located between the army of Egypt and the Jewish people.
During the entire night, the cloud gave light to the Jewish people, while it remained dark on the side of the pursuing army, so that the two groups never came near to each other throughout the entire night.

MŌSHE ACTS AND THE WATER PARTS

1911 378 14:21 Mōshe raised his hands toward the sea and G-d caused a powerful wind from the east to cause the water to recede.
The wind blew all night so the land was dry and the waters parted.

THE JEWISH PEOPLE START TO CROSS

1912 379 14:22 The Jewish people walked on dry land in the middle of the sea bed, and the waters became walls on each side of the rows of people.

Bishalaĥ - Section 3 - continued

The Army Chases Them

1913 380 14:23 The army chased the Jewish people and the army marched into the middle of the sea area.

1914 381 14:24 In the morning, G-d acted through the fire pillar and the cloud pillar and confused the army.

1915 382 14:25 G-d caused their chariot wheels to loosen and spin off.

   The soldiers said:

   "We need to run away from the Jewish people because G-d is fighting for them."

Bishalaĥ - Section 3 - Study Notes

---

[304] 14:15 "I have responded to your prayer" – This is the translation of Onkelos, who translated the Tōra into Aramaic, which was the spoken language of the Jewish people during the times of the Romans. Other commentators translate this verse as "Why pray to me?" However, Onkelos incorporates the fact that Mōshe just calmed the Jewish people. G-d is agreeing with Mōshe's assurance to the Jewish people, which is an implied request (i.e., prayer) to G-d.

[305] 14:19 "a divine agent" – Verse 13:21 states that G-d created the cloud pillar and the column of fire. See the note on verse 13:21 for a discussion of the implication of a divine agent, as opposed to G-d Himself.

Bishalaĥ - Section 4   - 32 verses

1916 383 14:26 G-d communicated to Mōshe (Moses):
"Raise your hand toward the sea so that the waters will pour down onto the attacking army."

ENEMY IS DROWNED

1917 384 14:27 Mōshe did so, and the sea returned to its natural state by morning.
The soldiers ran away from the rushing water, but G-d threw them into the sea.
1918 385 14:28 The waters returned to their natural state and covered the chariots and drowned the horsemen.
1919 386 14:29 But the Jewish people had walked on dry land[306] in the middle of the sea area.
The waters had been a wall on their right and left.
1920 387 14:30 This was how G-d saved the Jewish people from the enemy.
The Jewish people saw enemy soldiers lying dead on the shore.
1921 388 14:31 The Jewish people saw the great act of G-d and the people feared and believed in G-d and they believed in His agent Mōshe.

MŌSHE AND THE JEWISH PEOPLE PRAISE G-D

1922 389 15:1 Then Mōshe and the Jewish people praised G-d with this poem:[307]
1923 390 15:2 "I will sing to G-d because G-d is great.
"G-d threw horse and rider into the sea.
1924 391 15:3 "G-d is a warrior.
"G-d is His name.
1925 392 15:4 "G-d threw Pharaoh's chariots and army into the sea.
"Pharaoh's best soldiers sank into the Reed Sea (Red Sea).[308]
1926 393 15:5 "The waters covered them.
"Some of the soldiers sank like stones.
1927 394 15:6 "G-d: Your 'right hand' [309] has glorious power.
"G-d: Your strength dashed the enemy into pieces.

Bishalaĥ - Section 4 - continued

1928 395 15:7 "With the greatness of your excellence, You overthrow people who are against You.

"When You exercise Your anger, it destroys evil like stubble.

1929 396 15:8 "The sea waters parted because of a mere blast of Your 'nostrils.'[310]

"The waters became walls.

"The waters became solid.

1930 397 15:9 "The enemy said:

'I will overtake the Jewish people and take their possessions.

'I will satisfy my desire regarding them, namely, I will destroy them with my sword.'

1931 398 15:10 "You, G-d, caused the wind to blow the sea so that the waters covered them

"Some of them sank like lead weights in the turbulent waters.

1932 399 15:11 "G-d: There is no being or force as strong as You.

"You are glorious in Your holiness.[311]

"People are afraid to praise You because they are not able to understand or verbally express the full extent of your greatness.

1933 400 15:12 "You 'extended Your right hand'[312] and the earth swallowed the enemy.

1934 401 15:13 "You saved Your Jewish people and led them with love.

"You are leading them, utilizing Your powers, to the holy land of Israel.

1935 402 15:14 "Peoples of the world have heard, and will hear, about this and they will be afraid.

"Fear is already taking hold of the people in Pilash (Philistines).[313]

1936 403 15:15 "Leaders of Edōm[314] are afraid.

"Trembling has taken hold of the generals of Mōav.[315]

"The people in the land of Kinaan (Canaan)[316] are afraid.

Bishalaĥ - Section 4 - continued

1937 404 15:16 "Those peoples are very afraid and they are not able to do anything about it.
   "G-d, Your Jewish people will be traveling toward them, and past them into the land of Israel.
1938 405 15:17 "G-d, You are about to lead the Jewish people to Your special mountain which You have given to the Jewish people, and on which they will build the Holy Temple.[317]
1939 406 15:18 "G-d will rule forever.
1940 407 15:19 "The chariots, horses, and soldiers of Pharaoh sank into the sea when
G-d poured the waters back upon them, but the Jewish people had walked on dry land in the middle of the sea."

MIRYAM SINGS

1941 408 15:20 Miryam[318] (Miriam), the prophetess, the sister of Aharōn (Aaron), played her tambourine.
   The other women followed her lead and played their tambourines, and they danced.
1942 409 15:21 Miryam sang[319] the following poem to G-d:
   "Sing to G-d because he is great.
   "G-d threw horses and riders into the sea."

THE JEWISH PEOPLE STAY IN SHÙR: NO WATER FOR 3 DAYS

1943 410 15:22 Mōshe led the Jewish people onward to the wilderness called Shùr.
   They were in that wilderness for three days without water.

JEWISH PEOPLE ARRIVE AT MARATA: LAKE OF BITTER WATER

1944 411 15:23 They came to the place named Marata which had a lake, but the water was bitter and not drinkable.
   They called the place Mara.[320]
1945 412 15:24 Disgruntled people complained[321] to Mōshe:
   "What are we going to drink?"

Bishalaĥ - Section 4 - continued

G-D INSTRUCTS MŌSHE: SWEETEN THE LAKE WATER WITH A CERTAIN PLANT

1946 413 15:25 Mōshe prayed[322] to G-d.

G-d showed him a tree.

Mōshe threw the tree into the bitter lake and the water became sweet and drinkable.

At this location, G-d gave them laws to follow.

At this place, G-d tested the Jewish people.

G-D INSTRUCTS THE PEOPLE: BE LAW-ABIDING AND ETHICAL

1947 414 15:26 G-d communicated to them:

"If you obey G-d, behave ethically, and follow the commandments and laws, then I will not do to you any of the bad things that I did to the people of Egypt, because I am your doctor.[323]

Bishalaĥ - Section 4 - Study Notes

---

³⁰⁶ 14:29 "on dry land" – While the last of the Jewish people were still walking on dry land in the sea area, the waters at the other side of the sea poured down onto the oncoming army.

³⁰⁷ 15:1 "poem" – The following is an 18-verse poem of praise to G-d, largely addressed directly to G-d. Note that the original silent daily prayer, the Amēda, consisted of 18 blessings. Another blessing was added later, during times of trouble.

³⁰⁸ 15:4 "Reed Sea" – See note on verse 10:19.

³⁰⁹ 15:6 & 5:12 "right hand" – G-d is not physical. See note on 14:1.

³¹⁰ 15:8 "nostrils" – See note on 14:1.

³¹¹ 15:11 "glorious in Your holiness" – Usually, G-d's holiness is thought of in serene terms. But the Jewish people experienced the holiness of G-d even in the way that G-d metes out punishment.

³¹² 15:12 "extended Your right hand" – See note on 14:1.

³¹³ 15:14 "Pilash" – Philistine. See note on verse 13:17.

³¹⁴ 15:15 "Edōm" – Āsav (Esau), son of Isaac, was called Edōm after he sold his birthright to his brother Jacob for a bowl of red lentils (Brāshēt (Genesis) 25:30). The country to the east of Israel had been settled by a man named Sāêr. The land was called Sāêr. Āsav settled there later and it became know as the land of Edōm (Brāshēt 33:14).

³¹⁵ 15:15 "Mōav" – Mōav was a son of Lōt (Brāshēt 19:37), born from incest between Lōt and one of his own daughters. Lōt was the nephew of Avraham.

As a nation, Mōav hired a prophet to attempt to curse the Jewish people (Bamidbar (Numbers) Chapters 22-24). When that was unsuccessful, Mōav found a way to cause some Jewish people to sin, in the hopes of causing G-d to stop favoring the Jewish people (Bamidbar Chapter 25).

³¹⁶ 15:15 "Kinaan" – Kinaan was a grandson of Noah. As stated in Brāshēt 15:19-21, the land of Kinaan – the land of Israel - was occupied by 12 tribal nations. Brāshēt 15:19-21 lists 10 tribes: Ken, Kinēz, Kadmōn, Ĥet (Hittites), Prēz, Rifaim, Emôr, Kinaan (Canaanites), Gêrgash, and Yivūs. Shimōt (Exodus) 13:5 mentions the nation of Ĥiv (Hivites). Plus there was the tribe of Pilash (Plishtim = Philistines) in the Gaza (Aza) region. Gaza is fully part of Israel.

³¹⁷ 15:17 "mountain . . . Holy Temple" – Although Yerushalayim (Jerusalem) is not mentioned in Ĥumash (Five Books of Moses), the Jewish people were told by G-d that a special mountain (i.e., Jerusalem) is set aside for the Holy Temple.

³¹⁸ 15:20 "Miryam" - This is the first mention of her name. She is referred to as the sister of baby Mōshe in verse 2:3. She is mentioned again in Bamidbar (Numbers) 26:59.

³¹⁹ 15:21 "Miryam sang" – The women praised G-d in song and dance.
This shows that Jewish women are permitted to sing in public. For example, Talmud Tractate Sanhedrin states that when a rabbinical student took his ordination exam, and the word came that the student had successfully passed the test and is now a rabbi, women would line the street and sing songs of his praises as he walked home. In addition, early manuscripts of music written for synagogue services are scored for choruses of men and women.
Today, a difficulty has arisen due to a single statement in Talmud Tractate Braĥōt 24b, made by Shmūel who states: "the voice of a woman is indecent exposure."
This statement contradicts Jewish law and was clarified by the early rabbis. Rabbi Hai Gaon (939-1038) in his work Ōźar HaGaōnim (Braĥōt p. 30) interprets the above statement as follows: if a man feels aroused by a woman who is singing, he should not recite the Shima prayer while he can hear her. Both the Rif (Rabbi Yiźĥak Alfasi, 1013-1103) and Rambam (1135-1204) leave Shmūel's statement out of their legal codifications

because they reject such an unnecessary restriction. The Rush (Rabbi Yaakōv son of Asher, 1270-1343) and the Maharshal (1510-1573) both omit any prohibition of listening to a woman speak or sing.

An erroneous conclusion seen today is that many people believe that the statement in the Babylonian Talmud Tractate Braĥōt means that only singing is prohibited. However, in Tractate Kidushin (Laws of Betrothals) there is recorded an incident where someone refused to say hello to a woman because he accepted Shmūel's statement about a woman's voice, although no one else did.

The statement in the Babylonian Talmud reflects the fact that during that time period in Persia, Zoroastrians ruled. Zoroastrian law prohibits a woman from speaking in public. Jewish women were forced by gentile law to refrain from speaking or singing in public.

Similarly, the statement in Talmud Tractate Braĥōt 24b, which regards female hair as indecent exposure is rejected by Rif and Rambam. Tiferet Yisrael by Israel Lipschutz (1782-1860), when commenting on Mishna Nidarim 3:8 states: Gentile law in Persia required that girls and women cover their hair. Therefore, when Talmud Tractate Braĥōt 24a states that "female hair is indecent exposure" it means that hair is treated as if it is indecent exposure because the Zoroastrians, who ruled Persia during the time of the Talmud, forced girls and women, whether married or not, to cover their hair. See Art Scroll Mishna: Nidarim 3:8, p.64.

See the essay on the next page on the issue of comportment.

[320] 15:23 "Mara" – The Hebrew word *mara* means "bitterness."

[321] 15:24 "complained" – See note on verse 14:11. With this perplexing reaction so soon after the greatest miracle in history, Tōra emphasizes that living at a time of open overt miracles will not cause people to be more likely to believe and have faith. Rather, a person develops and strengthens his or her faith and beliefs based on conviction, study and understanding.

[322] 15:25 "prayed" – See note on verse 8:8 about prayer.

[323] 15:26 "doctor" – This assurance by G-d pairs with verse 23:25 which states that sincere prayer and service to G-d are linked to an assurance of good health.

Bishalaĥ - Section 4 - continued

Essay: Comportment

The following discussion defines Jewish law with regard to women's appearance and behavior. This includes:
a) uncovered hair,
b) singing in public,
c) head covering,
d) indecent exposure,
e) clothing coverage,
f) strict customs,
and g) modern orthodox appoach.

Caveat: There are people who adopt stricter views on these issues. But it is imperative to understand the baseline Jewish law. It is even more important for all people to respect one another, no matter what legitimate leniencies they have. On each page in Talmud, sages differed on major issues of Jewish law, but throughout Jewish history, they respected each other and each other's opinions. In today's varied and complex world, it is even more important for religious and social leaders to respect each other and their opinions. Only then can there be true unity that will usher in a time of lasting peace.

A. A woman's hair is not nakedness, and uncovered hair is not indecent exposure

1. Rabbi Yechiel Michel Epstein (1829-1908) in his work Arūĥ HaShulĥan (volume Ōraĥ Ĥīyim 75:5), states directly that a woman's hair is not indecent exposure.

2. Rabenu Alfasi (Rif) (1013-1103) in his comentary on Talmud, and Rambam (1135-1204) in his <u>Mishne Tora</u>, omit the statements about a woman's uncovered hair and her singing that are found in Talmud Tractate Braĥōt 24a. These omissions clearly show that Rif and Rambam reject the concept that a woman's hair is indecent exposure. They also reject the idea that a woman is forbidden to sing in public.

Bishalaĥ - Section 4 – continued

Essay: Comportment - continued

3. Ritva on Kidūshin 81b-82a: Nowadays, showing hair is not a behavior of promiscuity. It is normal and customary. Rashē also views this as the intent of the talmud (Broyde, p. 161).

4. The book <u>Tiferet Yisrael</u> by Israel Lipschutz (1782-1860), in his comments on Mishna Nidarim 3:8 states: Gentile law in Persia required that girls and women cover their hair. Hair covering for women is not a Jewish practice (Art Scroll Mishna: Nidarim 3:8, p.64).

When Talmud Tractate Braĥōt 24a states that "female hair is indecent exposure" it means that a woman's hair was treated as if it is indecent exposure because the Zoroastrians, who ruled Persia during the time of the Talmud, forced girls and women, whether married or not, to cover their hair. It is important to note that these statements in Talmud do not specify married women. This makes it clear that these are statements of Arab law which Jewish people in middleeastern countries were forced to follow.

5. Rabbi Yōsef Chaim in his book Ĥūkāt Nashim (17) states that in Western countries, women do not need to cover their hair, just as they do not wear veils.

6. Rashba on Braĥōt 24b quotes Rīvid (Raavad): A woman does not need to cover any body part that does not cause a man to be aroused (Broyde, p.119).

7. Ritva on Kidūshin 81b-82a: Men who are not aroused by looking at and/or speaking to women are permitted to do so (Broyde, pp.120, 161).

Bishalaĥ - Section 4 – continued

Essay: Comportment - continued

B. Women are permitted to sing in front of men

Shimōt 15:21 states that Miryam sang when the Jewish people crossed the Reed Sea. Women praised G-d in song and dance.

Talmud Tractate Sanhedrin states that when a rabbinical student took his ordination exam, and the word came that the student is now a rabbi, women would line the street and sing songs of his praises as he walked home.

Early manuscripts of music written for synagogue services are scored for choruses of men and women.

Today, a difficulty has arisen due to a single statement in Talmud Tractate Brahōt 24b, made by Shmūel who states: "the voice of a woman is indecent exposure."

This statement contradicts Jewish law and was clarified by the early rabbis. Rabbi Hai Gaon (939-1038) in his work Ōźar HaGaōnim (Brahōt) interprets the above statement as follows: if a man feels aroused by a woman who is singing, he should not recite the Shima declaration while he can hear her. Both the Rif (Rabbi Yiźĥak Alfasi, 1013-1103) and Rambam (1135-1204) leave Shmūel's statement out of their legal codifications because they reject such an unnecessary restriction (as mentioned above). The Rush (Rabbi Yaakov son of Asher, 1270-1343) and the Maharshal (1510-1573) both omit any prohibition against listening to a woman speak or sing.

Tractate Kidushin (Laws of Betrothal) records that there was one man who refused to say hello to a woman because he accepted Shmūel's statement about a woman's voice literally, although other people did not. The Talmud uses the term "voice" which includes speaking.

Shmūel's statement in the Babylonian Talmud reflects the fact that in Persia, Zoroastrian law prohibited a woman from speaking in public. Jewish women were forced by gentile law to refrain from speaking or singing in public.

Bishalaĥ - Section 4 – continued

Essay: Comportment - continued

C. In former times, married women wore head coverings

1. In all the Talmudic discussions about a woman's head covering, the term "hair" is never used. It is clear that the Talmud is dealing with a concern of social status and dignity, not indecency or modesty. A wife is expected to dress in public in a way that brings honor to herself and to her husband. Before the 1400's Jewish women did not wear a wedding ring. Wearing a head covering in public indicated that she was married.

2. According to Rush, what is considered modest depends on local practice and custom. In societies where woman do not cover their forearms and hair, they do not arouse men, and these practices are therefore permitted. (Broyde, p. 110).

3. The direct reading of the Shulĥan Aruch is that if social custom is to not cover one's head, it is not necessary for a woman to cover her hair. (Broyde p. 175).

4. Rashba on Talmud Tractate Braĥōt 24a states that hair that extends outside of a hat does not need to be covered. This includes bangs and hair that flows off her head.

5. The Rama on Ōraĥ Ĥīyim (75:2) states that hair that extends outside a kerchief need not be covered.

6. Even for people who want to be strict, Magen Avraham on Ōraĥ Ĥīyim (75:2) deals only about hair that is directly on a woman's head as needing to be covered. Therefore, bangs and hair that falls on a woman's shoulders do not need to be covered.

7. Maharam Alshakar, Even HaEzer 35: Everyone agrees that there is no Biblical prohibition for a woman to expose her hair. Women are permitted to expose hair that is normally exposed as long as she wears a hat (see Broyde, p. 107).

Bishalaĥ - Section 4 - continued

Essay: Comportment - continued

8. Yabēa Ōmer Vol. 4 Even HaEzer #3: Modest Jewish women are permitted to let their hair protrude from their hat, just as ruled by Maharam Alshakar 35 (Broyde, p.128).

D. Indecency, Modesty, and Social Status

1. Talmud Tractate Braĥōt 24a rules that a woman with no clothes on is permitted to perform the commandment of separating a portion of kneaded dough and she may recite the blessing, as long as she sits down, because by sitting down she is covering nakedness as defined by Tōra law.

When a woman wears a bikini outfit, she covers her nakedness both on the Biblical and rabbinic levels.

2. The Talmud and Jewish law make a distinction between three issues: indecency, modesty, and dignity. Any clothing that a woman wears in addition to a bikini outfit demonstrates modesty. Dressing in a way that is appropriate for the occasion is a matter of dignity. In former times, a person's hat was a sign of social status and dignity.

E. Areas that are normally covered

1. Tōsfōt on Talmud Tractate Kitūbōt 72 - Women do not have to cover their hair or wear a hat in a backyard or even going from yard to yard. Even for women who want to be strict, the requirement to wear a head covering pertains only to the marketplace (Broyde, p.113).

Bishalaĥ - Section 4 - continued

Essay: Comportment - continued

F. Strict customs have been a reaction of tragedies

After pogroms in Europe and Russia in the 1600s, the Hasidic movement grew out of the disaffected feelings of the discouraged Jewish people. Hasidim felt that Jewish people must be doing something wrong, otherwise these tragedies would not occur. Many strict customs developed in Hasidic circles, including forcing women to cover their hair, even though for 2,000 years Jewish women did not cover their hair unless forced to do so by Arabs.

Then, after World War I, Jewish communities had experienced terrible disruption. Certain ultra-orthodox groups decided that perhaps the custom of Hasidim - of women covering their hair - would prevent future difficulties. In actual fact, life in Europe in the 1930s only got worse.

In the 1980s and onward, more and more modern orthodox women – women whose religious mothers and grandmothers did not cover their hair – started covering their hair because of undue pressure from the ultra-orthodox.

G. Modern Orthodoxy

Throughout history, as is clearly evident in Talmudic discussions, Jewish leaders each had their ruling about Jewish law and custom. However, each leader respected the differing opinions of their colleages. This is a characteristic that is sorely lacking today. Ultra-orthodox leaders insist that people who do not rule the way they do are not following Jewish law. Nothing could be further from the truth. More and more orthodox people and synagogues are feeling tremendous pressure to conform to reactionary fundamentalist fanaticism.

The "modern orthodox" approach is not modern at all. It is an effort to revert to original traditional Jewish laws and customs.

Bishalaĥ - Section 5   - 11 verses

THE PEOPLE ARRIVE AT ĀLIM OASIS

1948 415 15:27 The Jewish people arrived at Ālim where there were 12 springs of water and 70 palm trees.

THE PEOPLE RESIDE IN ŹIN

1949 416 16:1 On day 15 of the second month after leaving Egypt, the Jewish people traveled from Ālim to the wilderness of Źin,[324] which is located between Ālim and Sēnī.

PEOPLE COMPLAIN ABOUT LACK OF FOOD

1950 417 16:2 Some people mutinied[325] against Mōshe (Moses) and Aharōn (Aaron) while in the wilderness.

1951 418 16:3 These people said to Mōshe and Aharōn:

"We would rather have perished by G-d in Egypt, where we used to eat well.

"You brought us to this wilderness where we will perish from hunger."

G-D PROMISES FOOD

1952 419 16:4 G-d communicated to Mōshe:

"I will rain food from the sky for you.

"The people will go out each day and collect a day's worth of food.

"Through this they will feel the need for the divine presence.

"They must follow My laws.

BISHALAḤ - SECTION 5 - CONTINUED

EACH PERSON MUST COLLECT TWICE AS MUCH ON FRIDAY

1953 420 16:5 "On Friday, the people will collect a two-day's amount of food." [326]

1954 421 16:6 Mōshe and Aharōn told the Jewish people:

"Tonight, you will know that G-d brought you out[327] of Egypt.

1955 422 16:7 "And in the morning you will see the glory of G-d.

"G-d has heard your complaints against Him.

"Who are Aharōn and I that you should complain against us?"

1956 423 16:8 Mōshe said:

"G-d will give you meat tonight, and food in the morning because G-d hears your complaints against Him.

"When you complain, you are not complaining to Aharōn and me, rather you are complaining against G-d."

1957 424 16:9 Mōshe told Aharōn:

"Announce[328] to the Jewish people:

'Come close to G-d because He has heard your complaints.' "

THE GLORY OF G-D APPEARS

1958 425 16:10 When Aharōn spoke to the Jewish people, they looked toward the wilderness and the glory of G-d appeared in the cloud.

Bishalaĥ - Section 5 - Study Notes

[324] 16:1 "Ālim to the wilderness of Źin" – This is recounted in Bamidbar (Numbers) 33:9-11.

[325] 16:2 "mutinied" – See note on verse 14:11 for a list and discussion of the many complaints.

[326] 16:5 "collect a two-day's amount of food" – This is described in verse 16:22.

[327] 16:6 "brought you out" – Throughout their journey through the wilderness, there were some difficult people, who, even after all the miracles and wonders, doubted that G-d had brought them out. Even during times when miracles and divine intervention are open and overt, people of little faith and trust still refuse to believe.

[328] 16:9 "announce" – Mōshe creates an opportunity to show the people that Aharōn is a special agent of G-d.

Bishalaĥ - Section 6   - 26 verses

1959 426 16:11 G-d communicated to Mōshe (Moses):
1960 427 16:12 "I have acknowledged the complaints of the Jewish people.
 "Tell them:
'In the late afternoon you will have meat to eat, and in the morning you will have food to eat.
'Through this you will realize that I am your G-d.' "

Food: Birds And Honey Wafers (Män)

1961 428 16:13 Toward evening, birds arrived in massive numbers.
In the morning there was a layer of moisture on the ground.
1962 429 16:14 When the moisture evaporated, there was food of fine flakes[329] of fine frost on the ground.
1963 430 16:15 The Jewish people did not know what it is and asked each other:
"What is this?" [330]
Mōshe answered them:
"This is the food that G-d has provided for you.
1964 431 16:16 "G-d instructed us:
'Collect a single day's amount of this food each morning for yourself and your family.' "
1965 432 16:17 The Jewish people did as instructed.
Some people collected a large amount of the food, while others collected a small amount.
1966 433 16:18 Each family found that they had just enough for their needs no matter how much or how little they had collected.
1967 434 16:19 Mōshe told them:
"No one should try to leave over food for the next day."

Non-Believers Try To Save Some Food For The Next Day

1968 435 16:20 Nonetheless, some people left some of the food over at night.
They found that in the morning it was infested with worms and was rotten.
Mōshe was very angry with those people.
1969 436 16:21 This daily routine continued each morning.
Once the sun rose, any food that had not been collected melted away.

BISHALAḤ - SECTION 6 - CONTINUED

SABBATH: DAY OF REST

1970 437 16:22 On Friday, the people collected twice as much food.[331]
The leaders were concerned [332] about this and confronted Mōshe.
1971 438 16:23 Mōshe explained to them:
"G-d has instructed that tomorrow is a solemn day of rest[333] to G-d.
"On Friday, you should bake and/or boil the food according to your desire, and to keep the leftovers for tomorrow."
1972 439 16:24 The Jewish people did as they were instructed, and the food did not rot the next morning.
1973 440 16:25 Mōshe told them:
"Eat today, because today is the day of rest (sabbath).
"Today[334] you will not find any food on the ground.
1974 441 16:26 "You will collect the food for six days, and on the seventh there will not be any on the ground."

NON-BELIEVERS LOOK FOR FOOD ON SABBATH

1975 442 16:27 But on the seventh day, some people went out to collect food, and they found that there was no food.
1976 443 16:28 G-d communicated to Mōshe:
"How long will people refuse to keep My commandments and laws?

Commandment 24: [335] Do Not Go Outside Of The Boundary On The Sabbath

1977 444 16:29 "G-d gave you the day of rest and you were able to collect double your needs on Friday.
"No one is permitted to go out of the boundary on sabbath."

ALL PEOPLE NOW ACCEPT THE SABBATH

1978 445 16:30 From that day onward, the people did rest on the seventh day.

Bishalaĥ - Section 6 - continued

THE PEOPLE NAME THE HONEY WAFERS: MÄN

1979 446 16:31 The Jewish people named the food män.[336]
It was white and tasted like honey wafers.
1980 447 16:32 Mōshe stated:
"G-d has instructed:
'Set aside one measure of this food so that future generations can see what you ate in the wilderness when I led you out of Egypt.'"
1981 448 16:33 Later, after the Tabernacle[337] had been constructed, Mōshe instructed Aharōn:
"Put one measure of this food in a jar and place it in front of G-d, to be kept forever.
1982 449 16:34 Aharōn placed it in the sacred box.
1983 450 16:35 Because eventually the Jewish people were not permitted to enter the promised land immediately, they ate män for forty years[338] in the wilderness until they arrived at the land of Israel.
1984 451 16:36 The unit of measure (ōmer) for the män is the volume of about 43 eggs, which is one-tenth the volume of the measurement known as an āfa.

Bishalaĥ - Section 6 - Study Notes

---

329 16:14 "flakes" – There are a number of different translations of word, including:
   Ramban: flakes
   Ibn Ezra: round balls
   Rashbam: hailstones
   Rashē: layered food
   Talmud Tractate Yōma 75b: a sticky food.

330 16:15 "What is this?" – In the verse, the word for "what" is "män." In Hebrew "mä" means "what." Män was translated into English as "manna."

331 16:22 "people collected twice as much food" – They had been instructed to do so in verse 16:5.

332 16:22 "leaders were concerned" – Either they had not heard Mōshe' previous instructions, or verse 16:5 had not been stated until now.

333 16:23 "solemn day of rest" – G-d performed the act of rest on epoch 7 of creation as recorded in Brāshēt (Genesis) 2:1-3, which is the source of the day of rest. Shabat is a sanctuary in the dimension of time (Holzer, 2011, p.250).
   The specific commandments of shabat in Tōra verses are:
     Commandment 24: Do not walk outside the city boundary on shabat (Shimōt 16:29).
     Commandment 31: Sanctify shabat by reciting the blessings of kidush and havdala (Shimōt 20:8) (Decaloge).
     Commandment 32: Do not perform prohibited activities on shabat (Shimōt 20:10).
     Commandment 83: Rest on shabat (Shimōt 23:12).
     Commandment 112: A court must not punish on shabat (Shimōt 35:30).
   But there is much more to the laws of shabat. Talmud Tractate Shabat 73a (mishna 7:3) lists the 39 categories of activities that are forbidden on shabat. They are derived from the work that was performed to build the tabernacle. Major activities forbidden on shabat include cooking, baking, lighting a fire, extinguishing a fire, and carrying objects in a public area.
   Verses that mention shabat include:

Shimōt 16:5, 16:22-30, 20:8-11 (Decaloge); 31:12-17; and 35:2-3.
Vayikra 19:3, 19:30, 23:3, 24:8, and 26:2.
Bamidbar 15:32-36 and 28:9-10.
Divarim 5:12-15.

In general society, the word Sabbath has incorrectly been interpreted as "holiday." It is important to realize that the word Shabat means rest – not celebration.

The concept of resting on the seventh also serves as the source for resting the land of Israel during the seventh Sabbatical year, as stated in numerous places including Shimōt 23:11 and 34:21.

[334] 16:25 "today . . . today . . . today" – The word today occurs 3 times in this verse that deals with meals on shabat. This is the source for having 3 meals on shabat. The first meal is on Friday night. Breakfast is considered to be more of a snack than a meal in Jewish law. Lunch on Saturday is the second meal. In order to honor this verse and to honor shabat, observant Jewish people make a special point of having another meal in the afternoon on shabat even on Saturdays when it gets dark early.

As a variant of this custom, because the third occurrence of the word "today" is connected to a negative phrase (i.e., "you will not"), some Jewish groups make the third shabat meal somewhat reduced. Instead of having bread at the meal, they eat cake instead. (This custom has nothing to do with Marie Antoinette.)

[335] Commandment 24 – Rambam Mishne Tōra: Book 3: Seasons: Laws of Sabbath.

[336] 16:31 "män" – See note on 16:5.

[337] 16:33 "Tabernacle" – Some commentators feel that at this point in time there was no intention for there to be a Tabernacle. Tōra includes a future fact here. Some commentators feel that the need for a Tabernacle arose because of the sin of the gold calf statue.

[338] 16:35 "they ate män for forty years" – They stayed in the wilderness for 40 years because they would later sin by believing negative reports by the scouts (Bamidbar (Numbers) 14:1). This is yet another instance of a future fact being stated in this section

Bishalaĥ - Section 7   - 13 + 3 verses

THE PEOPLE TRAVELED TO RIFĒDIM: NO WATER

1985 452 17:1 The Jewish people traveled from the wilderness of Żin in stages, as G-d instructed.[339]
 They stayed in Rifēdim.[340]
 There was no water.
1986 453 17:2 Some people demanded from Mōshe (Moses):
 "Give us water to drink."
 Mōshe responded to them:
 "Why do you fight with me?"
 "Why do you try to test G-d?"
1987 454 17:3 Some people were thirsty and confrontational.
 They complained to Mōshe:
 "Why did you lead us out of Egypt to have us, our children, and our cattle die of thirst?"
1988 455 17:4 Mōshe prayed [341] to G-d:
 "What should I do with these people? [342]
 "They are ready to stone me to death."

WATER FROM ROCK

1989 456 17:5 G-d communicated to Mōshe:
 "Stand in front of the Jewish people, have the leaders with you, and hold the staff with which you had ruined the waters of Egypt[343] by turning them into blood.
1990 457 17:6 "I will stand by you.
 "Hit the rock, water will pour out, and the people will have water to drink."
 Mōshe did so.
1991 458 17:7 This location was named Masa[344] (testing) and Mirēva (strife) because the Jewish people fought there and annoyed G-d by asking:
 "Is G-d with us or not?"

Bishalaĥ - Section 7 - continued

AMALĀK ATTACKS

1992 459 17:8 The army of Amalāk[345] attacked the Jewish people in Rifēdim.
1993 460 17:9 Mōshe said to Yihōshūa (Joshua):[346]
 "Select men for the army to fight Amalāk.
 "Tomorrow I will stand on the top of the hill holding the staff of G-d.

YIHŌSHŪA LEADS ARMY AGAINST THE ENEMY

1994 461 17:10 Yihōshūa led the army against Amalāk while Mōshe, Aharōn, and Ĥūr[347] went to the top of the hill.
1995 462 17:11 When Mōshe held up his hand, the Jewish army succeeded in battle, but when he let down his hand, Amalāk would succeed.
1996 463 17:12 Mōshe became tired and he was not able to keep his hands held up.
 Therefore, Aharōn and Ĥūr sat Mōshe on a stone and they held up his hands.
 They kept this up until sundown.
1997 464 17:13 Yihōshūa won the battle.

Bishalaĥ – Last Section

INSTRUCTION: ERADICATE THE MEMORY OF AMALĀK

1998 465 17:14 G-d communicated to Mōshe:
 "Include the following commandment in the Tōra and teach it to Yihōshūa:[348]
 'I promise to eradicate the memory of Amalāk.' " [349]
1999 466 17:15 Mōshe built an altar to G-d and named it "G-d Is My Flag."
2000 467 17:16 Mōshe said:
 "G-d has declared war against Amalāk from now on."

Bishalaĥ - Section 7 - Study Notes

---

[339] 17:1 "as G-d instructed" – Verses 40:36 & 37 make it clear that once the Tabernacle was built, the movement of the cloud of glory was the signal that G-d used to communicate whether they would travel that day. Verse 13:21 states that the cloud guided them. It is possible that G-d's instruction here is through the movement of the cloud.

[340] 17:1 "Rifēdim" – This is recounted in Bamidbar (Numbers) 33:14.

[341] 17:4 "prayed" – See note on verse 3:9, on the nature of prayer, and the note on verse 8:8 which lists the other instances of Mōshe praying.

[342] 17:4 "What should I do with these people?" - Mōshe feels that the people must be dealt with. However, G-d's response was not to punish people, but rather, to solve the problem. In contrast, at other points during the journey in the wilderness, G-d displays disappointment in the people.

[343] 17:5 "the staff with which you had ruined the waters of Egypt" – Note, however, this is also the staff with which Mōshe parted the waters of the sea, as stated in verse 14:16. The truth is that all the wonders that Mōshe performed, seemingly through his staff, were actually performed by G-d. By the will of G-d, the same staff that riuned waters, can produce pure water. A staff or any other implement was unnecessary. True believers understand this.

[344] 17:7 "Masa" – Mōshe mentions the incident at this location in Divarim (Deuteronomy) 6:16 and 9:22. Due to the way people contradicted Mōshe at Masa, Commandment 423: Do not unduly test a prophet, is derived from Divarim 6:16.

Later, after the passing of Miryam (Miriam), as recorded in Bamidbar chapter 20, the people complained about lack of water. This incident and its negative results are mentioned also in Divarim in verses 1:37 and 32:51.

[345] 17:8 "Amalāk" – Amalāk, the ancestor of this nation, was a grandson of Āsav (Esau) (Brāshēt (Genesis) 36:12). One of Amalāk's descendants was Haman, who plotted to exterminate the Jewish people.

³⁴⁶ 17:9 "Yihōshūa" – Originally, his name was Hōshāa (Bamidbar 13:8). Later, just before the Jewish people would have entered into the promised land, Mōshe gave him an extra blessing by modifying his name to Yihōshūa (Bamidbar 13:16), which can mean "be a salvation." With the help of that blessing, Yihōshūa, along with Kalāv (Caleb), did not give a bad report of the land, going so far as to even refute the report given by the 10 other scouts. Yihōshūa and Kalāv tried to convince the people to follow G-d's plan (Bamidbar 13:28-30, and 14:6-9).

There are examples of other name changes in Tōra. G-d modified Avram's name to Avraham (Brāshēt 17:5). G-d also modified Sarī's name to Sara (Brāshēt 17:15). Also, an adversary, possibly an angel, changes Yaakōv's name to Yisrael (Brāshēt 32:29), which means "struggles with G-d." G-d recognizes the name Yisrael as an additional name for Yaakōv in Brāshēt 35:10.

In this verse Tōra refers to Hōshāa by his future name, Yihōshūa, to have us recognize his greatness. He is mentioned also in verses 24:13, 32:17, and 33:11, where his integrity and devotion to Mōshe is apparent. Yihōshūa lived to be 110 years old (Book of Yihōshūa 24:29).

³⁴⁷ 17:10 "Ĥūr" – Ĥūr's grandson became the chief artisan for the Tabernacle.

³⁴⁸ 17:14 "Yihōshūa" – Here he is singled out for this particular role. Later, in Bamidbar 27:18-23, he is selected to be the leader after Mōshe.

³⁴⁹ 17:14 "eradicate the memory of Amalāk" – Commandments, according to Rambam, regarding Amalāk, are delineated in Divarim as follows:
Divarim 25:17 Commandment 602: Remember How Amalāk Attacked The Jewish People. Rambam considers this to be a commandment that is incumbent each moment of the day. It is similar to belief in G-d - a constantly operative commandment.
Divarim 25:19 Commandment 603: Eradicate the vestiges of Amalāk.
Divarim 25:19 Commandment 604: Do not forget how Amalāk viciously ambushed the Jewish people.

King Shaūl (Saul) was commanded to eliminate the Amalāk nation. See First Book of Shmūel (Samuel) Chapter 15. He did so except that he brought back the king of Amalāk to be executed publicly. Overnight, the king of Amalāk had relations with a slave girl, and her progeny survived and reproduced.

The Book of Esther Chapter 3 traces the lineage of the evil Haman to Amalāk. When the Book of Esther is read on the Jewish holiday of Purim (which occurs one month before the holiday of Passover), when the name "Haman" is read, people in the congregation make noise to "eradicate" his memory and thus fulfill commandment 603.

As part of Commandment 602 to remember what Amalāk did, on the shabat before Purim, a special public reading of the paragraph about the attack by Amalāk in Divarim Chapter 25 is chanted.

Yitrō - Section 1 - 12 verses   (Total: 75 verses)

(There are 16 commandments in this portion:
3 positive and 13 negative.)

2001 468 18:1 Yitrō (Jethro),[350] a spiritual leader in the land of Midyan and father-in-law of Mōshe (Moses),[351] heard about what G-d did for Mōshe and the Jewish people.
   Most notably, he heard that G-d brought the Jewish people out of the land of Egypt.

YITRŌ PREPARES TO TRAVEL TO MŌSHE

2002 469 18:2 Yitrō, as father-in-law of Mōshe, prepared to travel[352] to Mōshe to bring Żipōra, the wife of Mōshe, whom Mōshe previously had sent back[353] to Midyan,

2003 470 18:3 as well as their[354] two sons.
   The elder son was Gârshōm.[355]
   He was so named because at Gârshōm's birth, Mōshe declared:
   "I was a foreigner in a foreign place." [356]
2004 471 18:4 The younger son was Elēezer.[357]
   He was so named because at Elēezer's birth, Mōshe said:
   "The G-d of my father helped me and saved me from the sword of Pharaoh." [358]

YITRŌ TRAVELS TO MŌSHE AND BRINGS MŌSHE'S WIFE AND SONS

2005 472 18:5 Yitrō traveled and brought the sons and wife of Mōshe to Mōshe into the wilderness[359] at the mountain of G-d.[360]
2006 473 18:6 Yitrō sent a messenger to Mōshe to tell him:
   "I, your father-in-law,[361] Yitrō, along with your wife and two sons, are coming."

Yitrō - Section 1 - continued

Mōshe Travels To Meet Yitrō

2007 474 18:7 Mōshe went to meet his father-in-law.[362]
   Mōshe bowed and kissed him.
   Each asked about the other's welfare, and then entered into the tent.
2008 475 18:8 Mōshe told his father-in-law:
   (a) all the wonders that G-d had done to Pharaoh and the Egyptians for the sake of the Jewish people,
   (b) the difficulties that had occurred to the Jewish people during their travels,
   and (c) how G-d had saved the Jewish people.
2009 476 18:9 Yitrō was happy about all the good actions that G-d had performed for the Jewish people by saving them from the Egyptians.
2010 477 18:10 Yitrō said:
   "Blessed is G-d[363] who saved you from Egypt and from Pharaoh when He liberated you from the servitude of Egypt.
2011 478 18:11 "Now I know that G-d is greatest because G-d utilized the very plans and actions of the enemy to punish them."

Yitrō's Offerings To G-d

2012 479 18:12 Yitrō, the father-in-law of Mōshe, offered a burnt offering and other offerings to G-d.
   Aharōn and the elders came to dine with the father-in-law of Mōshe in the presence of G-d.

Yitrō - Section 1 - Study Notes

---

[350] 18:1 "Yitrō" - The first mention of the name Yitrō is 3:1, where he is already identified as the father-in-law of Mōshe and as a leader. See note on verse 2:18 for a discussion of the many names of Yitrō. The most previous time that Yitrō is mentioned is when Mōshe asks permission to return to Egypt (4:18).

[351] 18:1 "father-in-law of Mōshe" - Yitrō admired and was proud of his son-in-law and described himself in terms of his relationship to Mōshe. Mōshe, in turn, admired and revered Yitrō, as explained on verse 18:7.

[352] 18:2 "travel" –

Ramban: He arrived before the divine revelation at Sinai, so that this section is in chronological order. According to this opinion, Yitrō could have been part of the congregation that accepted Judaism, thus making him Jewish. The fact that the divine revelation is not mentioned among the events that he had heard about, nor the events that Mōshe told him about (verse 18:8), supports this opinion. Note that although the modern day Druze community traces their ancestry to Yitrō, he had many children, some of whom did not become Jewish (see Book of Judges 4:11).

Ibn Ezra: He arrived after revelation, so that this section is not in chronological order. According to this opinion, Mōshe's wife and their two sons did not witness the divine revelation, nor did they pledge to accept the Tōra. They became the first converts when they offered offerings as stated in verse 18:12.

[353] 18:2 "had sent back" – This earlier action is not stated in Tōra. He may have sent them back after their second son was born (after verse 4:26). Or it may be that Aharōn had told Mōshe not to bring his family into Egypt, which was a place of hardship. This would place his action at verse 4:28.

[354] 18:3 "their" - The verse uses the word "her," but the sons are both of theirs.

[355] 18:3 "Gârshōm" - His birth is recorded in verse 2:22.

³⁵⁶ 18:3 "foreigner in a foreign place" - This has been stated in verse 2:22. The Hebrew word "gâr" means "stranger". The Hebrew word "sham" means "there." Mōshe may have been referring to Egypt as the foreign land he had been in. Or he might mean that he felt like a foreigner (even) in Midyan.

³⁵⁷ 18:4 "Elēezer" - This is the first mention of their younger son's name.

³⁵⁸ 18:4 "from the sword of Pharaoh" - The fact that the pharaoh wanted to execute Mōshe is mentioned in verse 2:15. The derivation of his younger son's name is based on the fact that the Hebrew word "Elē" means "my G-d" and "the Hebrew word "ezer" means "helper."

³⁵⁹ 18:5 "wilderness" - Yitrō came despite the fact that the Jewish people were in the wilderness.

³⁶⁰ 18:5 "mountain of G-d" - This designation is used is verse 3:1 when Mōshe goes to graze the sheep, and again when Aharōn meets Mōshe coming to Egypt (4:27). It is Mount Sēnī (Sinai). It is also called Ĥōreb. See note on verse 3:1 concerning the different opinions about Ĥōreb.

³⁶¹ 18:6 "your father-in-law" - Yitrō exhibits humility and implies that even though he may be unworthy to come to this holy place, he is bringing Mōshe's family, and therefore, should be allowed to come.

³⁶² 18:7 "father-in-law" - Tōra could have used shorter wording by simply using his name, Yitrō. Tōra thus teaches that Mōshe regarded Yitrō as a great man and took pride in describing himself in terms of his relationship to Yitrō, just as Yitrō was proud of Mōshe (see note on 18:1).

³⁶³ 18:10 "blessed is G-d" – The first (and until now, the only) person to use this expression was Malkē Źedek (Brāshēt 14:20).

Yitrō - Section 2 - 11 verses

MŌSHE PRESIDES AS JUDGE

2013 480 18:13 On the next day[364] Mōshe (Moses) presided as judge and teacher.

People waiting for their case or question to be heard, stood in front of Mōshe from morning until evening.

2014 481 18:14 When the father-in-law of Mōshe saw this, he asked Mōshe:

"What are you doing to the people?

"Why do you sit while people stand from morning until evening?"

2015 482 18:15 Mōshe replied to his father-in-law:

"The reason is that the people come to me to ask about G-d and His ways.

2016 483 18:16 "When they have a question they come to me.

"I judge people's cases according to the laws of G-d."

2017 484 18:17 The father-in-law of Mōshe said to him:

"The manner in which you are doing this is not good.

2018 485 18:18 "Both you and the people will wear down because it is too difficult for you to do this alone.

2019 486 18:19 "Follow my advice[365] as long as you feel that it is consistent with G-d's will.

"Certainly, you should be the intermediary of G-d to the people

2020 487 18:20 "by teaching them the laws, how to behave, and what to do.[366]

YITRŌ - SECTION 2 - CONTINUED

YITRŌ ADVISES TO APPOINT JUDGES

2021 488 18:21 "In addition, select capable[367] people who fear G-d, are truthful, and despise wrongful gain.

"Place these people over thousands, hundreds, fifties, and tens.[368]

2022 489 18:22 "They will preside as a court[369] to judge cases throughout the year.

"Important cases will be brought to you, while lesser cases[370] will be brought to them.

"This will ease your burden.

2023 490 18:23 "If you do this, assuming that G-d agrees, then you will endure and the people will live in peace."

Yitrō - Section 2 - Study Notes

---

³⁶⁴ 18:13 "next day" – See note on verse 18:1 that explains the two opinions as to when Yitrō had arrived. There are two basic opinions as to what day is described here as the next day:

Ibn Ezra, Ramban: The day after Yitrō had arrived.

Rashē: The day after The Day of Atonement, which is when Mōshe descended the mountain with the second set of stone slabs.

³⁶⁵ 18:19 "my advice" – In Divarim (Deuteronomy) 1:9-18, Mōshe describes this episode as Mōshe telling the people to appoint judges, and the people agree in response. In Divarim, he stresses how he found it too difficult to be the only judge. He does not mention Yitrō.

In a similar vein, in Bamidbar 11:14, Mōshe admits that he cannot be the only prophet leader.

³⁶⁶ 18:20 "how to behave, and what to do" – These extra words reveal that Yitrō innovates that ethical and moral behavior, and acts of kindness must be part of the Jewish legal system, as stated in Talmud Tractate Bava Metzēa page 30b.

³⁶⁷ 18:21 "capable" - There are many opinions (see Kaplan, p.347) among the commentators as to the meaning of this quality, including:

Rambam: Laws of Supreme Court 2:7 – A judge must exhibit superior self-control, morality, & leadership.

Tanĥūma: A judge must be confident.

Meĥilta, Rashē: A judge must be wealthy so as not to be tempted by bribes or favors.

Rashbam: A judge must be a person of high social status.

Ibn Ezra: A judge must be physically strong, knowledgeable, wise, wealthy and have integrity.

Ramban: A judge must be efficient so that cases do not pile up. Otherwise justice will be delayed.

Māam Lōāz: A judge must exhibit initiative.

Rabbi Samson Hirsch: A judge must be resourceful so that he or she can handle the wide variety of cases and the varied types of people who come to court.

These traits are not mutually exclusive. Ideally a judge should possess all these traits. However, it may be very difficult to find such people. Therefore, each commentator lists what is of uppermost importance.

³⁶⁸ 18:21 "thousands, hundreds, fifties, tens" - There are various opinions as to the meaning of these numbers, including:

Rashē: There were 600 of judges of thousands, one for each of the 600 thousand men. There were proportionally more judges of hundreds, etc.

Others: A judge of thousands had at least 1,000 students. There were very few such people, but there were many teachers who had 100 students, for example.

Others: A judge of thousands had at least 1,000 servants, etc.

³⁶⁹ 18:22 "court" – A Jewish court consists of a panel of ordained rabbis who have attained the necessary experience to judge cases. Civil cases are heard by a court of three rabbis. Decisions follow majority rule.

Capital cases are heard by a court of 23 judges. In a capital case, there must be a majority of at least 2 judges in order to convict (verse 23:2, commandment 76).

The Jewish Supreme Court, known as the Sanhedrin, is made up of 71 rabbis. Verse 24:1 and 24:9 mention that there were 70 leaders. Later, when Mōshe states that that he can no longer lead the people by himself, G-d communicates that the 70 learned elders will help lead the Jewish people along with Mōshe (Bamidbar 11:16), thus creating a court of 71.

Appointing judges is Jewish commandment 489, as stated in Divarim (Deuteronomy) 16:18.

Under no circumstance is a person or group of people permitted to take the law into their own hands. If someone witnesses a crime, it is that person's responsibility to report it to an official authority. Today, when living under countries that are governed by rule-of-law, laws of the country must be abided by. The Talmudic sage and chief rabbi of Persia, Shmūel, in 300 C.E., stated in the Talmud: the law of the land must be followed.

One of the universal commandments given to all mankind is for each society to develop a code of social and civil law and institute a system of courts to enforce laws. See Table 8a for a list of these universal commandments. Table 8b shows which of these commandments are found in ancient codes of law.

These universal commandments are derived from the communication G-d had with Nōaĥ (Noah) after the flood (Brāshēt (Genesis) chapter 9). Talmud Tractate Sanhedrin p. 56a explains universal commandments, which are:
1. Do not eat an animal while it is still alive (Brāshēt 9:4)
Of the 613 commandments, this is commandment 450
(Divarim 12:23).
2. Do not commit suicide (Brāshēt 9:5)
3. Do not commit murder (Brāshēt 9:6)
This is commandment 35 (Shimōt 20:13).
4. Establish courts of law (Brāshēt 9:6)
This is commandment 489 (Divarim 16:18).
5. Have children (Brāshēt 9:7)
This is commandment 1 (Brāshēt 1:28).
6. Do not blaspheme G-d.
This is commandment 68 (Do not curse G-d) (Shimōt 22:27).
7. Do not worship idols.
The note on 1:17 list the commandments against idolatry.
8. Do not commit adultery.
This is commandment 208 (Vayikra 18:20).
9. Do not seal.
This is embodied in commandments 227 and 229
(Vayikra 19:11 & 13).

Comparing these universal commandments to those of other ancient cultures (as also shown in Table 8):
The Hammurabi code explicitly prohibits
murder, adultery, and theft; and it institutes a court of law.
The ancient Hittite Code prohibits
murder, adultery, theft, and assault; and it institutes a court of law.
The ancient Assyrian laws prohibit
murder, adultery, theft, and blasphemy; and it institutes a court of law.

[370] 18:22 "lesser cases" – Yitrō feels that cases that do not involve much monetary value can be handled by ordinary judges. When Mōshe enacts this decentralized system, he stipulates that it is not the amount of money at stake in the case that determines how capable a judge should be assigned to

the case. Rather, it is the legal difficulty of the case that determines the rank of the judge selected to preside over the case (verse 18:26). This concept of competence is made part of Jewish law in commandment 80, verse 23:7.

Yitrō - Section 3   - 4 verses

Mōshe Follows Yitrō's Advice

2024 491 18:24 Mōshe (Moses) took the advice of his father-in-law and implemented his suggestions.

2025 492 18:25 Mōshe selected capable people[371] from among the Jewish nation and appointed them as judges over the nation.

He placed these people as leaders of thousands,[372] hundreds, fifties, and tens.

2026 493 18:26 These people administered justice regularly.

They brought the difficult cases[373] to Mōshe, and judged the other cases themselves.

Yitrō Travels Back To His Home

2027 494 18:27 Mōshe helped his father-in-law pack, and Yitrō (Jethro)[374] traveled back to his homeland.

Yitrō - Section 3 - Study Notes

[371] 18:25 "capable people" – See note on 18:21.

[372] 18:25 "of thousands" – See note on 18:21.

[373] 18:26 "difficult cases" – Yitrō's original advice was to base the selection of a judge on the monetary value of the case being tried (verse 18:22). In contrast, Mōshe instructed that the level of capability of the judge selected must be based on the difficulty of the case. This becomes part of Jewish law in commandment 80, verse 23:7.

[374] 18:27 "Yitrō" - See Bamidbar (Numbers) 10:29-32, where Ĥōvav, son of Riūâl, expresses his desire to return home even though Mōshe urges him to come with them to the land of Israel.

    Rashē, Rashbam, Ramban: Ĥōvav is another name of Yitrō.

    Ibn Ezra: Ĥōväv was the son of Yitrō. He was the brother-in-law of Mōshe.

Yitrō - Section 4   - 6 verses

THE JEWISH PEOPLE ARRIVE AT MOUNT SĒNĪ

2028 495 19:1 On the first day of the third month[375] after they left Egypt, the Jewish people came to the wilderness known as Sēnī (Sinai).
2029 496 19:2 They had departed from Refēdim and arrived at Sēnī, camping in the wilderness across from the mountain.

MŌSHE'S FIRST ASCENT UP MOUNT SĒNĪ

2030 497 19:3 Mōshe (Moses) walked up[376] the mountain to G-d.
   G-d called[377] to him from the mountaintop and communicated:
   "Say this to the House of Yaakōv (Jacob = Israel)[378] and the Jewish people:

WINGS OF EAGLES

2031 498 19:4 'You saw what I, G-d, did in Egypt, namely, I carried you as if on the wings of eagles[379] and brought you to Me.
2032 499 19:5 'If you obey Me and keep My covenant, I will consider you to be My special treasure, even though I possess the whole world.
2033 500 19:6 'Be a kingdom of priests and a holy nation to Me.'
   "These are the statements you must tell the Jewish people."

Yitrō - Section 4 - Study Notes

[375] 19:1 "first day of the third month" – According to the sages in Talmud Tractate Shabat, page 86a, this was the first day of Sēvan, which was a Monday. This was 46 days after the exodus. This includes 15 days of Nēsan after the exodus (the month of Nēsan was 30 days long), plus 30 days of Ēyar, plus the first day of Sēvan.

Divine revelation (verses 20:1-14) will occur on the next shabat (Sabbath), the sixth day of Sēvan, which is 51 days after they left Egypt. See Tables 3 and 5a for a calendar. A six day period is mentioned in verse 24:16, which some commentators believe are these 6 days.

Note that Vayikra 23:15-21 define that 50 days after the start of Passover is the holiday of Shavūōt. Vayikra 23:16 states that farmers present their new grain on Shavūōt. However, although Shavūōt is actually 1 day earlier than when the revelation took place, it has come to be associated with divine revelation at Sinai.

Note that the current Jewish calendar sets the month of Nēsan as 30 days long, and sets Ēyar as 29 days long. Originally, whether a month was 29 or 30 days depended on when the new crescent moon was seen. Physically, a lunar month is approximately 29.5 days long.

[376] 19:3 "Mōshe walked up" - Shimōt chapter 24 adds details, which according to Rashē, occurred at about this time period, before the divine revelation. Table 4 presents one possible integration of the details of Chapters 19, 20 and 24 based on combining some of the many different understandings by traditional commentators (see Miller, 2003, pp. 467 & 504). Words in braces indicate implied understandings by commentators that are not stated in the verses. Note that a completely different approach is taken by Ramban, who believes that all of these verses are presented in chronological order.

[377] 19:3 "G-d called" - Tōra expresses actions of G-d in terms that people can understand. But even the verbs such as "called," "communicated" and "descended" are more physical than the sublime spiritualness of G-d. Similarly, when Tōra describes physical attributes such as "arm," "hand" or "feet" with regard to G-d, it is purely metaphysical because people experience the greatness of G-d in a physical manner that they can understand and relate to.

[378] 19:3 "House of Yaakōv" - There are two opinions in Talmud Tractate Sanhedrin as to who these are, in contrast to the next phrase: "the Jewish People." One opinion is that House of Yaakōv is the high court, which needs to know more intricate detail of law than the rest of the population. The other opinion is that House of Yaakōv refers to the women, who need to be instructed in a manner that is appropriate for them.

[379] 19:4 "eagles" – In Divarim 32:11 (Portion Haazēnū, Section 2) Mōshe describes G-d as protectively hovering above the Jewish people

Yitrō - Section 5 - 13 verses

Mōshe's First Descent Down Mount Sēnī

2034 501 19:7 Mōshe came back and summoned the elders and told them everything that G-d had communicated.

Elders: We Will Obey

Mōshe's Second Ascent Up Mount Sēnī

2035 502 19:8 They responded by saying:
"All that G-d has spoken, we will obey." [380]
Mōshe went back up the mountain and conveyed the people's response to G-d.
2036 503 19:9 G-d communicated to Mōshe:
"I will come to you in a thick cloud so that everyone will hear when I speak to you.
"Then they will believe in you forever."
Mōshe told G-d the people's response.[381]
2037 504 19:10 G-d communicated to Mōshe:
"Go to the people and sanctify them today and tomorrow.
"They should wash their clothing
2038 505 19:11 "and be ready on the third day.
"On the third day, G-d will reveal Himself to the people, on Mount Sēnī (Sinai).
2039 506 19:12 "Set boundary posts around the mountain and tell the people:
'Be careful not to walk onto the mountain.[382]
'Any person or animal that touches the mountain will not live.
2040 507 19:13 'No one is permitted to touch a living thing that touches the mountain during that time.
'Rather, such a being must be stoned or shot with an arrow.
'This remains true until the sound of the horn is heard.' "

Yitrō - Section 5 - continued

Mōshe Descends Mount Sēnī

2041 508 19:14 Mōshe walked down the mountain and sanctified the people.

The people washed their clothes.

2042 509 19:15 He told the people:

"Be ready for the third day: do not have intimate relations."

2043 510 19:16 On the third day in the morning there was thunder and lightning and a thick cloud on the mountain.

The sound of the horn was loud, and the people trembled.[383]

2044 511 19:17 Mōshe asked the people to come out of their tents[384] so they can encounter G-d.

The people stood at the foot of the mountain, at a distance.[385]

2045 512 19:18 The mountain was enveloped in black smoke because G-d had descended onto it in a fire.

The smoke went up into the air, and the mountain quaked.

2046 513 19:19 The sound of the horn became progressively louder.

Mōshe spoke and G-d answered.

Yitrō - Section 5 - Study Notes

[380] 19:8 "obey" – The Hebrew word in the verse can be translated as "perform" or "act." They are ready to obey whatever G-d will request. It connotes that they are committed to perform all positive commandments, and it can also mean that they are committed to refrain from violating negative commandments.

In this verse the leaders make this declaration. Later, in verse 24:3, all the Jewish people make this declaration. In verse 24:7 the Jewish people amplify this declaration by stating: "we will obey and study all the laws."

According to Rashē, the events stated in chapter 24 occurred during these few days before the divine revelation (See Table 4).

[381] 19:9 "Mōshe told G-d the people's response." - Rashē interprets this repetitive phrase as a new response by the people. Some commentators take this to be a request by the people for them to hear G-d directly rather than overhear G-d communicating to Mōshe. Based on this, some commentators interpolate an extra walk down the mountain and then a walk up the mountain, which is not stated in the verses (see Miller, 2003 pp. 467 & 504). Thus, the explicit second descent in the verse becomes the third descent, as noted in Table 4.

[382] 19:12 "not to walk onto the mountain" – Mōshe is told to warn them again in verse 19:21.

[383] 19:16 "the people trembled" – This is stated again in 20:15. Mōshe recounted this in his retelling of the event in Divarim (Deuteronomy) 5:5.

[384] 19:17 "out of their tents" – This is the rendition according to Ibn Ezra. The people were apprehensive of all the thunder and smoke. Therefore, they understandably waited in their tents until Mōshe assured them that it is safe for them to come toward the mountain.

[385] 19:17 "at a distance" – Verses 20:15 & 18 also state that the people stood far from the mountain. There are two approaches in the commentators about this. One opinion is that they were understandably being careful about the strict warnings not to step onto the mountain.

An alternative understanding is that they stood further from the mountain than needed because they were terrified of the direct communication by G-d, as is stated in verse 20:16.

Yitrō - Section 6   - 20 verses

MŌSHE ASCENDS MOUNT SĒNĪ

2047 514 19:20 G-d descended onto the mountain and requested Mōshe (Moses) to come.

Mōshe walked up to the top of the mountain.

2048 515 19:21 G-d communicated to Mōshe:

"Walk back down the mountain and warn the people not to come onto the mountain to try to get a look at G-d, because if they do so, they will perish.

2049 516 19:22 "The firstborn men[386] who do come closer to G-d must sanctify themselves, otherwise G-d will punish them."

2050 517 19:23 Mōshe responded to G-d:

"The people will not go onto the mountain because you had already commanded us:

'Place boundary marks around the mountain and sanctify it.' "

MŌSHE DESCENDS MOUNT SĒNĪ

2051 518 19:24 G-d communicated to him:

"Walk back down, and later you and Aharōn (Aaron) will come up.[387]

"But the first-born men and other leaders will not stand higher on the mountain to come to G-d, because G-d would be angry with them."

2052 519 19:25 Mōshe walked down[388] to the people and informed them.

Yitrō - Section 6 - continued

Decaloge
2053 520 20:1 G-d communicated[389] these commandments:[390]

Commandment 25:[391] Know That There Is G-d
2054 521 20:2 "I[392] am G-d who led you out of slavery in Egypt.

Commandment 26: Do Not Believe That There Are Other Deities
2055 522 20:3 "Do not have any other deities.

Commandment 27:[393] Do Not Form Idols
2056 523 20:4 "Do not form idols[394] of any type.

Commandment 28: Do Not Worship Idols in Their Manner

Commandment 29: Do Not Worship Idols the Way Jewish People Worship G-d
2057 524 20:5 "Do not bow down to idols, and do not worship idols,[395] because I am G-d Who punishes sinners for many generations
2058 525 20:6 "but I am merciful[396] for many generations to those who love Me and keep My commandments.

Commandment 30:[397] Do Not Speak G-d's Name Unnecessarily
2059 526 20:7 "Do not speak G-d's name unnecessarily because that is a sin.

Commandment 31:[398] Sanctify the Sabbath By Reciting Blessings
2060 527 20:8 "Remember[399] to make shabat (Sabbath)[400] a day of holiness.
2061 528 20:9 "Work for the first six days[401] of the week

Yitrō - Section 6 - continued

Commandment 32: Do Not Perform Forbidden Activities on The Sabbath

2062 529 20:10 "but the seventh day of the week is a day of rest to G-d.
   "Do not perform those activities[402] that are forbidden on shabat.
   "This applies to you, your family, your servants and your animals.
   "This also applies to converts[403]
2063 530 20:11 "because G-d created the universe during 6 days and He rested on day 7.
   "G-d blessed shabat and made it holy.

Commandment 33:[404] Honor Your Father and Mother

2064 531 20:12 "Honor[405] your father and mother.
   "If you do, G-d will enable you to live a long life[406] in the land of Israel which G-d is giving you.

Commandment 34:[407] Do Not Murder A Human Being

2065 532 20:13 "Do not murder people.

Do Not Have Intimate Relations With Another Man's Wife

   "Do not have intimate relations with another man's wife.[408]

Commandment 35:[409] Do Not Kidnap A Human Being

   "Do not kidnap[410] a person.

Commandment 36:[411] Do Not Lie

   "Do not tell a lie.

Commandment 37:[412] Do Not Scheme to Take Other People's Property

2066 533 20:14 Do not scheme[413] to take someone else's house, wife, servants, animals, or any other possessions that belong to other people.

Yitrō - Section 6 - Study Notes

386 19:22 "firstborn men" – The firstborn had been designated as the spiritual leaders. After the sin of the gold statue, the Levites were appointed instead (verse 32:29). See note on verse 11:5 for the role of first born in Jewish life.

387 19:24 "you and Aharōn will come up" – This might be the same as that stated in verse 24:1, which is recorded as having taken place in verse 24:9 (see Table 4).

388 19:25 "Mōshe walked down" – In Divarim (Deuteronomy) 5:5, Mōshe tells the people that he stood between them and G-d. See note on 19:1 as to the date this occurred.

389 20:1 "G-d communicated" – Rambam derives 13 commandments from these verses. Verse 34:28, and Divarim (Deuteronomy) 10:4 refers to them as the 10 statements (i.e., Decaloge (Ten Commandments)):
    1. verse 2 - I am G-d.
    2. verses 3-6   - There are no other deities.
               (Rambam: 4 commandments:
               do not believe in other deities;
               do not form idols;
               do not worship idols in their manner;
               do not worship idols the way G-d is worshipped.)
    3. verse 7   - Do not speak G-d's name in vain.
    4. verses 8-11 - Sanctify the shabat day
         (Rambam: this is accomplished by reciting a blessing).
    5. verse 12   - Honor your father and mother.
    6. verse 13   - Do not murder.
    7. verse 13   - Do not commit adultery.
               (Rambam: this is commandment 208 is in Vayikra 18:20.)
    8. verse 13   - Do not steal. (Rambam: do not kidnap)
    9. verse 13   - Do not lie.
    10. verse 14 - Do not scheme to take away other people's possessions.

[390] 20:1 "commandments" – When Mōshe reviews the history of the Jewish people to the new generation who are about to enter the land of Israel, he repeats these 10 principles that the people heard, but he makes a few changes in the wording (see Divarim 5:6-18).

An interesting fact to ne aware of is that in this portion there is no mention of stone slabs (comminly translated as tablets). Stone slabs are no even mentioned until verse 24:12 (toward the end of portion Mishpatim). G-d provides the slabs to Mōshe in verse 31:18 (portion Kē Tēsa, section 2). The fact that there will be a second pair of stone slabs as recorded in verses 34:1-4 (portion Kē Tēsa, section 5) does not mean that the wording in Mōshe's retelling of the Decaloge are the words on the second pair of slabs.

[391] Commandments 25 & 26 – This is explained by Rambam in his Mishne Tōra Book 1 Fundamentals: Fundamentals of Tōra

[392] 20:2 "I" – This verse and verses 5 and 6 are stated in the first person ("I" and "Me"), whereas verses 7, 10, and 11 are written in the third person (i.e., "G-d"). Similarly, Divarim 5:4 states that the Jewish people heard the Decaloge directly from G-d, while in Divarim 5:5 Mōshe states that he had spoken the words of G-d to the Jewish people.

There are two opinions as to what people heard directly from G-d. One opinion is that they heard the entire Decaloge directly from G-d.

The other opinion is that the Jewish people heard the first two directives of the Decaloge directly from G-d. Then, because they were frightened, as stated in verses 20:15-16, the people asked Mōshe to relate the rest to them. This could explain why the third item in the Decaloge is stated in the third person, even though it would be more consistent to have been stated in the first person.

Note that in verse 20:17, Mōshe tells the people to hear all the revelation directly from G-d. Tōra does not state whether the people agreed to do so. The first opinion above believes that they did agree.

[393] Commandments 27-29 - Book 1: Fundamentals: Laws of Idolatry

[394] 20:4 "Do not form idols" – Although a basic concept of monotheism innately forbids idols, the weakness of human nature is such that even the

Jewish people, soon after hearing the commandments from G-d, as soon as they felt vulnerable, demanded that a statue be formed for them (verse 32:1).

[395] 20:5 "do not worship idols" – The inverse is stated in Divarim 12:31 – do not worship G-d in ways that idol worshippers worship idols.

[396] 20:6 "punish . . . merciful . . ." – This pair of phrases reflect two of the thirteen attributes of G-d's mercy (see verses 34:6-7), namely:
    Attribute 9 – G-d transfers merits to later generations
    Attribute 13 – G-d punishes descendants severely if they continue to sin.

[397] Commandment 30 – Book 6: Oaths: Laws of Oaths.

[398] Commandments 31 & 32 – Book 3: Seasons: Laws of Shabat.

[399] 20:8 "remember" – In Mōshe's restatement (Divarim 10:4), he uses the verb "safeguard." The term "remember" refers to performing the positive laws for observing shabat, whereas safeguard refers to refraining from performing actions forbidden by the negative laws of shabat. Many commentators state that both the terms "remember" and "safeguard" were stated as part of the Decaloge during divine revelation.

[400] 20:8 "shabat" – See note on 16:23.

[401] 20:9 "Work for the first six days" – This is the source of the Jewish work ethic. Verses 23:12, 31:15, 34:21, and 35:2 stress the importance of having a job or profession and earning an honest living. The sages in the Talmud each had professions and supported themselves.

[402] 20:10 "Do not perform those activities" – This is the negative commandment to refrain from forbidden work activities on the Sabbath. Positive commandment 83, to "actively" rest on shabat, is stated in verse 23:12.

[403] 20:10 "converts" – See note on verse 12:48.

[404] Commandment 33 – Book 14: Judges: Laws of Insurgents.

[405] 20:12 "honor" – Honor your parents is stated again in Divarim 5:16 as part of Mōshe's retelling of the Decaloge. Commandment 213 is to fear you parents (Vayikra (Leviticus) 19:3). Commandment 46 is not to hit your parents (Shimōt 21:15), and commandment 47 is not to curse your parents (Shimōt 21:17). The prohibition against cursing your parents is stated again in Vayikra 20:9.

There is also a commandment to honor Tōra scholars and Tōra teachers, as stated in Vayikra 19:32 (commandment 258).

[406] 20:12 "long life" – Other verses that promise long life are:
Divarim 5:16 Honor your father and mother...
Divarim 5:30 Follow the commandments...
Divarim 22:7 Shoo away a parent bird before taking the eggs or chicks...
Divarim 22:15 Have accurate weights and measures...

[407] Commandment 34 – Book 11: Damages: Laws of Theft.

[408] 20:13 "Do not have intimate relations with another man's wife" – Rambam does not include this verse as one of the 613 commandments. The prohibition not to commit adultery, according to Rambam, is found in Vayikra verse 18:20 as commandment 208. The prohibition not to have relations with an unmarried woman is found in Divarim verse 23:18 as commandment 570.

The verse here is stated in the <u>Book Of Education,</u> as: do not indecently expose another man's wife, as it's commandment 35. Although the <u>Book of Education</u> is largely based on Rambam, there are a number of differences between it and the Rambam's list of commandments.

Another example is that the <u>Book of Education</u> derives the law of circumcision from Brāshēt (Genesis) 17:11 (portion Leĥ Liĥa, section 7) where Avraham is commanded. In contrast, Rambam derives it from the explicit directive in verse Vayikra 12:3 (portion Tazrēa, section 1).

[409] Commandment 35 – Book 11: Damages: Laws of Murder and Preservation of Life.

[410] 20:13 "do not kidnap" - Rambam renders the words in this verse "do not steal" as "do not kidnap."

Rambam derives commandment 228, do not steal stealthily, from verse Vayikra 19:11.

And Rambam derives the prohibition not to rob openly as commandment 229 from Vayikra 19:13.

There are a number of ways to steal that are included as negative commandments.

[411] Commandment 36 – Book 14: Judges: Laws of Evidence.

[412] Commandment 37 – Book 11: Damages: Laws of Robbery and Lost Objects.

[413] 20:14 "Do not scheme" – This prohibition is against making plans to take other people's property. The prohibition against the desire to own someone else's belongings is negative commandment 415 stated in Divarim 5:18. There is no prohibition to desire to purchase goods that other people have (e.g., keeping up with the Jones'). However, Tōra teaches that a rich person is one who is happy with what he or she has (Chapters of the Fathers Chapter 4). This principle is not against healthy ambition, but rather advocates having a balanced attitude and state of mind concerning the material aspects of life

Yitrō - Section 7   - 4 + 5 verses

2067 534 20:15 Before the declaration of these commandments, the Jewish people had experienced the thunder, lightning, sound of the horn, and smoke on the mountain.
    The people had trembled[414] and stood far from the mountain.[415]
2068 535 20:16 They had told Mōshe (Moses):
    "You tell us what G-d communicates.
    "But we do not want G-d to communicate with us directly[416] because we feel like we would perish[417] if He does."
2069 536 20:17 Mōshe told them:
    "Do not be afraid.[418]
    "G-d is doing this in order to
        a. make you honored [419] among the peoples of the world,
        b. get you accustomed to G-d,[420] and
        c. instill His fear in you so that you will not sin."

2070 537 20:18 The people had stayed far from the mountain, and Mōshe walked into the thick darkness toward G-d.[421]

Yitrō - Last Section

2071 538 20:19 G-d communicated to Mōshe:
    "Tell the Jewish people:
    'All of you have experienced that I, G-d, have communicated with all of you from the spiritual world.

Commandment 38:[422] Do Not Form Human Statues, Even Just For Decoration

2072 539 20:20 'Do not form idols.
2073 540 20:21 'Build an altar of soil [423] on which you will offer offerings to Me.
    'I, G-d, will be with you and I will bless you.

Commandment 39:[424] Do Not Use Metal Tools When Building an Altar

2074 541 20:22 'If you build a stone altar, do not use metal tools[425] to form it.

Yitrō - Section 7 - continued

Commandment 40: Do Not Have Steps Leading to The Top of An Altar

2075 542 20:23 'Do not make steps that lead up to the top of the altar.
    'Steps would cause indecent exposure of private parts[426] when walking up.
    'Therefore, a ramp, not steps, should lead up to the altar.' "

Yitrō - Section 7 - Study Notes

---

[414] 20:15 "trembled" – as had been stated in 19:16. Mōshe recounts this in Divarim (Deuteronomy) 5:5.

[415] 20:15 & 18 "far from the mountain" – as had been stated in verse 19:17.

[416] 20:16 "we do not want G-d to communicate with us directly" – Mōshe recounts this in Divarim 18:16. Tōra does not state whether G-d and/or Mōshe consented to their request.

[417] 20:16 "we would perish" – Divarim 18:17 states that G-d agrees with the Jewish people with respect to this. Mōshe states there that this is the reason why each generation will have prophets and sages to guide them.

[418] 20:17 "Do not be afraid" – See note on 20:2 concerning how many verses the people heard directly from G-d. This verse indicates that Mōshe may very well have convinced the people to hear the entire Decaloge directly from G-d.

[419] 20:17 "honored" – This is the meaning of the verse according to Rashē.

[420] 20:17 "accustomed to G-d" – This is the meaning of the phrase according to Ramban.

[421] 20:18 "Mōshe walked into the thick darkness toward G-d" – Details of events that took place before divine revelation are described in verses 24:7-24:18 (see Table 4 and note on verse 19:3). The events that occur after the Decaloge are described starting with verse 31:18.

[422] Commandment 38 – Rambam Mishne Tōra: Book 1: Fundamentals: Laws of Idolatry

[423] 20:21 "altar of soil" – Siforno: A simple altar of earth is enough to worship G-d.

[424] Commandments 39 & 40: Book 8: Service To G-d: Laws of the Temple.

[425] 20:22 "do not use metal tools" –

Rashbam & Siforno: A rough stone as an altar is all that is needed to worship G-d.

Ramban: Metal tools sever and estrange. They are not appropriate for an altar whose purpose is to effect reconciliation between people and G-d.

[426] 20:23 "indecent exposure of private parts" – In line with having a ramp rather than steps, pants are part of the priestly garments, as stated in verse 28:42. Also see notes on verses 28:4 and 6.

Mishpatim[427] - Section 1 - 19 verses   (Total: 118 verses)
[There are 52 commandments in this portion:
23 positive and 29 negative.]

ALL JEWISH LAWS ARE DIVINELY GIVEN

2076 543 21:1 You, Mōshe (Moses), should teach these laws, which were given at Sēnī (Sinai),[428] to the Jewish people in ways that they will understand and remember.[429]

Commandment 41:[430] Properly Purchase a Jewish Indentured Manservant

2077 544 21:2 If a Jewish man[431] steals but is unable to pay back, and a court sells him[432] to you as an indentured servant,[433] then het must serve you for six years.

At the start of his seventh year of his servitude he will be freed.

2078 545 21:3 If he started his term of servitude unmarried, then his master may not give him a gentile woman as a wife if it is against his will.

If he started his term of servitude as a married man,[434] the master must support the servant's family[435] as well.

When a married indentured servant is freed, his family leaves along with him.

2079 546 21:4 If a master had given his married Jewish servant a gentile woman as a wife, then, when he is freed, the gentile maidservant and her children remain as servants of the master.

A Jewish indentured servant leaves without them when he is freed.

2080 547 21:5 If, when the seventh year of servitude arrives, a Jewish indentured servant declares:

"I love my master, my wife, and my children. I refuse to be free."

2081 548 21:6 Then the master should bring that Jewish indentured servant to the judges of the court, and stand him upright at the doorpost[436] of the door.

The master must pierce that indentured servant's right earlobe[437] and he will be his indentured servant until the Jubilee year, which is year 50 of the national cycle.

MISHPATIM - SECTION 1 - CONTINUED

IF A FATHER ARRANGES FOR HIS YOUNG DAUGHTER TO BE A WARD

2082 549 21:7 If a man is so poor that he cannot support his daughter who is younger than twelve years old,[438] he can arrange for her to be a ward to a Jewish family.

The manner in which she goes free is not the same as for a male servant in that she is freed when she reaches maturity if that occurs before the seventh year.

Commandment 42: Redeem A Jewish Maidservant

Commandment 43: Betroth A Jewish Maidservant

Commandment 44: Do Not Sell a Jewish Maidservant

2083 550 21:8 If the ward is not pleasing to the man (i.e., master) who had agreed to support her, then he must allow her to be redeemed at a discounted price.

However, because she feels deceived because he changed his mind about marrying her, he is not permitted to espouse her to anyone else.

2084 551 21:9 If the son of the master marries her, with his and her consent, then the son must treat her as a full wife.

Commandment 45:[439] Do Not Withhold Your Obligations from Your Wife

2085 552 21:10 If a woman's husband marries another wife in addition to her, he is not permitted to diminish his first wife's food, clothing, and conjugal rights.

2086 553 21:11 If a master does not marry his ward, and he does not espouse her to his son, and she is not redeemed, then the master must free her once she reaches maturity.

INTENTIONAL ASSAULT THAT RESULTS IN DEATH

2087 554 21:12 If a person intentionally attacks someone, and the attacked person dies from the wound, the attacker must be severely punished by the court.

Mishpatim - Section 1 - continued

Accidental Death

2088 555 21:13 A person who kills someone accidentally must travel to a haven city[440] which G-d will specify.

Premeditated Murder

2089 556 21:14 A person who intentionally murders someone, must be severely punished by the court, even if the perpetrator is a priest.

Commandment 46:[441] Do Not Hit Your Father or Mother

2090 557 21:15 Anyone who hits or wounds[442] his or her father or mother must be severely punished by the court.

Kidnapping

2091 558 21:16 A kidnapper who sells, or is caught with, the kidnapped person, must be severely punished by the court.

Commandment 47: Do Not Curse Your Father or Mother

2092 559 21:17 Anyone who curses[443] his or her father or mother must be severely punished by the court.

Commandment 48:[444] A Court Must Litigate Against Injury And Damages

2093 560 21:18 If two people fight and one strikes the other with a stone or fist, and the injured person does not die, but is confined to a bed, then
2094 561 21:19 if the injured person recuperates and can walk, then the perpetrator is let out of prison, but must pay the lost wages and the medical expenses of the injured person until the person is completely healed.

Mishpatim – Section 1 – Study Notes

---

427 "Mishpatim" - The Hebrew word *mishpatim* means "laws."
The technicalities of Tōra laws, which can only be decided by courts of law, are fully explained in various tractates of the Talmud. Literal translations of Tōra verses can be very misleading. The rendition in Tōra Study Bible provides only a basic starting point for further study. For the best treatment of the technical details of the laws, see the translation and notes in Chumash by Rabbi Chaim Miller (2003). Also see note on 18:22 concerning the structure and authority of Jewish courts.

428 21:1 "at Sēnī" - This verse is rendered based on Rashē's interpretation.

429 21:1 "understand and remember" - This rendition is based on Rashē.

430 Commandments 41-44 – These commandments are explained by Rambam in his Mishne Tōra: Book 12: Acquisition: Laws of Indentured Servants.

431 21:2 "Jewish man" - There also are laws about indentured servants who are gentiles. The text in this section does not indicate whether the servant is Jewish or not. We know that this section is dealing only with Jewish servants because in Divarim (Deuteronomy) 15:12, the text specifies that only a Jewish indentured servant is freed in his seventh year of servitude.
A gentile indentured servant abides by the basic Tōra laws. When the master decides to free the gentile servant, the servant becomes fully Jewish. This is another factor that contributes to the fact that Jewish-ness is not defined solely by genealogy.

432 21:2 "a court sells him" - There are two situations in which a Jewish man is sold as a servant: either he stole and cannot pay back, thus forcing the court to sell him (e.g., see verse 22:2); or he is so poor and unable to support himself (see Vayikra 25:39), that he decides to sell himself as a servant. There are some laws that are different between these two types of servants. The verses here deal with a man who was sold by a court to pay for what he stole.

433 21:2 "indentured servant" - Ibn Ezra: Laws of servitude teach that if you

do not understand a particular law, then follow it just as a servant follows a master.

Ramban: Laws of servitude remind us that we had been slaves, but now we serve G-d.

Note that most English translations translate the word as "slave." However, Tōra law does not permit someone to mistreat, disrespect, or be condescending to a servant, whether Jewish or gentile. Therefore, the word "slave" is not appropriate.

[434] 21:3 "married" - This is a Jewish man married to a Jewish woman.

[435] 21:3 "family" - Rashē: The master is obligated to support a Jewish servant's Jewish wives and children.

Ramban: The servant's dependents are expected to provide services to the master, but a dependent of a servant has the right to leave whenever he or she wants.

[436] 21:6 "doorpost" - Just before the exodus, the Jewish people placed a sign of freedom on their doorpost. This servant does not appreciate that freedom.

[437] 21:6 "earlobe" - The Jewish people heard G-d with their own ears: "You are servants of G-d (not man)." This servant does not appreciate this.

[438] 21:7 "twelve years old" - The actual law specifies puberty. Twelve years old is used in this rendition as a typical age when maturity occurs. In addition, a father is not permitted to make such a transaction until the daughter is at least three years old.

[439] Commandment 45 - Book 4: Women: Laws of Marriage.

[440] 21:13 "haven city" – This is discussed at length in Bamidbar (Numbers) 35:10, Divarim 19:1, and Yihōshūa (Book of Joshua) 20:1.

Sifōrnō: Until these cities were designated, a person who unintentionally murdered would live near the altar, probably in the camp of the Levites.

[441] Commandments 46 & 47 – Book 14: Judges: Laws of Insurgents

[442] 21:15 "hits or wounds" – See note on 20:12 concerning other commandments (honor and fear) with regard to one's parents.

[443] 21:17 "curses" - Other prohibitions against cursing include:
Commandment 68 – do not curse G-d (do not blaspheme) (Shimōt 22:27).
    Vayikra 22:32 prohibits profaning the name of G-d.
    In Vayikra 20:11, someone curses G-d and is punished.
Commandment 69 – do not curse judges.
Commandment 70 – do not curse leaders.
Commandment 232 – Do not curse a deaf person or any good person (Vayikra 19:14).

Related commandments include:
Commandment 238 – Do not speak derogatorily about people (Vayikra 19:16).
Commandment 329 – Do not embarrass someone.
Commandment 241 – Do not hate someone (Vayikra 19:17).
Commandment 242 – Do not take revenge (Vayikra 19:18).
Commandment 243 – Do not hold a grudge.

[444] Commandment 48 – Book 11: Damages: Laws of Robbery and Lost Objects

Mishpatim[445] - Section 2 - 21 verses

Commandment 49:[446] A Court Must Carry Out Capital Punishment by Sword When Necessary

IF A MASTER INJURES A GENTILE SERVANT

2095 562 21:20 If a man hits his gentile servant or maid with an object[447] and the servant or maid dies because of it, that man must be punished by the court.

2096 563 21:21 If the victim lived for two days after the incident, then the master is not as culpable.

Commandment 50:[448] Do Not Oppress Weak People

IF BRAWLING MEN INJURE A PREGNANT WOMAN

2097 564 21:22 If people are fighting with each other and accidentally hit a pregnant woman and cause her to lose the baby, but do not cause her any other wounds, then the perpetrator must pay a fine[449] to her as determined by the court.

2098 565 21:23 If the perpetrator caused her bodily harm, then the perpetrator must compensate her based on the extent and severity of the damage.

If the injured woman dies, the perpetrator will be severely punished[450] by the court.

COMPENSATION FOR INJURY

2099 566 21:24 If he hurt her eye or tooth or hand or foot, he compensates her accordingly.

2100 567 21:25 If he caused an injury that heals, the perpetrator must pay for medical bills, pain suffered, disfigurement, and loss of wages.

IF A MASTER CAUSES SERIOUS INJURY TO A GENTILE SERVANT

2101 568 21:26 If a master blinds a gentile servant or maid, the servant or maid goes free.

2102 569 21:27 If a master seriously injures a limb or knocks out a tooth of his gentile servant or maid, he or she goes free.

Mishpatim Section 2 - continued

Commandment 51:[451] Do Not Benefit from A Condemned Animal

Commandment 52:[452] A Court Must Assess Damages Caused By A Goring Animal

2103 570 21:28 If an animal kills a person, the animal must be put to death. It cannot be used as food.[453]

Its owner is not punished,[454] but cannot benefit from the animal.

2104 571 21:29 If it was known that the animal attacks, and the owner had been formally warned to pen the animal, but the owner had not adequately done so, and the animal killed a person, then the owner must be punished by the court.[455]

2105 572 21:30 If the court decides that he must pay a fine as a substitute for his execution, he must do so.

2106 573 21:31 The above laws apply whether the animal kills a Jewish man or woman or child.

2107 574 21:32 The owner of an animal that kills a gentile servant or maid, must pay to the master an appropriate penalty[456] as determined by the court.

Commandment 53: A Court Must Assess Damages Caused by A Pit In Public Area

2108 575 21:33 If someone opens an existing pit or digs a new pit and leaves it uncovered and an animal falls into it,

2109 576 21:34 the perpetrator must pay the owner of the animal the value of the animal less the value of the animal's hide, which still belongs to the animal's owner.

IF AN ANIMAL KILLS SOMEONE'S ANIMAL

2110 577 21:35 If one person's animal kills another person's animal of the same value, both the live and dead animals must be sold, and the money must be split between the two owners.

Mishpatim Section 2 - continued

2111 578 21:36 If the owner of an animal that killed another animal knew that his own animal was dangerous, yet did not adequately pen it up, then he must pay the value of the dead animal less the value of the dead animal's hide, which still belongs to the owner of the dead animal.

Commandment 54:[457] A Court Must Judge A Thief

IF SOMEONE STEALS OX OR SHEEP AND KILLS OR SELLS IT

2112 579 21:37 A person who steals an ox, then kills or sells it, must pay the owner five times its value.

A person who steals a sheep, then kills or sells it, must pay four times its value.

IF SELF-DEFENSE RESULTS IN A PERSON BEING KILLED

2113 580 22:1 Someone who kills a night burglar, and it is apparent that the burglar would have killed the victim if the burglar would have found it necessary to do so, is not liable for murder because it is self-defense.

CAUSING DEATH WHEN NOT MORTALLY THREATENED

LAWS OF THEFT

2114 581 22:2 Someone who kills a burglar where it is obvious that the intruder could not or would not have done bodily harm, has committed murder.

Someone who breaks in and steals must pay back the value of what he or she stole.

If the thief does not own enough to pay back, then the court must arrange for the thief to become an indentured servant.

2115 582 22:3 If a stolen item is found in the thief's possession,[458] the thief must pay the owner double its value.

Mishpatim – Section 2 – Study Notes

---

[445] "Mishpatim" - As stated in the first note of Mishpatim Section 1, the laws that derive from these verses are explained in lengthy discussions in Talmud. Tōra Study Bible presents a basic rendition which requires further study.

[446] Commandment 49 - This commandment is explained by Rambam in his Mishne Tōra: Book 14: Judges: Laws of Courts and Punishments.

[447] 21:20: "object" - If he used a stick or stone, and especially if he used a lethal weapon such as a knife, sword or firearm, and the servant dies, the criminal must be executed by the court.

[448] Commandment 50 – Book 1: Fundamentals: Laws of Character.

[449] 21:22 "pay a fine" – According to Jewish law, abortion, whether intentional or accidental, is not murder. It is forbidden in most circumstances, but it is not murder. Abortion that is done other than for sdaving the life of the mother is forbidden, but it is not murder.

[450] 21:23 "severely punished" - Some sages rule that the perpetrator is executed, while other sages rule that the perpetrator pays compensation to her husband because there was no intention to kill anyone.

[451] Commandment 51 – Book 5: Holiness: Laws of Forbidden Food

[452] Commandment 52 & 53 – Book 11: Damages: Laws of Property Damage.

[453] 21:28 "food" – An animal that is not slaughtered in a kosher manner is forbidden for consumption. This phrase teaches an added law, namely, if after the animal was declared by a court to be stoned, but someone kosher slaughtered the animal before the animal could be stoned, it is still forbidden to be eaten.

[454] 21:28 "owner is not punished" – This phrase teaches that if the animal that killed a person, has killed "only" one or two people, the owner does

not pay to the bereaved family.

This is different than the laws concerning an animal that causes damages. An owner must pay for half the damages that his or her animal caused when the animal damages once or twice.

[455] 21:29 "punished by the court" - If an animal damages a third time, then the owner must pay full damages. If an animal kills a third person, then in addition to killing the offending animal, the owner of that animal must pay a fine to the bereaved family.

[456] 21:32 "appropriate penalty" – The verse specifies 30 shekels of silver. See note on 30:13 for the weight and value of a shekel.

[457] Commandment 54 – Book 11: Damages: Laws of Theft.

[458] 22:3 "found in the thief's possession" – As opposed to the person admitting his crime.

Mishpatim[459] - Section 3   - 23 verses

Commandment 55:[460] A Court Must Assess Damage by A Grazing Animal

2116 583 22:4 A person who allows his or her animal to eat or damage someone else's crops must pay for the damage with the best of his or her own crops.
    The same applies to a vineyard.

Commandment 56: A Court Must Assess Damage by Fire

2117 584 22:5 Someone who starts a fire on his or her own property and it spreads to a neighboring property, must pay for the damage done.

Commandment 57:[461] A Court Must Judge Cases of An Unpaid Guard

2118 585 22:6 Someone who is found to have stolen an item that was being guarded by someone else, must pay the owner double the value of the item stolen.
2119 586 22:7 If the item being guarded is not found, the guardian must formally swear in court that he or she did not steal it.

Commandment 58:[462] A Court Must Judge Cases of a Plaintiff

2120 587 22:8 All cases of embezzlement must be decided by a court of judges.
    The punishment is to pay double the value of what was stolen.

Commandment 59:[463] A Court Must Judge Cases of Hired Worker And Guard

2121 588 22:9 A paid guardian who is watching an animal, but it dies or is hurt or is chased away during the care of the paid guardian,
2122 589 22:10 must solemnly swear in court that he or she did not cause the mishap.
2123 590 22:11 If the item being guarded for payment had been stolen, the guardian must pay its value to the owner because a paid guardian should take better precautions against theft.
2124 591 22:12 A guardian of an animal that was killed by a wild animal should bring evidence or witnesses to that effect in order to avoid paying for the loss of the animal.

Mishpatim Section 3 - continued

Commandment 60:[464] A Court Must Judge Cases of Borrower

2125 592 22:13 Someone who borrows an animal which then gets hurt or dies must pay its value to the owner.
2126 593 22:14 If the owner of the borrowed animal is with the person who borrowed the animal during the mishap, then no payment for the animal is made.

Commandment 61:[465] A Court Must Judge Cases of Seduction

2127 594 22:15 If a man seduces[466] an underage unmarried girl, then he must pay her dowry and marry her, if she consents.
2128 595 22:16 If the girl's father refuses to allow him to marry her, then the seducer must give the dowry money to her father.

Commandment 62:[467] A Court Must Judge Cases of Indulging in Witchcraft

2129 596 22:17 Do not allow someone who engages in witchcraft[468] to remain alive.
2130 597 22:18 Anyone who is intimate with an animal[469] must be severely punished by a court.
2131 598 22:19 Anyone who offers to idols must be punished.

Commandment 63:[470] Do Not Cheat A Convert

Commandment 64: Do Not Insult or Harm A Convert

2132 599 22:20 Do not annoy or wrong a righteous gentile or a convert[471] because you had been visitors in Egypt.
2133 600 22:21 Do not wrong widows, orphans, or any defenseless people.
2134 601 22:22 If you do so and they pray[472] to Me, I will listen to their prayer
2135 602 22:23 and I will be angry at you, and I will severely punish you.

Mishpatim Section 3 - continued

Commandment 65:[473] **Lend Money to Jewish People Who Need Funds**

Commandment 66: Do Not Demand Repayment from Someone Who Is Poor

Commandment 67: Do Not Be Involved in An Interest Loan Among Jewish People

2136 603 22:24 When you lend money to a fellow Jew who is poor, do not insist on being paid back and do not charge interest.[474]

2137 604 22:25 If a poor person cannot repay a loan and you take an essential item of his or hers as collateral, you must provide that item back[475] to him or her when he or she needs it

2138 605 22:26 because that poor person needs the item.

If that poor person prays[476] to Me, I will acknowledge and act on that prayer.

Mishpatim – Section 3 – Study Notes

[459] "Mishpatim" - As stated in the first note of Mishpatim Section 1, the laws that derive from these verses are explained in lengthy discussions in Talmud. Tōra Study Bible presents a basic rendition which requires further study.

[460] Commandments 55 & 56 - These commandments are explained by Rambam in his Mishne Tōra: Book 11: Damages: Laws of Property Damage.

[461] Commandment 57 – Book 13: Judgement: Laws of Creditor and Debtor.

[462] Commandment 58 – Book 13: Judgement: Laws of Plaintiff and Defendant.

[463] Commandment 59 – Book 13: Judgement: Laws of Hiring.

[464] Commandment 60 – Book 13: Judgement: Laws of Borrowing and Depositing.

[465] Commandment 61 – Book 4: Women: Laws of Women.

[466] 22:15 "seduces" – The case of a man who forces himself on a woman against her will is dealt with in Divarim (Deuteronomy) 22:29.

Tōra prohibits each type of crime against women. Today, people take ethics and morality as a benchmark norm. It is easy to forget that Tōra is the source of modern ethics and morality. Yet many people wonder why there is no verse specifically prohibiting crimes against children. The reason is that in Jewish law there is no concept of "consenting adults." All our interactions among people must be based on decency and respect.

[467] Commandment 62 – Book 14: Judges: Laws of Courts and Punishments.

[468] 22:17 "witchcraft" – Witchcraft is forbidden as commandment 509 in Divarim 18:10.

[469] 22:18 "intimate with an animal" – This is restated in Vayikra (Leviticus) verses 18:23, 20:15, and 20:16.

[470] Commandments 63 & 64 – Book 12: Acquisition: Laws of Purchase Transactions.

[471] 22:20 "righteous gentile or convert" – See note on verse 12:48.

[472] 22:22 "pray" – See Essay 7 on the nature of prayer.

[473] Commandments 65-67 – Book 13: Judgement: Laws of Creditor and Debtor.

[474] 22:24 "interest" – A Jewish person is permitted to charge the going interest rate when loaning money to gentiles.

[475] 22:25 "provide that item back" – Similar statements are made in Divarim (Deuteronomy) from which Rambam derives the following commandments:
    Divarim 24:6 – commandment 583: do not take utensils used for preparing food as collateral for a loan.
    Divarim 24:10 – commandment 585: do not forcibly take back a pledge for a loan.
    Divarim 24:12 – commandment 586: do not delay returning a pledge when the owner needs it.
    Divarim 24:13 – commandment 587: return collateral items to the owner when the owner needs them.
    Divarim 24:17 - commandment 590: Do not ask for collateral when you make a loan to a widow.

[476] 22:26 "prays" – See Essay 7 on the nature of prayer.

Mishpatim[477] – Section 4 - 9 verses

Commandment 68:[478] Do Not Blaspheme

Commandment 69:[479] Do Not Curse Judges

Commandment 70: Do Not Curse Leaders

2139 606 22:27 Do not blaspheme G-d or judges.
   Do not curse judicial, educational, social, political, or spiritual leaders.

Commandment 71:[480] Set Aside Tithes in The Proper Sequence

2140 607 22:28 Perform the produce tithing processes in the correct order.[481]
   Redeem your firstborn son[482] 30 days after his birth.
2141 608 22:29 Redeem your firstborn animal 8 days after its birth.

Commandment 72:[483] Do Not Consume Meat from An Injured Animal

2142 609 22:30 Be holy by not eating meat of an injured animal,[484] because it is not kosher.
   You can use non-kosher meat to feed your livestock and pets.

Commandment 73:[485] Do Not Listen to Claims Unless All Parties Are Present

Commandment 74:[486] Do Not Accept Testimony from Someone Who Is A Sinner

2143 610 23:1 Do not listen to only one side of a case.
   Do not accept testimony from a person who is a verified sinner.

Mishpatim - Section 4 - continued

Commandment 75:[487] **Decide Court Cases by Majority Vote**

Commandment 76: Do Not Decide Capital Cases by Majority Of Only 1 Vote

Commandment 77: Once A Judge Acquits, He Cannot Argue for Conviction

2144 611 23:2 Do not make a capital case ruling based on a majority of one vote.

Rather, a majority of at least two votes is required.

If you feel that most of the judges[488] are mistaken, do not refrain from casting your vote based on your convictions.

Judge Fairley And Impartially

2145 612 23:3 Do not show favoritism to someone just because he or she is poor and needs a favorable legal decision.

Return A Stray Animal

2146 613 23:4 If you see an animal gone astray, you should return[489] the animal to the owner.

This is true even if you are not on good terms with the owner.

Commandment 78:[490] Help Unburden an Animal

2147 614 23:5 If someone's animal is struggling under a too-heavy burden, you must help[491] the owner or handler to unburden the animal.

This is true even if the animal owner or handler is not friendly to you.

As long as the owner or handler is involved in the process of unburdening the animal, then you must help.

You must help in such a case even if it must be performed multiple times.

Mishpatim – Section 4 – Study Notes

[477] As stated in the first note of Mishpatim Section 1, the laws that derive from these verses are explained in lengthy discussions in Talmud. Tōra Study Bible presents a basic rendition which requires further study.

[478] Commandment 68 - This commandment is explained by Rambam in his Mishne Tōra: Book 1: Fundamentals: Laws of Idolatry.

[479] Commandments 69 & 70 – Book 14: Judges: Laws of Courts and Punishments.

[480] Commandment 71 – Book 7: Produce: Laws of Gifts to Priests.

[481] 22:28 "correct order" – The basic law is that for the first six years of the seven-year cycle, farmers in Israel first set aside a small part of their harvest as *trūma* for priests. Then they set aside one-tenth of what is left for Levites. After that, one-tenth of what is left is set aside either for the poor or for eating in Jerusalem, depending on what year of the seven-year cycle it is.

[482] 22:28 "Redeem your firstborn son" – This was stated in verse 13:2, which also includes firstborn animals.

[483] Commandment 72 – Book 5: Holiness: Laws of Forbidden Food

[484] 22:30 "injured animal" – Divarim (Deuteronomy) 14:21 states commandment 470: Do not eat meat of an animal that had not been ritually slaughtered. Divarim 12:21 states commandment 448: Ritually slaughter animals.

[485] Commandment 73 – Book 14: Judges: Laws of Courts and Punishments.

[486] Commandment 74 – Book 14: Judges: Laws of Evidence.

[487] Commandments 75-77 – Book 14: Judges: Laws of Courts and Punishments.

[488] 23:2 "judges" – Jewish courts are made up of a panel of judges as explaine in the note on 18:22.

[489] 23:4 "return" – Commandment 538: Return Lost Objects is derived from Divarim 22:1. Commandment 539: Do not ignore a lost object is derived from Divarim 22:3.

[490] Commandment 78 – Book 11: Damages: Laws of Murder and Preservation of Life.

[491] 23:5 "help" – Both commandments 542: Help a person load his or her animal, and commandment 541: Do not abandon someone who needs help, are derived from Divarim 22:4.

Mishpatim[492] – Section 5 - 14 verses

Commandment 79:[493] Do Not Disfavor A Habitual Offender

2148 615 23:6 Do not show favoritism and do not disregard someone based on external factors.

Commandment 80: Do Not Base A Capital Case On Circumstantial Evidence

2149 616 23:7 A judge must not speak in a way that leads to distorted testimony.

If a case is too difficult for a judge, the judge must give the case over to a more competent legal authority.[494]

If a guilty party goes free, G-d will exact punishment.

Commandment 81: A Judge Must Not Accept Any Gifts

2150 617 23:8 A judge must not accept any gift because gifts distort a person's thinking and decision-making process.

2151 618 23:9 Do not insult or cheat a righteous gentile or a convert.[495]

You know how it feels to be different because you had been an outsider in Egypt.

2152 619 23:10 Farm the land of Israel[496] for 6 years and harvest the produce,

Commandment 82:[497] Allow The Land To Re-fertilize During the Year 7

2153 620 23:11 but let the land rest during year 7.

Anyone can take produce that grows on its own throughout year 7.

All animals also can eat whatever grows on its own.

Commandment 83:[498] Rest On The Shabat

2154 621 23:12 Work throughout the first 6 days of the week,[499] but rest[500] on day 7 so your livestock, servants, and converts can become refreshed.

Commandment 84:[501] Do Not Lead A City's Population To Worship Idols

Commandment 85: Do not Take An Oath In The Name Of An Idol

2155 622 23:13 Follow my laws.

Do not speak the name of idols.[502]

Mishpatim - Section 5 - continued

Commandment 86:[503] Celebrate The 3 Holy Festivals: Pesaĥ, Shavūōt, and Sūkōt

2156 623 23:14 Celebrate the 3 holy festivals.[504]
2157 624 23:15 Observe the holy festival of Pesaĥ (Passover).

If you eat food prepared from grain during this seven-day holy festival, only eat unleavened foods.

Pesaĥ must occur during the spring[505] because you left Egypt in the spring.

Each person must offer offerings during this holy festival.
2158 625 23:16 The next holy festival is Shavūōt[506] when the first fruits are harvested and offered.

The third holy festival is Sūkōt[507] when produce is harvested before the rainy season.

This marks the end of the agricultural year.
2159 626 23:17 Each year, people must offer offerings to G-d.

Commandment 87:[508] Do Not Offer The Pesaĥ Offering Until All Leaven Is Gone

Commandment 88: Do Not Leave Leftovers Of Pesaĥ Offering Overnight

2160 627 23:18 Do not offer the Pesaĥ offering until all leaven has been removed from your possession.

Once the Pesaĥ offering is offered, do not allow any leftovers to remain past sunrise.

Commandment 89:[509] Set Aside The First Fruits Of The 7 Types Of Produce

Commandment 90:[510] Do Not Ingest Meat And Dairy Products Together

2161 628 23:19 There are 7 types of produce[511] whose first fruits[512] must be offered to G-d.

Do not ingest meat and dairy[513] products together.

Mishpatim – Section 5 – Study Notes

[492] As stated in the first note of Mishpatim Section 1, the laws that derive from these verses are explained in lengthy discussions in Talmud. Tōra Study Bible presents a basic rendition which requires further study.

[493] Commandments 79-81 - These commandments are explained by Rambam in his Mishne Tōra: Book 14: Judges: Laws of Courts and Punishments.

[494] 23:7 "more competant legal authority" – Mōshe had instructed that a more difficult case must be handed over to a more experienced and competent judge (18:26), regardless of how much or how little an amount of money is at stake in the case.

[495] 23:9 & 12 "righteous gentile or convert" – See the note on verse 12:48 and Essay 5 about the role of conversion in Judaism.

[496] 23:10 "land of Israel" – See note on 3:8 and Essay 6 for the promise that G-d made to the Jewish people about the land of Israel.

[497] Commandment 82 – Book 7: Produce: Laws of Sabbatical and Jubilee Years.

[498] Commandment 83 – Book 3: Seasons: Laws of Shabat.

[499] 23:12 "work throughout the first 6 days of the week" – See note on verse 20:9.

[500] 23:12 "rest" – This is the positive commandment. The negative commandment to not perform forbidden activities on the Sabbath is commandment 32, verse 20:10. See note on 16:23 concerning the nature of commandments and laws of shabat.

[501] Commandments 84 & 85 – Book 1: Fundamentals: Laws of Idolatry.

[502] 23:13 "Do not say the name of idols." – Rambam derives two commandments (i.e., 84 & 85) from this prohibition.

The specifics about a city that has largely worships idols is found in Divarim (Deuteronomy) 13:13-18, from which Rambam derives the following commandments:

Commandment 463: The buildings and property of a city of idol-worship must be burned.

Commandment 464: Do not rebuild such a city.

Commandment 465: Do not derive benefit from buildings and items of a city of idol worship.

[503] Commandment 86 – Book 9: Offerings: Laws of Pilgrim Offerings.

[504] 23:14 "holy festivals" – Festivals are mentioned in:
verses 34:18-25,
Vayikra (Leviticus) 23:2-43,
Bamidbar (Numbers) 28:16-31,
Bamidbar 29:1-39,
and Divarim 16:1-17.

In addition to the 3 central holy festivals, there are the New Year (Rōsh Hashana) and the Day of Atonement (Yōm Kipur). Neither of these two holy days require people to make a pilgrimage.

[505] 23:15 "spring" – See note on verse 13:4 concerning the lunar year and the Jewish leap month that enables the Jewish holidays to fall out during the same season each year.

[506] 23:16 "Shavūōt" – The Festival of Weeks. On this holy festival, farmers bring their first fruits to the Temple, when the Temple stood. It takes place 50 days after the first day of Passover.

Counting the days and weeks from Passover to Shavūōt is Commandment 305 stated in Vayikra 23:15.

After the exodus, the divine revelation at Sinai took place 51 days later (see note on verse 19:1). Nonetheless, Shavūōt is treated as the anniversary of the divine revelation at Mount Sinai.

Shavūōt is mentioned also in verse 34:22.

[507] 23:16 "Sūkōt" – The Festival of Tabernacles. This holy festival commemorates that fact that G-d protected the Jewish people throughout

their many years traveling in the wilderness.

[508] Commandments 87 & 88 – Book 9: Offerings: Laws of Pascal Offering.

[509] Commandment 89 – Book 7: Produce: Laws of First Fruits.

[510] Commandment 90 – Book 5: Holiness: Laws of Forbidden Food.

[511] 23:19 "7 types of produce" – They are enumerated in Divarim 8:8 as:
wheat,
barley,
grapes,
figs,
pomegranates,
olives,
and dates.

[512] 23:19 "first fruits" – This is expanded upon in Divarim chapter 26 with a description of the ceremony that accompanies the giving of first fruits in the Temple.

Shimōt 34:22 links first fruits with the holy festival day of Shavūōt (Festival of Weeks, which takes place 7 weeks after the start of Passover). This teaches that Shavūōt marks the start of the year for first fruits.

Shimōt 34:26 describes the offering as the best fruits.

Bamidbar 18:13 states that each family can eat the first fruits that they bring to the Temple.

Vayikra 2:14 specifies how the first harvest of barley should be offered. It is offered on the second day of Passover.

Vayikra 23:17 specifies how the first harvest of wheat should be brought as loaves of bread.

[513] 23:19 "meat and diary" – This phrase occurs three times in Tōra. Here, it instructs not to eat them together. In verse 34:26, commandment 111, it instructs not to cook them together (even if there is no intention of eating the resulting food). Divarim 14:21 teaches not to derive any benefit from food that results in cooking meat and dairy together.

Mishpatim - Section 6 - 6 verses

2162 629 23:20 "I,[514] G-d, will be appointing a protective agent[515] to lead you to the land of Israel.
2163 630 23:21 "Listen to that agent and do not rebel against him because he will have the power to punish.
"The agent has My authority.
2164 631 23:22 "If you follow the agent whom I will appoint, I will be an enemy to your enemies.
2165 632 23:23 "My agent will lead you to the land where gentile nations currently reside, and I will displace them."
2166 633 23:24 Do not bow to their idols and do not worship them.
You must destroy the idols in the land of Israel.

Commandment 91:[516] Pray[517] To G-d Daily

2167 634 23:25 Worship and serve G-d.
G-d wants you to pray[518] for prosperity, good health, and recovery from disease.

Mishpatim – Section 6 – Study Notes

[514] 23:20 "I" – These four verses are somewhat distinct in that G-d speaks in the first person.

[515] 23:20 "agent" – Here, G-d informs Mōshe that, instead of G-d leading them directly, an agent who has the power to bring them to, and settle them into, the land, will lead them. However, this agent cannot pardon sin. Later, G-d informs Mōshe that having an agent is a good thing because now, the agent to be appointed will not destroy people the way G-d Himself would if the people sin (32:34 and 33:2-3). But Mōshe expresses dissatisfaction with having a mere agent (33:12), and G-d then agrees to imbue the agent with some of His divine glory (33:14). Yet Mōshe states that such an agent will not possess enough divine glory to make it clear to the world that the Jewish people are not merely conventionally conquering the land of Israel. Also, such as agent cannot show that he, Mōshe, is not just an ordinary leader (33:15). Finally, Mōshe asks again (34:9), and G-d agrees to lead the Jewish people Himself (34:10).

A contributing reason why Mōshe is so insistent is that Mōshe's first encounter with a divine agent was at the burning bush (see note on verse 3:2). After getting Mōshe's attention, G-d communicates with him directly. Thus, Mōshe experienced the big difference between G-d and a mere divine agent.

[516] Commandments 91 - This commandment is explained by Rambam in his <u>Mishne Tōra</u>: Book 2: Love G-d: Laws of Prayer.

[517] Commandment 91: Pray – Rambam interprets the word "worship" in verse 23:25 as prayer, as the talmud states: prayer is how people serve G-d with their hearts.

People can express their acknowledgement of G-d, their praise of G-d and their thankfulness G-d. But prayer is specifically a request that people make of G-d.

The sages instituted morning prayer based on Avraham (Abraham) in Brāshēt (Genesis) verse 18:23. They instituted the afternoon prayer based on Yiẑhak (Isaac) in Brāshēt 24:63. The evening prayer is based on Yaakōv in Brāshēt 32:10. See Essay 7 on prayer and the note on verse 3:9.

[518] 23:25 "pray" – This verse, along with the next verse, is rendered to teach prime examples of what people should pray for. The topic of this verse pairs with verse 15:26 where G-d describes Himself as the doctor or healer of the Jewish people. Jewish law expects and requires people to seek medical help when necessary but asking help from G-d is an essential element of faith.

Mishpatim – Section 7   - 23 + 3 verses

2168 635 23:26 Pray[519] that no woman will miscarry.
   Pray that no one will be unable to have children.
Pray that everyone will live a full life.
2169 636 23:27 "I, G-d, will displace your enemies.
2170 637 23:28 "G-d will make sure that your enemies will not be able to fight against you.
2171 638 23:29 "I will not displace the current inhabitants of the land of Israel all at once because wild animals would overpopulate and run rampant.
2172 639 23:30 "I will displace them gradually, as your population grows."

Borders of the Land of Israel
2173 640 23:31 The borders[520] of the land of Israel are:
   southern boundary: the Reed (Red) Sea,[521]
   western boundary: the Mediterranean Sea,
   northern boundary: the wilderness,[522] and
   eastern boundary: the Frat (Euphrates) River.[523]
2174 641 23:32 Do not make treaties with idol worshipers who reside in the land of Israel.
   Do not worship their idols.

Commandment 92:[524] Do Not Allow Idol Worshipers To Live In The Land Of Israel
2175 642 23:33 Do not allow idol worshipers to live in the land of Israel[525] because they will cause you to sin.

2176 643 24:1 G-d communicated to Mōshe (Moses):[526]
   "You, Aharōn (Aaron), Nadav, and Avēhū, and the 70 leaders[527] should come onto the mountain.[528]
   "They will stay only part of the way up.
2177 644 24:2 "Only Mōshe will walk up to the top of the mountain."

Mishpatim - Section 7 - continued

THE JEWISH PEOPLE PROCLAIM: "WE WILL OBEY"

2178 645 24:3 Mōshe told the Jewish people all the instructions and laws that G-d had communicated.

The entire Jewish people responded:

"All the things that G-d commanded, we will obey." [529]

MŌSHE BUILDS AN ALTAR AND 12 COLUMNS

2179 646 24:4 Mōshe wrote down the words of G-d in Book Of The Covenant.[530]

Mōshe awoke early and built an altar at the foot of the mountain, and he set up 12 columns, one for each tribe.

2180 647 24:5 Mōshe directed the firstborn men[531] to offer animal offerings.

2181 648 24:6 Mōshe poured half the blood into buckets and dashed the other half onto the altar.

MŌSHE READS THE BOOK OF THE COVENANT TO THE PEOPLE

THE JEWISH PEOPLE RESPOND: "WE WILL OBEY AND STUDY"

2182 649 24:7 Mōshe read the Book Of The Covenant aloud to the people.

When the people heard these commandments, they responded:

"Everything that G-d has commanded, we will obey and will apply ourselves to understand the laws[532] so that we will know how to correctly observe them."

2183 650 24:8 Mōshe then sprinkled blood of the offerings onto the people, and said:

"This blood ratifies the solemn promise that G-d promises you because you have agreed to follow His commandments."

2184 651 24:9 Mōshe, Aharōn, Nadav, and Avēhū,[533] and the 70 leaders walked onto the mountain.

2185 652 24:10 They experienced the presence of G-d.

Metaphysically, there was sapphire stone under His feet, and there was a clear sky.

Mishpatim - Section 7 - continued

2186 653 24:11 Although people would normally perish by having such an experience, G-d made sure that they did not perish, because they were worthy of this vision.

They rejoiced while having this divine experience.

2187 654 24:12 G-d communicated to Mōshe:[534]

"Come up to the top of the mountain and beyond.

"I will give you the stone slabs[535] along with the Tōra and the commandments which I have written[536] so that you can teach them."

2188 655 24:13 Mōshe and Yihōshūa (Joshua)[537] walked onto the mountain of G-d.[538]

2189 656 24:14 Mōshe told the leaders:

"Stay here until we come back to you.

"Aharōn and Ĥùr[539] will be here.

"If there are any problems, go to them."

MŌSHE ASCENDS THE MOUNTAIN

2190 657 24:15 Mōshe[540] walked up the mountain[541] and the cloud covered the mountain.

Mishpatim – Final Section

2191 658 24:16 The glory of G-d was on Mount Sēnī (Sinai).

The cloud covered the mountain for 6 days.[542]

On day 7, G-d called to Mōshe from the cloud.

2192 659 24:17 The glory of G-d was a devouring fire[543] on the top of the mountain and the Jewish people could see it.

MŌSHE STAYS ON MOUNT SĒNĪ FOR FORTY DAYS

2193 660 24:18 Mōshe walked into the cloud and walked up to the top of the mountain.

Mōshe was on the mountain for 40 days and nights.[544]

Mishpatim – Section 7 – Study Notes

[519] 23:26 "pray" – This verse is a continuation of previous verse 23:25. This verse is rendered as examples of what people can and should pray for. See Table 7 on the nature of prayer.

[520] 23:31 "borders" – Table 3 compares the verses that define the borders of Israel.

[521] 23:31 "Reed Sea" – Known today as the Red Sea. Divarim (Deuteronomy) 1:7 and 11:24 state that the Negev desert is the southern border. Our verse here elucidates that the Negev, down to the area around the modern city of Eilat is included in Biblical Israel. See note on verse 10:19 for more facts about the Reed Sea.

[522] 23:31 "wilderness" – The northern boundary of Israel is stated as Lebanon in Divarim 1:7 and 11:24.

[523] 23:31 "Frat (Euphrates) River" – Arabic: al Farat. The Euphrates River is stated as a border of the Land of Israel in Brāshēt (Genesis) 15:18 when G-d promises the land to Avraham. It is stated again as the eastern border of Israel in Divarim (Deuteronomy) 1:7 and 11:24. However, the Yardān (Jordan) River is mentioned as the east border in Bamidbar (Numbers) chapter 34, where a detailed list of borders is specified.

[524] Commandments 92 - This commandment is explained by Rambam in his Mishne Tōra: Book 1: Fundamentals: Laws of Idolatry.

[525] 23:33 "Do not allow idol worshipers to live in the land of Israel" - When the Jewish people, led by Yihōshūa (Joshua), entered into the land of Israel, they did not automatically battle against the inhabitants. Commandment 525 in Divarim (Deuteronomy) 20:10 states that the Jewish people must offer peace terms to a city. Yihōshūa sent a messenger to each town with the following statement: "This land is holy to G-d. You may continue to live here in peace as long as you stop worshipping idols and destroy your idols. If you do not want to give up idol worship, then you must leave this holy land. If you choose not to do either, then we must

enter into battle against you."

[526] 24:1 "G-d communicated to Mōshe" – According to Rashē, these events took place before the divine revelation and align with what has already been described in chapter 19, adding details (see Table 4).

Ramban and Ibn Ezra explain that the events recorded here took place after the revelation.

[527] 24:1 and 24:9 "70 leaders" – The note on verse 18:22 explains the role and context of these leaders.

[528] 24:1 "should come onto the mountain" – This is stated as occurring in verse 24:9.

[529] 24:3 "obey" – See verse 19:8. In verse 24:7, the people amplify their pledge.

[530] 24:4 "Book Of The Covenant" – According to Ramban and Ibn Ezra, this book is made up at least of chapters 20-23.

[531] 24:5 "firstborn men" – This is the rendition of Rashē.
See note on verse 11:5 as to reason firstborn were singled out.
Alternate interpretations include:
Ibn Ezra: the sons of the 70 elders.
Ramban: unmarried men.

[532] 24:7 "we will obey and will apply ourselves to understand the laws" – When the people previously stated that they will obey (19:8 and 24:3), they make an unconditional pledge to follow the laws of Tōra. Here they amplify their commitment by pledging to observe the laws even before knowing what those laws are.

Note, however, that in Divarim 5:24, Mōshe states that at this time the people had said that they will "listen and obey."

Another way to render this two-part pledge is:
"we will perform" the positive commandments,
and "we will refrain" from trespassing the negative commandments.

533 24:9 "Nadav, and Avēhū" – These two oldest sons of Aharōn were designated to be leaders. However, later, they severely violated divine instructions and they perished during the consecration ceremony (see Vayikra (Leviticus) chapter 10).

534 24:12 "G-d communicated" – At this point, the narrative continues after the divine revelation of the Decaloge, as shown in Table 4.

535 24:12 "I will give you the stone slabs" – Most translations translate the Hebrew word for these slabs as "tablets."
This is the first time that slabs are mentioned. During the entire detailed description of the first 6 days at Mount Sēnī, including the dramatic divine revelation, no mention is made of slabs. The next time the slabs are mentioned, G-d specifies that they must be placed in the sacred box (verses 25:16 & 21). Verse 40:20 states that this was done.
This verse does not directly state what, if anything, will be engraved on the slabs. When this verse mentions "Tōra" and "a commandment" along with the stone slabs, they may or may not be referring to what was engraved on the slabs. Verse 31:18 states that G-d engraved commandments on the first stone slabs, although it does not specify which commandments. Verse 34:1 (portion Kē Tēsa section 5) elucidates that the second pair of slabs will have the same engraving as the first. Finally, verse 34:28 states that it is the Decaloge that was engraved on the second slabs. Therefore, the first slabs did also. As a side note: even though when Mōshe recounts the Decaloge to the new generation as told in Divarim, he makes small changes to the wording, this is not because the second pair of slabs were engraved differently than the first pair.
There are two approaches as to the role of the slabs. In one approach, G-d intended all along to give slabs, but there was no need to mention them until now. The other approach feels that the need for physical stone slabs is a reaction to human behavior, in that people need artifacts to prevent them from sliding off the path of righteousness. Along these lines, there are traditional commentators who believe that even the Tabernacle became necessary because people had demanded that a statue be made for them as recorded in chapter 32.
G-d gives the stone slabs at the end of Mōshe' first 40-day stay on the mountain (31:18). The first slabs had been fashioned by G-d as stated

in verse 32:16. Mōshe throws down those first slabs (32:19). According to Radak (Rabbi David Kimchi), based on verses 25:16 & 21, the broken pieces of the first slabs were eventually placed in the sacred box. Note, however, when King Shlōmō (Solomon) dedicates the Temple, the existence of the first slabs are not mentioned. (See Kings I 8:9).

Mōshe, at the direction of G-d (34:1), forms the second pair of blank stone slabs and carries them up Mount Sēnī (34:4).

Verse 34:28 states that Mōshe engraved the Decaloge on the second slabs. But in verse 34:1 G-d states that He will engrave them. Divarim 10:2-4 corroborates that G-d had engraved them.

Mōshe carried the engraved second pair of stone slabs down to the people (34:29). Mōshe placed the second stone slabs into the sacred box (40:20). This is recounted by Mōshe in Divarim (Deuteronomy) 10:1-5.

[536] 24:12 "along with the Tōra and the commandment which I have written" – It is not clear what were were engraved on the slabs. It is not until verse 34:28 that the Decaloge is specified as the words engraved on the second pair of slabs.

In terms of the inclusion of the word Tōra here, perhaps it refers to the Decaloge. Or perhaps G-d gave or dictated the Tōra parchment that included all verses up to this point. A third possibilty that it refers to the Book of the Covenant mentioned in verse 24:4.

It is not clear what the wotd "commandment" in the singular refers to here. Perhaps the first commandment of the Decaloge, is "the" commandment.

[537] 24:13 "Yihōshūa" – Yihōshūa is first mentioned when he was selected to lead the army against Amalek (17:9-14). See note on verse 17:9 for more information about Yihōshūa.

[538] 24:13 "mountain of G-d" – See note on verse 3:1 for the references of Sēnī as mountain of G-d.

[539] 24:14 "Ĥùr" – Ĥùr is also mentioned in 17:10, and 31:2.

[540] 24:15 "Mōshe" – Yihōshūa stayed partly up the mountain. Therefore, both Mōshe and Yihōshūa were not present during the incident of the gold

calf statue.

[541] 24:15 "walked up the mountain" – As shown in Table 4, based on the opinion of Rashē, this is Mōshe's sixth ascent up the mountain.

[542] 24:16 "6 days" –Some commentators state this is part of the 40 days. Others state that these 6 days occurred before the divine revelation, and the 40 days occurred after revelation.

[543] 24:17 "devouring fire" – No one could live among that fire. That is a contributing reason why later, some people thought that Mōshe was no longer alive (verse 32:23).

[544] 24:18 "40 days and nights" – There are multiple approaches among the commentators with regard to this duration. One approach is that the 40-day duration was G-d's original intention. However, the text does not indicate whether anyone was told of this intended duration. Some commentators feel that the people were told, and they knew what to expect. This is the approach and opinion taken by Tōra Study Bible. Later, when some people erroneously thought that the 40 days were up and Mōshe should be back, some people panicked and insisted on a replacement for Mōshe.

A different approach is that Tōra is simply stating what ended up happening, namely, in response to the fact that the people sinned, G-d instructed Mōshe to leave the mountain, although the original intention was for Mōshe to be on the mountain for a longer period of time. See notes on verses 32:1 and 32:7.

There are three 40-day durations. First Mōshe was on the mountain for 40 days after the revelation as stated here. Verse 34:28 states that Mōshe did not eat or drink during this period. That took place right after revelation until the day 17 of Tamūz (which now is observed as a fast day).

The second 40-day period was from the next day (Tamūz 18) onward.

The third 40-day period was from Elūl 1 until the day now known as the Day of Atonement, Yōm Kipur, which is Tishrā 10. Mōshe descended with the second pair of stone slabs on that special and holy day.

Much later, when speaking to a new generation, Mōshe tells the people that he had fasted for those first 40 days (Divarim 9:9). There, he mentioned that he prayed for forgiveness for the sin of the gold statue for another 40 days and fasted during that 40-day period as well (Divarim 9:18). Mōshe mentions this also in Divarim 10:10.

The 5 parts of Table 7, one part for each of the consecutive months of Sēvan, Tamūz, Av, Elūl, and Tishrā, show the sequence of these events

Trūma[545] - Section 1   - 16 verses   (Total: 96 verses)
[There are 3 commandments in this portion:
                    2 positive and 1 negative.]

DONATIONS FOR THE TABERNACLE

2194 661 25:1 G-d communicated[546] to Mōshe (Moses) as follows:
2195 662 25:2 Ask the Jewish people to voluntarily contribute donations
2196 663 25:3 of the following types of materials:
  1 gold,
  2 silver,[547]
  3 copper,[548]
 2197 664 25:4
  4 blue[549] wool,
  5 red[550] wool,
  6 wool colored with dye from a crimson[551] animal,[552]
  7 fine linen,[553]
  8 goat hair,[554]
2198 665 25:5
  9 ram skins dyed red,
  10 skins of a wild animal,[555]
  11 acacia wood,
2199 666 25:6
  12 pure olive oil for lamps,[556]
  13 spices[557] for the anointing[558] oil,
  14 fragrances[559] for the sweet incense,
2200 667 25:7
  15 two onyx stones[560] for the apron,
     and twelve various stones[561] for the breastplate.

Commandment 93:[562] Build A Sanctuary

2201 668 25:8 They must build a sanctuary[563] for Me through which I will reside within the Jewish people[564] and accept their prayers.[565]
2202 669 25:9 You must build the sanctuary and its furniture according to the plan that I am showing[566] you.

Trūma - Section 1 - continued

Sacred Box

2203 670 25:10 The Jewish people must construct a box[567] of acacia wood that is 5 feet[568] by 3 feet by 3 feet high.

2204 671 25:11 You must line its inside by placing a gold box into it, which has an outward lip to cover the thickness of the wood.
Also, place the sacred box into a gold box that just fits it.
On the top of the outer gold box make a crown of gold.

2205 672 25:12 Make four rings of gold and attach them to the upper part of the outer gold box: two on one side and two on the opposite side.

2206 673 25:13 You must make two poles of acacia and cover them with gold.

2207 674 25:14 You must place the rods through the rings and hold up the sacred box by holding the rods when the box needs to be moved.

Commandment 94:[569] Do Not Remove The Rods From The Sacred Box

2208 675 25:15 The rods must always stay in the rings of the sacred box and they should never be removed.[570]

2209 676 25:16 You should place the stone slabs[571] of evidence which I will give you, into the sacred box.

Trūma - Section 1 – Study Notes

⁵⁴⁵ The Hebrew word *trūma* means "donation." In its more specific technical use, trūma refers to the gift that a farmer gives to a priest. This enabled priests to concentrate on serving G-d and teaching Tōra to the people. Similarly, farmers gave tithe to the Levites who also devoted themselves to serving in the sanctuary and teaching people Tōra.

⁵⁴⁶ 25:1 "communicated" - The communications from G-d contained in portions Mishpatim, Trūma, Teźave, and Kē Tēsa took place while Mōshe was on the mountain before he came down and broke the stone slabs. For example, in the following verses, G-d shows Mōshe the form of an object while he is on the mountain:
a) 25:40 candelabra,
b) 26:30 how the pieces of the tabernacle fit together,
and c) 27:8 altar.

See note on verse 24:18 and Table 4. Table 7 presents a calendar that shows the sequence of the three 40-day periods. Also, Table 5 summarizes the events over the first year-and-a-half after the exodus.

There are two major opinions in the commentators as to the nature of the commandment to have a tabernacle. One opinion is that G-d intended all along for the Jewish people to have a tabernacle, and eventually, the Holy Temple.

The alternate opinion is that G-d instituted a tabernacle in response to people having formed a gold calf statue. A tabernacle enables people to focus and direct their prayers to G-d. It is a concession to human weakness. According to this opinion, G-d communicated this portion (i.e., Trūma) and the next portion (i.e., Tiźave) on the fortieth day after the calf was formed. This would place these portions just before verse 32:7.

After this first verse, the entire rest of portion Trūma is a quote by G-d. Therefore, quotation marks have been omitted.

⁵⁴⁷ 25:3 "silver" - Silver, in the form of a half-shekel coin was a mandatory contribution from each adult man. See note on 30:13 for the weight and value of a shekel.

Verse 38:26 states that 603,550 half-shekels were collected. The purpose was to provide silver for the socket foundation pieces for the Tabernacle, but it served secondarily as a population count. The Jewish people are instructed not to count people directly, but rather for each person to give a coin and the coins are then counted (verses 30:11-16). See study note on verse 38:26 for the role of this count in terms of the detailed census described in Bamidbar (Numbers).

There are various opinions as to why silver is included in the list of voluntary donations:

Sadya Gaon, Rashē: Silver was also given voluntarily and used for forming various dishes and utensils. The wording in verse 35:24 supports this view. There is a tradition that there are 15 different types of materials that were voluntarily donated. If silver is included as a voluntary donation, then all the gemstones can be considered as a single type, as is seen in this list.

Ibn Ezra: No voluntary silver was given. There was enough silver from the half-shekel donations for all silver needed for the tabernacle. Tōra includes silver in the list here even though it doesn't technically belong. According to this opinion, the fifteenth item could be achieved by treating the pair of onyx stones as a separate type of item from the other gemstones.

[548] 25:3 "copper" – According to most opinions, it is copper. Other opinions include:

Ibn Ezra, Rambam: gold-colored brass.
Septuagint: bronze.

[549] 25:4 "blue" – For technical details and opinions about each of the many materials listed in these verses, see Kaplan, 1981, pp. 380-384. Various opinions as to what shade of blue this is, include:

Septuagint:	hyacinth blue
Josephus, Sadya, Rambam:	sky-blue
Talmud Tractate Menahot:	midnight blue indigo
Menachem as quoted by Rashē:	deep blue
Rashē, Ibn Ezra:	greenish blue aquamarine
Radak:	ultramarine azure

There is also discussion as to the source of the blue dye:

Septuagint: purpura snail

Rabbi Yiẑhak Herzog, 1919: Janthina deep water snails that produce a light violet-blue dye.

Physical evidence: Dye-works in various archeological sites of ancient

Tyre, Phoenicia, Athens, and Pompeii include snail shells of both the Purpura and Murex genus.

⁵⁵⁰ 25:4 "red" – There are various interpretations as to what this dye is. Not all commentators treat the word as a color. Opinions include (see Kaplan):
    Septuagint: Deep crimson from Purpura snails.
          Note that Aristotle in his Animal Biology 5:15 states that snails found along the northern Israel coast are blue; those along the southern coast are red. Other sources state that whether the extract of purpura snails produce blue or red depends on extent of sunlight exposure during processing.
    Rambam: Mishne Tora: Laws of the Utensils of the Temple: 8:13; and
    Radak: purplish red
    Rīvid (Raavad): three-colored threads twisted together
    Ibn Ezra: dark red
    Zōhar (Book of Splendor): iridescent, with green overtones.

⁵⁵¹ 25:4 "crimson" – As mentioned in the footnotes in Kaplan:
    Septuagint, Sadya, Radak, Ramban: crimson
    Pesikta Rabasi 20:3:   orange
    Zohar (2:139a):   pink

⁵⁵² 25:4 "animal" – As mentioned in the footnotes in Kaplan:
    Tōsefta Menahôt 9:16   red mountain worm
    Sadya Gaōn: Kermes biblicus
    Ralbag: conchineal insect

⁵⁵³ 25:4 "linen" - The word used for linen also means "six."
    Sadya: the linen cloth was made of six-ply Egyptian linen, which looks like silk.

⁵⁵⁴ 25:4 "goat hair" - As mentioned in the footnotes in Kaplan:
    Ibn Ezra, Rashbam: goats' hair.
    Sadya, Rashe, Abarbanel: angora.
    Māam Lōaz: mohair.

⁵⁵⁵ 25:5 "wild animal" - Discussions in the Talmud indicate that the animal

was multi-colored, somewhat spotted, and had horns. Some scholars identify it as a giraffe, which had horn-like protrusions. A giraffe is a kosher animal because it has true hooves and it chews its cud.

[556] 25:6 "lamps" - The lamps of the menora (verses 25:37-38).

[557] 25:6 "spices" – Spices for anointing oil are specified in verses 30:23-24.

[558] 25:6 "anointing" –The list of items and people to be anointed are stated in verses 30:26-30. The oil itself as a voluntary donation is part of the olive oil listed above, as is indicated in verse 35:28.

[559] 25:6 "fragrances" – Fragrances for incense are listed in verse 30:34.

[560] 25:7 "two onyx stones" – They are agate quartz with alternating red and white bands. Their use is described in verses 28:9-12.

The fact that onyx stone is precious is evident because it is mentioned in Brāshēt (Genesis) 2:12. Tōra describes the greater middle-eastern region in terms of the 4 great rivers and the lands they run though. The first river is Pēshōn and its land is Ĥavēla. Opinions as to what Pēshōn and Ĥavēla are include (see Kaplan, 1981, p.9):
    a. Nile River – Egypt, or
    b. Ganges River – India, or
    c. Karun River – Persian Gulf.
Tōra states that Ĥavēla is a land that has gold, pearls, and onyx.

[561] 25:7 "twelve various stones" – They are described in verses 28:17-21.

[562] Commandment 93 – This commandment is explained by Rambam in his <u>Mishne Tōra</u>: Book 8: Service To G-d: Laws of the Holy Temple.

[563] 25:8 "sanctuary" – The sanctuary in the wilderness is called the Tabernacle. Later, King David set aside the area for the Temple, which was constructed by his son, King Solomon.

[564] 25:8 "reside within the Jewish people" – There is a mistaken tendency to believe that G-d resides in a place or building, where prayers will be

accepted. Tōra teaches that G-d resides throughout the entire universe and beyond. Because it s easy to forget that G-d permeates the universe, it is people who need houses of worship.

565 25:8 "accept their prayers" – This is the rendition of Siforno.

G-d accepts sincere prayer from any location. It is considered especially meritorious to pray with a group. In times of the Tabernacle and the Holy Temple, the service to G-d that took place in these special locations played a unique role. However, prayer today is no less valid than when the sanctuary stood. Verses 34:24 and 34:26 refer to a central house of worship. See Essay 7 on the nature of prayer and for the occurrences of prayer.

566 25:9 "showing" - Other verses where G-d "showed" are:
 a) 25:40 candelabra,
 b) 26:30 how the tabernacle pieces fit together,
 and c) 27:8 altar.

The note on 25:1 states that the instructions about the tabernacle took place during Mōshe's first 40-day stay on the mountain.

567 25:10 "box" – This is referred to by Tōra as the Box of Evidence or the Box of Testimony because the stone slabs were placed inside. It is commonly translated as "ark." A better descriptive rendition is Sacred Box or Sacred Container.

568 25:10 "feet" - The verse uses the Hebrew term *ama*, commonly translated as "cubit." An *ama* is described as 6 handbreadths long. A medium-sized man's handbreadth is a length of 3 inches, while a large handbreadth is 4 inches. Thus, an *ama* may be anywhere from 18 to 24 inches long. This rendition selects 2 feet as the lengtht of an *ama*.

569 Commandment 94 – Book 8: Service To G-d: Laws of Temple Furniture, Utensils, and Caretakers.

570 25:15 "should never be removed" – Radak (Rabbi David Kimchi): King Shlōmō (Solomon) had longer rods made for the sacred box and once they were in place in the Holy Temple, they were never removed (see Kings

I:8:8).

[571] 25:16 "stone slabs" - This is the second mention of slabs. Here, G-d states for the first time that the stone slabs will be placed in the sacred box. It is not until verse 34:28 that a verse states what was engraved on the slabs. See study note on verse 24:12 concerning the details about the stone slabs.

Trūma - Section 2   - 14 verses

LID OF THE SACRED BOX

2210 677 25:17 You must make a gold lid[572] for the sacred box. It must measure 5 feet[573] by 3 feet.

2211 678 25:18 You must make two gold statues on the top of the lid, one at each end of the lid.

2212 679 25:19 You must make the statues as part of the lid.
The statues must not be formed first and attached afterward.

2213 680 25:20 Each statue must have wings projecting upward,[574] shadowing the lid with their wings.
The faces of the statues must face each other and be oriented somewhat downward toward the lid.

2214 681 25:21 You must place the lid on the sacred box.
First, you must place the stone slabs, which I will give you,[575] into the sacred box.[576]

2215 682 25:22 Whenever I will communicate with you it will be from the point between the two statues on top of the sacred box of the testimony.

TABLE

2216 683 25:23 You must construct a table of acacia wood that is 4 feet long by 2 feet wide.
Its legs must be almost 3 feet high so that the table top will be 3 feet off the ground.

2217 684 25:24 You must cover it with gold and make a gold crown around the top of the base.

2218 685 25:25 You must make a frame that is 4 inches high, that will go around the table and make a crown that goes around the frame.

2219 686 25:26 You must make four gold rings, one on each leg.

2220 687 25:27 The rings must be on the outer side of the frame so that rods can be inserted for carrying the table.

2221 688 25:28 You must make the rods of acacia and cover them with gold and the table will be carried using them.

Trūma - Section 2 – continued

Dishes For The Table

2222 689 25:29 You must make:
 a. the metal dishes in which the multi-surfaced bread is baked,
 b. the gold dishes on which the bread will be transferred until it is placed onto the tubes of the table,
 c. the two gold spoons in which incense will be placed,
 d. the open half circle gold tubes that will cover the bread on the table, and
 e. its gold supports.

Commandment 95:[577] Prepare The Showbread

2223 690 25:30 You must continually place the multi-surfaced bread on the table."

Trūma - Section 2 – Study Notes

[572] 25:17 "lid" - Talmud Tractate Sūka: The cover was 4 inches thick.

[573] 25:17 "feet" – See note on 25:10 concerning the length calculations.

[574] 25:20 "wings projecting upward" - Talmud Tractate Sūka: The wings reached to 40 inches above the cover.

[575] 25:21 "which I will give you" – G-d formed and etched the first pair of stone slabs. Mōshe prepared the second pair.

[576] 25:21 "place the stone slabs . . . into the sacred box" – The second pair of slabs were placed in the sacred box (40:20; Divarim 10:2-5). Radak (Rabbi David Kimchi) states that even the broken pieces of the first pair of stone slabs were placed into the sacred box. See study note on verse 25:12 for details about the slabs.

[577] Commandment 95 – This commandment is explained by Rambam in his Mishne Tōra: Book 8: Service To G-d: Laws of Regular and Additional Offerings.

Trūma - Section 3   - 24 verses

CANDELABRA MENŌRA

2224 691 25:31 "You must make the candelabra, beaten from a single block of gold,[578] including its base, middle branch, and decorative cups, knobs, and flowers.

2225 692 25:32 It must have six branches which emerge from the main central branch, three on one side and three on the other side.

2226 693 25:33 Each branch must have a decoration consisting of three cups, a knob, and a flower.

2227 694 25:34 The central branch must have four cups, a knob, and a flower.

2228 695 25:35 There must be a knob at each of the three points where the side branches emerge from the central branch.

2229 696 25:36 All parts of the candelabra must be fashioned out of a single block of gold.

2230 697 25:37 You must construct its seven lamps.
  The priest will light the lamps.
  The opening of each side lamp must face toward the central branch.

2231 698 25:38 The tongs and scoops for the candelabra must be made of gold.

2232 699 25:39 The candelabra and its implements must be made from a large block of gold.

2233 700 25:40 Construct the candelabra based on the form you are being shown[579] on the mountain.

ROOF

2234 701 26:1 You must make a tabernacle cover of 10 fabric panels made of linen, blue wool, purple wool, and red wool.
  Each fabric panel must have cherub images woven into them.

2235 702 26:2 Each fabric panel must be 56 feet[580] long by 8 feet wide.

2236 703 26:3 Two large fabric panels must be made by sewing together five panels together along their long edges.

2237 704 26:4 You must make loops of blue wool along the lengthwise edges of each of the large fabric panels.

2238 705 26:5 You must make 50 loops on the lengthwise edge of each large fabric panel.

Trūma - Section 3 - continued

2239 706 26:6 You must make 50 golden hooks, with which you must attach the large fabric panels together by their loops.

2240 707 26:7 You must make 11 panels as a top cover made from goat hair[581] over the tabernacle.

2241 708 26:8 Each goat hair panel must be 60 feet long by 8 feet wide.

2242 709 26:9 You must attach five of the goat hair panels together and six goat hair panels together.
You must fold over the sixth goat hair panel at the end of the tent.

2243 710 26:10 You must make 50 loops on the edges of each of the large goat hair panels.

2244 711 26:11 You must make 50 copper hooks with which to join the two large goat hair panels via their loops.

2245 712 26:12 You must drape half of the overhang of the top cover over the back of the tabernacle.

2246 713 26:13 The extra 2 feet on each side of the top cover must drape over the sides of the tabernacle cover.

2247 714 26:14 You must make a third cover of ram skin and a fourth cover of wild animal skins." [582]

Trūma - Section 3 – Study Notes

---

[578] 25:31 "gold" – The law is that the menora must be made of a single block of material. In the Tabernacle and in first Temple, it was made of gold.

[579] 25:40 "are being shown" - Other verses where G-d shows Mōshe are:
    a) 25:9 the completed tabernacle and its furniture,
    b) 26:30 how the tabernacle pieces fit together,
and c) 27:8 altar.

The note on 25:1 states that the instructions about the tabernacle took place during Mōshe's first 40-day stay on the mountain.

[580] 26:2 "feet" – See note on 25:10 concerning the length calculations.

[581] 26:7 "goat hair" – This is the second layer of the roof.

[582] 26:14 "wild animal skins" – See note on verse 25:5 concerning the identity of the wild animal species.

Trūma - Section 4 - 16 verses

WALLS

2248 715 26:15 "You must make the beams of the tabernacle out of acacia trees with the grain lengthwise.

2249 716 26:16 Each beam must be 20 feet[583] long by 3 feet wide.

2250 717 26:17 Each beam is carved with two prongs at its bottom.

2251 718 26:18 You must make 20 beams for the south wall of the tabernacle.

2252 719 26:19 You must make 40 silver rectangular socket bases for the 20 beams.
Place 2 sockets under each beam for the two prongs.

2253 720 26:20 There must be 20 beams for the north side of the tabernacle

2254 721 26:21 as well as 40 silver sockets, two for each beam.

2255 722 26:22 You must make 6 beams for the west side of the tabernacle.

2256 723 26:23 You must make 2 corner beams, one for the northwest corner and one for the southwest corner.

2257 724 26:24 All beams must fit next to each other with no gaps along the bottom.
The top of each beam must have notches for a square ring to fit into, which holds adjacent beams together.
This is true for the corner beams as well.

2258 725 26:25 As mentioned just above, there will be 8 beams with 16 silver sockets.
Two sockets must be placed under each beam.

2259 726 26:26 You must make 5 rods of acacia wood for the beams on one wall of the tabernacle

2260 727 26:27 and 5 rods for the beams of the opposite wall of the tabernacle, and 5 rods for the west wall of the tabernacle.

2261 728 26:28 A middle rod that will fit in the center of the beams will extend from one end of a wall to the other.

Trūma - Section 4 -continued

2262 729 26:29 You must cover the beams with gold.
Each beam must have rings of gold on the front side which will serve to hold the rods.
You must cover the rods in gold.
2263 730 26:30 You must put the tabernacle together based on its design as you are being shown[584] on the mountain."

Trūma - Section 4 – Study Notes

[583] 26:16 "feet" – See note on 25:10 concerning the length calculations.

[584] 26:30 "are being shown" - Other verses where G-d shows Mōshe are:
    a) 25:9 the completed tabernacle and its furniture,
    b) 25:40 candelabra,
and c) 27:8 altar.

The note on 25:1 states that the instructions about the tabernacle took place during Moshe's first 40-day stay on the mountain.

Trūma - Section 5   - 7 verses

CURTAIN AT THE ENTRANCE OF THE HOLIEST ROOM

2264 731 26:31 "Weave a cloth that will serve as an entrance curtain.
   It must be made of blue, red, and crimson wool yarn woven with linen thread.
   Images of the Cherubin must be woven into the curtain such that they are visible on both sides of the cloth.

2265 732 26:32 Hang the curtain on four gold-covered acacia pillars that each have gold hooks.
   The four pillars must be set into silver bases.

SACRED BOX RESIDES IN THE HOLIEST ROOM

2266 733 26:33 Align the curtain along the line of fasteners that join the two roof tapestries and hang it from them.
   Place the sacred box in the holiest area, behind the curtain.
   The curtain separates the holy area of the sanctuary and its holiest area.

PLACING THE LID ON THE SACRED BOX

2267 734 26:34 After the sacred box is in place, place the cover on it.

POSITIONING THE TABLE AND THE CANDELABRA

2268 735 26:35 Place the table along the north wall.
   Place the candelabra opposite the table along the south wall.

FRONT ENTRANCE CURTAIN

2269 736 26:36 Make a drape for the entrance of the sanctuary.
   It must be made of blue, red, and crimson wool with linen.
   It must be embroidered.

COLUMNS AT THE ENTRANCE

2270 737 26:37 Make five acacia wood pillars on which to hang the drapery.
   Cover the pillars in gold and place golden hooks on them.
   Make a copper base for each pillar.

Trūma - Section 6 — 8 verses

OUTER ALTAR

2271 738 27:1 Craft the altar out of acacia wood.
The altar must be 10 feet[585] square and 6 feet high.
2272 739 27:2 Include, in the process of crafting the altar, protrusions on each top corner as an integral part of the altar.
Cover the entire altar with copper.

INSTRUMENTS OF THE OUTER ALTAR

2273 740 27:3 Craft pots which must be used to remove ashes.
Craft scoops, basins, pokers, and pans that must be utilized for the various processes of offerings on the altar.
All these instruments must be made of copper.

SCREEN AROUND THE OUTER ALTAR

2274 741 27:4 Craft a copper screen which will go around the altar.
Put four copper rings on the four corners of the screen.
2275 742 27:5 The screen must be placed below the decorative border of the altar.
The screen must be hung such that the bottom of the screen will reach the middle of the altar.

POLES FOR CARRYING THE OUTER ALTAR

2276 743 27:6 Craft two acacia poles covered with copper that must be used when carrying the altar.
2277 744 27:7 Insert the poles into the rings of the altar when it is carried.
2278 745 27:8 The altar itself is hollow, although it must be filled with earth when set down and utilized.
You, Mōshe (Moses), must construct it as you are being shown[586] on the mountain.

Trūma - Section 6 – Study Notes

[585] 27:1 "feet" – See note on 25:10 concerning the length calculations.

[586] 27:8 "are being shown" - Other verses where G-d shows Mōshe are:
a) 25:9 the tabernacle and its furniture,
b) 25:40 candelabra,
and c) 26:30 tabernacle.

The note on 25:1 states that the instructions about the tabernacle took place during Mōshe's first 40-day stay on the mountain.

Trūma - Section 7   - 8 + 3 verses

COURTYARD ENCLOSURE

2279 746 27:9 The following specifies how to craft the outer wall of the courtyard of the tabernacle.
The south wall must be made of woven linen netting.
It must be 200 feet[587] long.

2280 747 27:10 The south wall curtain must be held up by 10 pillars, each inserted into a copper base.
Each pillar must have silver hooks for the curtain, and bands to fasten the hooks to the pillars.

2281 748 27:11 The wall for the north side must be constructed with exactly the same materials and measurements as the south wall.

2282 749 27:12 For the west side, the curtain must be 100 feet long, held up by 10 pillars, each pillar in its base.

2283 750 27:13 The total length on the east side also must be 100 feet long.

2284 751 27:14 On one side of the entrance, the wall must be 30 feet long.
It must be held up by three pillars, each in its base.

2285 752 27:15 The wall on the other side of the entrance must also be 30 feet long, held up by three pillars, each pillar in its base.

ENTRANCE

2286 753 27:16 The entrance must have an embroidered curtain that is 40 feet long.
The entrance curtain must be made of blue, dark red, and crimson wool, with twisted linen.
It must be held up by four pillars, each with its own base.

Trūma - Last Section

2287 754 27:17 Each pillar of the courtyard must have silver hoops, silver hooks, and a copper base.
2288 755 27:18 The courtyard must be 200 feet by 100 feet.
The pillars holding up the curtain wall around the courtyard must be 10 feet high, and their bases must be made of copper.
2289 756 27:19 All equipment used to fashion the tabernacle must be made of copper.
The stakes for the tabernacle and the stakes for the outer wall must be made of copper.

Trūma - Section 7 – Study Notes

[587] 27:9 "feet" – See note on 25:10 concerning the length calculation.

Tiźave[588] - Section 1 - 14 verses (Total 101 verses)

[There are 8 commandments in this portion: 4 positive and 4 negative.]

OIL FOR THE LAMP

2290 757 27:20 Command[589] the Jewish people to donate[590] pure olive oil[591] to be used to light a nightly-lit candelabra menōra lamp.[592]

Commandment 96:[593] Light The Candelabra Lamps Every Day

2291 758 27:21 Aharōn (Aaron) and his sons must pour enough oil each evening to last throughout the night into the continually burning candelabra menōra lamp.

The menōra lamp is located in the tent of meeting which is on the holy side of the special curtain[594] that hides the stone slabs[595] that are in the presence of G-d.

This is an eternal decree[596] for the Jewish people.

DESIGNATING WHO WILL BE THE PRIESTS

2292 759 28:1 After the tabernacle is completed, you should consecrate Aharōn and his sons Nadav, Avēhū, Elazar, and Ētamar as priests to Me.

COMMANDMENT 97:[597] PRIESTS MUST WEAR PRIESTLY CLOTHES FOR THE SERVICE

2293 760 28:2 Guide the preparation of the holy clothes of glory and splendor to be worn by Aharōn your brother.

2294 761 28:3 Ask the skilled artisans[598] to make the clothes for Aharōn to sanctify him so that he will be able to function in the role of priest.

2295 762 28:4 The garments are a breastplate, apron, robe, checkered tunic, hat, and belt.[599]

They should make these clothes for Aharōn your brother and for his sons[600] so they can officiate as priests.

2296 763 28:5 They should use the gold,[601] blue wool, purple wool, red wool, and linen in the preparation of these clothes.

APRON

2297 764 28:6 They should make the apron[602] for the high priest, as an artistically patterned brocade out of gold thread,[603] blue wool, purple wool, red wool, and linen.

Tiżave - Section 1 - continued

2298 765 28:7 The apron must have two shoulder straps attached in the back to which, in the front, the breastplate will be attached[604] to create a single article of clothing.
2299 766 28:8 The apron must have its own attached belt woven with the same yarn as the apron.

ENGRAVED STONES ON THE APRON

2300 767 28:9 Engrave the names of the sons of Yisrael[605] (Israel = Jacob) on two onyx stones:[606]
2301 768 28:10 six names on each stone, in birth order.
2302 769 28:11 A skilled jeweler must engrave the stones with the names of the sons of Yisrael and then set the stones in a gold setting.
2303 770 28:12 Attach two gold settings, each containing an engraved onyx stone, on the shoulder straps of the apron such that the onyx stones sit on the shoulder of the high priest.

Thus Aharōn will carry their names on his shoulders in the presence of G-d.

Tiżave - Section 1 – Study Notes

[588] The Hebrew word *tiżave* is the imperative verb "you should command." It has the same root as the noun *miżva*, commandment.

[589] 27:20 "command" - This entire weekly portion is a quote of G-d to Mōshe (a continuation of the last portion). All direct commands and occurrences of the term "you," refer to Mōshe. Interestingly, Mōshe's name does not appear at all in this portion (it appeared only twice in the previous portion), although Aharōn's name does appear in portion Tiżave. Aharōn's name does not appear at all in the previous portion.

[590] 27:20 "donate" - Olive oil was already listed as one of the types of items that people should donate (verse 25:6).

[591] 27:20 "pure olive oil" - Each select olive was crushed in a mortar and only the first few ultra-clear drops were used for the lamp oil.

[592] 27:20 "nightly-lit candelabra menōra lamp" – This lamp is the candelabra mentioned in verses 25:31-40, and 26:35. Here it is called the Constant Lamp (Hebrew: *nâr tamid*). Verses 30:7-8 specify that the high priest must light it each evening. The priests poured enough oil each late afternoon to last until morning (as stated in the next verse). Some say that the flames, or at least the center flame, miraculously lasted for 24 hours. Today, as a remembrance of the lamp in the Tabernacle and Holy Temple, every synagogue has a (electric) light that is kept on continuously. It is usually located in front of the Tōra ark.

[593] Commandment 96 – This commandment is explained by Rambam in his Mishne Tōra: Book 8: Service To G-d: Laws of Regular and Additional Offerings.

[594] 27:21 "holy side of the special curtain" – The special curtain (verses 26:31-32) separated the holiest area of the tabernacle from the holy area. The menōra, along with most of the furniture and utensils were located in the holy area (verse 26:35). The sacred box was located on the holiest side.

[595] 27:21 "stone slabs" – They were to be placed in the sacred box. The

sacred box (verses 25:10-22) was placed in the holiest area on the other side of the special curtain (26:33-34).

The first slabs were broken (verse 32:19). According to commentary Radak (Rabbi David Kimchi), the broken pieces of the first slabs were placed in the sacred box.

Mōshe, at the direction of G-d, wrote new slabs (verse 34:1-4, and :28) and placed them in the sacred box (verse 40:20). This is recounted by Mōshe in Divarim (Deuteronomy) 10:1-5.

[596] 27:21 "eternal decree" - The commandment involving lighting an oil lamp only applies when there is a Holy Temple. This is true for a vast number of commandments. When the temple is rebuilt, this law goes into effect again.

[597] Commandment 97 – Book 8: Service To G-d: Laws of Temple Furniture, Utensils, and Caretakers.

[598] 28:3 "skilled artisans" – Mōshe spoke to individuals to determine who were truly skilled at each craft.

[599] 28:4 "breastplate, apron, robe, checkered tunic, hat, and belt" - This verse lists only 6 garments. The high priest wore 8 garments. The pants and headband are the other two.

[600] 28:4 "and his sons" - Regular priests wore only 4 of the garments: pants, tunic, belt, and hat. There are opinions that each of these articles of clothing for the regular priest were fashioned somewhat differently than those for the high priest.

[601] 28:6 "gold" – Gold threads were used only for the high priest clothes. Regular priests' clothes were of linen only.

[602] 28:6 "apron ..." As a reference, these are the Hebrew words for the priest clothes:
    Āfōd   apron
    Afūdatō   belt of the apron
    Avnāt   belt   - also for regular priest

Ĥāshev	integrated belt of the apron
Ĥōshen	breastplate
Kitāfa	shoulder piece of the apron
Kūtōnes tunic	- also for regular priest
Miēl	robe (sleeveless)
Miĥnasīyim short pants	- also for regular priest
Migba	hat (same as miźnefet) - also for regular priest
Miźnefet	hat (same as migba)
Żiż	gold headband

[603] 28:5 "thread" – Yarn was made from the following:
    6 strands of blue wool with 1 strand of gold thread, and
    6 strands of purple wool with 1 strand of gold thread, and
    6 strands of red wool with 1 strand of gold thread, and
    6 strands of linen with 1 strand of gold thread.
    These 4 strands were twisted together to make the yarn of the apron.

[604] 28:7 "attached" – This is described in verse 28:25.

[605] 28:9 "sons of Yisrael" – Some commentators state that actually, the names of the twelve tribes were inscribed. That would leave out Yōsef, and include his two sons. It also excludes Lāvē.

[606] 28:9 "onyx" - agate quartz with alternating red and white bands.

Tiżave - Section 2 - 18 verses

BREASTPLATE

2304 771 28:13 Make gold settings for the two onyx stones for the breastplate.[607]

2305 772 28:14 Make chains of braided strands of gold which will be attached at the upper corners of the breastplate.

2306 773 28:15 Make the Breastplate of Judgment artistically.

Make it out of the same materials as the apron: gold, blue wool, purple wool, red wool, and linen.

2307 774 28:16 The breastplate will be a rectangle that is folded over to make a square.

Each side of the square will be 1 foot[608] long.

STONES ON THE BREASTPLATE

2308 775 28:17 Attach the engraved stones, each in its gold setting, to the breastplate as four rows - three different types of stones make up the top row,

2309 776 28:18 three other types of stones make up the second row,

2310 777 28:19 three other types of stones make up the third row,

2311 778 28:20 and three other types of stones make up the bottom row.

2312 779 28:21 Each stone will be engraved with one name of a son of Yisrael (Israel = Jacob), in birth order.

ATTACHING THE BREASTPLATE TO THE APRON

2313 780 28:22 Make chains of braided strands of gold for the breastplate that will be attached at the upper corners of the breastplate.

2314 781 28:23 Make gold rings attached to the upper corners of the breastplate.

2315 782 28:24 Put one gold ring through one of the gold rings and the other chain through the other gold ring.

Tiżave - Section 2 - continued

2316 783 28:25 One chain must be attached to one stone setting and the other chain must be attached to the other.

The stone settings must be attached to the outer surface of the loose ends of the shoulder straps[609] of the apron.

ATTACHING THE BOTTOM OF THE BREASTPLATE

2317 784 28:26 Make two gold rings and attach them to the two bottom corners of the breastplate which will be positioned near the front of the apron.

2318 785 28:27 Make two other gold rings and attach one to each outer edge of the straps in the back of the apron.

Commandment 98:[610] Do Not Loosen The Breastplate From The Apron

2319 786 28:28 The breastplate will be stabilized by tying a blue thread from the right gold ring on the breastplate to the gold ring attached to the back of the right shoulder strap of the apron.

So too must a blue thread be tied for the left side as well.

NAMES ON THE BREATSPLATE

2320 787 28:29 Aharōn (Aaron) will carry the names of the sons of Yisrael on the breastplate of judgment when he enters the sanctuary.

It will be a constant reminder in the presence of G-d.

HOLY NAME

2321 788 28:30 Place the parchment with G-d's holy name written on it into the slot of the breastplate of judgment that is created by folding over the breastplate.

The parchment is the Ūrim and Tūmim.[611]

The holy name will be on Aharōn's heart when he comes before G-d.

Aharōn will thus always carry the decisions[612] concerning the Jewish people on his heart in the presence of G-d.

Tiżave - Section 2 – Study Notes

⁶⁰⁷ 28:13 "two onyx stones for the breastplate" – See note on verse 25:7. They are described as being either for the apron or for the breastplate because it was part of the design that attached the breastplate to the apron.

⁶⁰⁸ 28:16 "foot" – See note on 25:10 concerning length measurements.

⁶⁰⁹ 28:25 "shoulder straps" – The shoulder strap attachment is described for the structure of the apron in verse 28:7.

⁶¹⁰ Commandment 98 – This commandment is explained by Rambam in his Mishne Tōra: Book 8: Service To G-d: Laws of Temple Furniture, Utensils, and Caretakers.

⁶¹¹ 28:30 "Ūrim and Tūmim" – The word Ūrim comes from the Hebrew word for "light." The word Tūmim comes from the Hebrew word for "complete." The holy parchment brought questions to light, and completed the understanding of answers to questions.

The blessing that Mōshe gave to the tribe of Lāvē includes the fact that they manage the Ūrim and Tūmim (Divarim 33:8).

⁶¹² 28:30 "decisions" - The letters of the names engraved on the stones that are set on the breastplate would light up in response to a question that the high priest would ask G-d. It was the parchment with G-d's holy name, inserted in the fold of the breastplate, placing it under the engraved stones that enabled the letters to light up.

Tiźave - Section 3 — 13 verses

Robe

2322 789 28:31 Make the fabric of the robe[613] entirely out of blue wool.

Commandment 99:[614] Do Not Tear The Priestly Clothes

2323 790 28:32 The opening for the head must have a hem that encircles the opening and is folded toward the inside.
    It must be woven.
    It has an open circle for a person's head in the center of the robe.
    But it is hemmed so that it will not tear.
2324 791 28:33 Make decorative pomegranate shaped spheres out of blue wool, purple wool and red wool for the bottom hem of the robe.
    Make gold bells for the bottom hem of the robe.
2325 792 28:34 Attach bell-pomegranate pairs around the entire perimeter of the bottom hem of the robe.

High Priest Must Wear Holy Clothes When Entering The Sanctuary

2326 793 28:35 The bells will sound when Aharōn enters the sanctuary in the presence of G-d, and they will sound when he leaves.
    The high priest must be wearing all the high priest clothes whenever he enters the sanctuary.
        Otherwise he will perish.

Headband

2327 794 28:36 Make a gold headband and engrave on it 'Holy to G-d.'
2328 795 28:37 Slide a thread of blue wool through a hole in the middle of the headband and tie it to the hat.
2329 796 28:38 The headband will be placed on Aharōn's forehead.
    Aharōn will forgive the sin of bringing an impure animal offering that Jewish people might mistakenly bring.
    He must touch the headband often in order to remind himself that it is on his forehead.

Tiżave - Section 3 - continued

Tunic, Hat, Belt

2330 797 28:39 Make the tunic of checkered linen material.
   Make a hat of linen.
   Make an embroidered belt.

Clothes For Regular Priests

2331 798 28:40 The regular priests shall wear four garments: tunic, belt, hat for glory and splendor, (and linen short pants).

Anointing Priests

2332 799 28:41 With these holy clothes you will clothe Aharōn your brother and his sons.
   Anoint them, inaugurate them, and sanctify them.
   By doing so they will become priests to Me.

Short Pants

2333 800 28:42 Make linen short pants[615] to cover their privates, including their hips and thighs.

2334 801 28:43 All the relevant clothes must be worn by Aharōn and his sons when they enter the Tabernacle and when they approach the altar to serve in holiness.
   By wearing these clothes they will not sin.
   This is an eternal law for him and his descendants.

Tiżave - Section 3 – Study Notes

[613] 28:31 "robe" – There are many opinions about the robe. Some commentators believe it had sleeves, while others believe that it did not. Some believe that it was a closed robe that only slipped over the head, while others believe that it was slit entirely along the front. Still others believe that it was slit up to, but not including, the neck hem, along the front. See Kaplan, 1981, pp. 426-427.

[614] Commandment 99 – This commandment is explained by Rambam in his <u>Mishne Tōra</u>: Book 8: Service To G-d: Laws of Temple Furniture, Utensils, and Caretakers.

[615] 28:42 "linen short pants" – Pants cover private parts. This goes along with the instruction to have a ramp leading up to the altar, rather than steps, as stated in verse 20:23.

Tiżave - Section 4   - 18 verses

SANCTIFYING THE PRIESTS

2335 802 29:1 This is how you will sanctify them as priests in My service:
You will take a young unblemished bull and two unblemished rams
2336 803 29:2 and 10 each of the following three types of unleavened baked flour foods (maźa):
(a) boiled dough (dough is boiled, then slightly baked, and then fried in oil),
(b) baked dough (dough is mixed with oil, then baked), and
(c) wafers (dough is baked and then oil is poured onto them),
each made from fine flour.
2337 804 29:3 Then place all the cakes in one basket and bring them into the tabernacle courtyard along with the bull and two rams on the day the tabernacle is initiated.
2338 805 29:4 Then bring Aharōn (Aaron) and his sons to the door of the tent of meeting.
Have them bathe first.

CLOTHE THE PRIESTS

2339 806 29:5 Then take the clothes and dress Aharōn with the tunic, robe, apron, and breastplate.
Beautify him with the belt of the apron.
2340 807 29:6 Then place the hat on his head and put the holy headband on the hat.
2341 808 29:7 Then pour the anointing oil on his head.
2342 809 29:8 Then bring his sons to the entrance of the tabernacle and place tunics on them.
2343 810 29:9 Then put belts on Aharōn and his sons and put hats on them and they will be priests forever, and you will thus consecrate Aharōn and his sons.

TIŻAVE - SECTION 4 - CONTINUED

OFFERING THE MALE COW

2344 811 29:10 Then bring the bull in front of the tabernacle and Aharōn and his sons will place their hands on the head of the bull.

2345 812 29:11 Then kill the bull in the presence of G-d at the entrance of the tabernacle.
2346 813 29:12 Then take some of the blood of the bull and smear it with your finger on the top of the corner protrusions of the altar and pour the rest of the blood onto the base of the altar.
2347 814 29:13 Then burn on the altar all the inner fat, diaphragm, two kidneys, and fat that is on the kidneys.
2348 815 29:14 But you must burn the muscle, skin and dung of the bull outside of the camp as a sin-offering.

OFFERING THE FIRST RAM

2349 816 29:15 Then take one of the rams.
    Aharōn and his sons must place their hands on the head of the ram.
2350 817 29:16 Then kill the ram, take its blood, and dash it onto two opposite corners of the altar so that all sides have blood on them.
2351 818 29:17 Then cut the ram into pieces, wash its inside and legs, and put them with other pieces and its head.
2352 819 29:18 Then burn up the entire ram on the altar as a burnt-offering to G-d.
    It is a pleasing fragrance as a fire-offering for G-d.

Tiżave - Section 4 – Study Notes

29:1 "sanctify them as priests" – Starting in Vayikra (Leviticus) chapter 8, the events of the installation of priests are described.

Tiźave - Section 5 - 19 verses

OFFERING THE SECOND RAM

2353 820 29:19 Then take the second ram.

Aharōn (Aaron) and his sons must place their hands on the ram's head.

2354 821 29:20 When you offer the ram, place some of its blood on the right upper earlobes, right thumbs and right big toes of Aharōn and his sons.

2355 822 29:21 Then mix ram's blood from the altar with anointing oil and sanctify them by sprinkling it on Aharōn and his sons and their clothes.

2356 823 29:22 Then, from the ram of consecration, take its fat, tail fat, inner fat, liver, both kidneys along with their fat, and right thigh.

2357 824 29:23 And also take a maźa,[616] oil maźa,[617] and a wafer out of the basket that is set aside for maźa.

2358 825 29:24 Place these offerings in the hands of Aharōn and his sons who will offer them.

You must place your hands beneath theirs.

Thus you will act in the role of the priest.

This is a wave-offering[618] to G-d.

2359 826 29:25 Then take the offerings from their hands and place them on the altar.

2360 827 29:26 Wave the upper meat of the ram brought by Aharōn, to G-d.

This will be for you.

2361 828 29:27 Sanctify the wave-offering and the thigh of the heave-offering of the ram, of Aharōn and of his sons.

2362 829 29:28 The breast and shoulder of every peace-offering will belong to the priests as a heave-offering.

2363 830 29:29 The high priest clothes must be worn by his descendants who are selected to be high priest.

2364 831 29:30 There will be a 7-day preparation period for consecrating a high priest.

If a son of the previous high priest is worthy, then he must be given preference as the next high priest.

2365 832 29:31 The consecration ram offering for the high priest inauguration must be eaten in a holy area.

Tiżave - Section 5 - continued

Commandment 100:[619] Priests Should Eat The Offerings That Are For Them

2366 833 29:32 The priests must eat their offerings in a holy area.

Commandment 101: Non-Priests Must Not Eat Holy Offerings

2367 834 29:33 Priests will eat the atonement offerings, but non-priests must not eat these holy offerings.
2368 835 29:34 Burn, before sunrise, any leftovers of offerings.
2369 836 29:35 There is a 7-day consecration period.
2370 837 29:36 Offer a sin-offering bull each day.
    Purify the altar when you perform atonement.
    Anoint and sanctify the altar.
2371 838 29:37 Perform atonement for the altar for 7 days.

Tiżave - Section 5 – Study Notes

[616] 29:23 "maża" – Unleavened bread. See verse 29:2 for how each type of maża is prepared. For this food item, Tōra uses the term "bread." However, in Vayikra (Leviticus) 8:26, it uses the term maża for this item. In addition, Vayikra 6:10 prohibits leavened bread for offerings. Rambam states this as as two commandments:
a) Do not use fruit juice or leaven on offerings, which is commandment 114 derived from Vayikra 2:11, and
b) Do not allow meal offerings to leaven, which is commandment 134 derived from Vayikra 6:10.

[617] 29:23 "oil maża" – Here also the term bread is used. And in Vayikra 6:10, the term bread is also used for this item. However, commandment 134 informs that this meal offering is also unleavened.

[618] 29:24 "wave-offering" – Wave offerings are moved horizontally. Heave-offerings are moved up and down. Other verses that mention wave offering include Vayikra 7:30; 8:27 & 29; 9:21; and 10:14.

[619] Commandments 100 & 101 – Rambam: Mishne Tōra: Book 8: Service To G-d: Laws of Offerings Procedures.

Tiźave - Section 6   - 9 verses

MORNING AND LATE AFTERNOON DAILY OFFERING

2372 839 29:38 Each day, offer 2 lambs that are less than a year old.
2373 840 29:39 Offer 1 lamb in the morning, and 1 in the late afternoon.
2374 841 29:40 With each morning lamb, add flour and oil.
     In addition, offer a drink-offering by pouring wine into the bowls that are above the altar.
2375 842 29:41 Do the same thing for the late afternoon lamb.
2376 843 29:42 These will be daily offerings everyday from now on.
2377 844 29:43 I, G-d, will be with the Jewish people there.
2378 845 29:44 I will sanctify the tabernacle, the altar, Aharōn (Aaron), and his sons.
2379 846 29:45 I will be with the Jewish people and I will be their G-d.
2380 847 29:46 They will realize that I am the G-d who had led them out of Egypt.

Tiźave - Section 7   - 7 + 3 verses

INCENSE ALTAR

2381 848 30:1 Build the incense altar out of acacia wood.
2382 849 30:2 Make it 2 feet[620] square and 4 feet high.
   It must have a protrusion at each top corner, each of which is a single solid part of the entire altar.
2383 850 30:3 Overlay it with gold.
   Make a gold crown for it.
2384 851 30:4 Form two gold rings under the crown, at two opposite vertices.
2385 852 30:5 Form two acacia wood rods for the altar, and overlay them with gold.
2386 853 30:6 Place the incense altar opposite the sacred box, but on the other side (i.e., the holy area) of the curtain that separates the holiest area from the rest of the tabernacle.

Commandment 102:[621] Burn Incense Every Day

2387 854 30:7 Aharōn will burn incense on the incense altar each morning when he cleans the candelabra.

Tiźave – Last Section

2388 855 30:8 Also, when Aharōn lights the candelabra lamps in the evening,[622] he will offer more incense.

Commandment 103:[623] Do Not Burn Anything But Incense On The Gold Altar

2389 856 30:9 Do not offer any offerings other than those specified.[624]
2390 857 30:10 Once a year, on the Day of Atonement,[625] Aharōn will atone the Jewish people by offering a sin-offering on the incense altar.

Tiżave - Section 7 – Study Notes

---

[620] 30:2 "feet" – See note on verse 25:10 concerning length measurements.

[621] Commandment 102 - Rambam: Mishne Tōra: Book 8: Service To G-d: Laws of Regular and Additional Offerings

[622] 30:8 "when Aharōn lights the candelabra lamps in the evening" – Verses 27:20-21 state that a priest must clean the candelabra each late afternoon and fill the cups with enough oil to last until morning.

[623] Commandment 103 –Book 8: Service To G-d: Laws of Temple Furniture, Utensils, and Caretakers.

[624] 30:9 "Do not offer any offerings other than those specified" –Nadav and Avēhū, the oldest two sons of Aharōn tragically violated this command, as described in Vayikra (Leviticus) 10:1.

[625] 30:10 "Day of Atonement" – Yōm Kipur. This ceremony is described and specified in chapter 16 of Vayikra

Kē Tēsa[626] - Section 1 - 45 verses (Total: 139 verses)

[There are 8 commandments in this portion: 4 positive and 4 negative.]

2391 858 30:11 G-d communicated to Mōshe (Moses) as follows:
2392 859 30:12 "When you take a census of the Jewish people, each man must give a coin to G-d so that there will not be a plague.[627]

Commandment 104:[628] Give A Half-Shekel Every Year

2393 860 30:13 "Each adult man must give a half-shekel[629] coin, which equals 20 gāra, to G-d.
2394 861 30:14 "Every man from age 20 years and older must give the coin to G-d.
2395 862 30:15 "No one is permitted to give more or less than one half-shekel coin, which is an atonement for the soul.
2396 863 30:16 "Take the atonement coins from the Jewish people for the tabernacle as a memorial for the Jewish people in the presence of G-d to atone for you."
2397 864 30:17 G-d communicated to Mōshe as follows:

Washing Basin

2398 865 30:18 "You must make a basin of copper, with a base of copper, for washing.
  "Place the basin in the area between the tabernacle and the altar.
  "Put water in the basin.

Commandment 105:[630] Priests Must Wash Before Service

2399 866 30:19 "Aharōn (Aaron) and his sons must wash their hands and feet - the right hand and foot simultaneously and the left hand and foot simultaneously.
2400 867 30:20 "When they enter the tabernacle they must wash so as not to perish.
  "And when they come to the altar to offer an offering
2401 868 30:21 "they must wash their hands and feet, so as not to perish.
  "This is a law to them and their descendants."
2402 869 30:22 G-d communicated to Mōshe as follows:

KĒ TĒSA - SECTION 1 - CONTINUED

INGREDIENTS FOR THE ANNOINTING OIL

2403 870 30:23 "Take the main spices:[631]
          500 shekel weight of myrrh
          500 shekel weight of sweet aromatic cinnamon in 2 equal batches
          250 shekel weight of sweet aromatic calamus
2404 871 30:24 "500 shekel weight of cassia root
    and a volume of olive oil
2405 872 30:25 "to be used for anointing.
    "All the ingredients are finely mixed in the oil into a perfume which will be the anointing oil.
2406 873 30:26 "Use this oil to anoint the tabernacle, the sacred box of testimony,
2407 874 30:27 "the table with its vessels, the candelabra with its vessels, the incense altar,
2408 875 30:28 "the offering altar with its vessels, and the wash basin with its base.
2409 876 30:29 "Sanctify them as most holy.
    "Anyone who touches them must be in a state of holiness.[632]
2410 877 30:30 "Anoint Aharōn and his sons and sanctify them so they can serve Me in the priesthood.

Commandment 106:[633] Prepare Anointing Oil

2411 878 30:31 "Inform the Jewish people:
    'This will be the holy anointing oil for Me throughout your generations.

Commandment 107: Do Not Duplicate Anointing Oil

Commandment 108: Do Not Use Anointing Oil For Personal Use

2412 879 30:32 " 'It must not be used on non-priests.[634]
    "You are not permitted to prepare other oil with this recipe.
    "It is holy and you must treat it as being holy.
2413 880 30:33 "Anyone who prepares this recipe and anyone who pours it on a non-priest will be punished with divine excision from the people."

Kē Tēsa - Section 1 - continued

Ingredients of Incense

2414 881 30:34 G-d communicated to Mōshe as follows:
"Mix together equal amounts of the following ingredients:[635]
sweet balsam sap,
sweet aromatic herb root,
a pungent spice,
other sweet spices,
and incense.
2415 882 30:35 "Prepare the ingredients as incense.
"It is a perfumer's mixture that must be mixed well.[636]
"It is pure and holy.
2416 883 30:36 "Grind it finely.
"Burn it each day on the incense altar in the tabernacle where I will meet you.
"It is very holy to you.

Commandment 109: Do Not Duplicate Incense

2417 884 30:37 "The incense that you prepare using this recipe, you must not prepare for your own use because it is holy to G-d.
2418 885 30:38 "Anyone who prepares it this way for a mundane purpose such as smelling its aroma, will be punished with divine excision from the people."

KĒ TĒSA - SECTION 1 - CONTINUED

BIŻALEL AND AHALĒAV, HEAD CRAFTSMEN FOR THE TABERNACLE

2419 886 31:1 G-d communicated to Mōshe as follows:

2420 887 31:2 "I have singled out Biżalel[637] son of Ūrē son of Ĥūr[638] of the tribe of Yihūda (Judah).

2421 888 31:3 "I filled him with the spirit of G-d in terms of wisdom, understanding, knowledge, and craftsmanship

2422 889 31:4 "in skillful work of gold, silver, copper,

2423 890 31:5 "gem cutting, and wood carving.

2424 891 31:6 "With him I have also appointed Ahalēav[639] son of Aĥēsamaĥ of the tribe of Dan.

"I have also imparted wisdom to other worthy people so that they can craft the items that I have commanded

2425 892 31:7 "regarding the tabernacle:

the sacred box of testimony, its lid,

and all the furniture of the tabernacle, including:

2426 893 31:8 "the table with its vessels,

the candelabra with its vessels,

the incense altar,

2427 894 31:9 "the offering altar with its vessels,

the wash basin with its base,

2428 895 31:10 "the carrying sacks,

as well as the holy clothes for Aharōn the priest,

the clothes of his sons which they wear when they minister as priests,

2429 896 31:11 "the anointing oil, and

the incense of sweet spices for the holy place.

"Each of these according to all that I have commanded you for them to make."

KĒ TĒSA - SECTION 1 - CONTINUED

SABBATH

2430 897 31:12 G-d communicated to Mōshe as follows:

2431 898 31:13 "Speak to the Jewish people as follows:

'Keep My shabat[640] because it is a bond between Me and you throughout your generations so that you understand that I am G-d who sanctifies you.

2432 899 31:14 'Keep the shabat because it is holy to you.

'Anyone who publicly profanes shabat must be severely punished by the court.

'Anyone who performs activities that are forbidden on the Sabbath will be excised from the people.

2433 900 31:15 'Perform work for six days.[641]

But the seventh day is shabat of solemn rest.[642]

'Shabat is holy to G-d.

'Anyone who publicly does forbidden work on shabat must be severely punished by a court.

2434 901 31:16 'The Jewish people must keep shabat and observe the shabat throughout the generations as a perpetual covenant.

2435 902 31:17 'It is a sign between Me and the Jewish people forever because in six days G-d willed into existence the spiritual universe and the physical universe.

'On the seventh day He ceased from work, and instead, rested.' "

Kē Tēsa – Section 1 – Study Notes

[626] "Kē Tēsa" - The Hebrew phrase *kē tēsa* means "when you take."

This first section of the portion and the next section are uncharacteristically very long sections in Tōra. On shabat, the person who is called to the Tōra for the reading of the first section is someone who is a priest (*kōhān*). The second person to be called up for the reading of the second section is a Levite. The second section tells how all the Levite men responded to Mōshe's call to action. Therefore, the sages made the first section long so that the events in which the Levites responded would go to a Levite, so that a non-Levite would not feel embarrassed that perhaps his ancestor did not respond to Mōshe.

[627] 30:12 "census . . . coin . . . so that there will not be a plague" – Do not treat a person like a number and do not think of a population as a total count. Every person is unique, and every group of people must be viewed in human terms.

[628] Commandment 104 - This sommandment is explained by Rambam in his <u>Mishne</u> <u>Tōra</u>: Book 3: Seasons: Laws of Shekel.

[629] 30:13 "shekel" – Shekel as a unit of weight, based on ancient manuscripts, is about 5,000 years old, making it a well-established unit by the time of Avraham (Abraham). It was the weight of a certain number of grains of barley, totaling 11 grams (.35 troy ounces). (American commemorative silver dollars have 1 troy ounce of silver.) Ancient shekel coins weigh about 13 grams because other metals need to be added in order to make the silver harden as a coin. Shekels found in archeological sites are about the size of today's American quarter. Ancient half-shekel coins weigh 7 grams and are about the size of today's American nickel.

[630] Commandment 105 – Book 8: Laws of Entering the Holy Temple.

[631] 30:23 "spices" – They were specified as items to be donated in verse 25:6.

[632] 30:29 "state of holiness" – This is the meaning according to Rashbam.

[633] Commandments 106-109 - Book 8: Service To G-d: Laws of Temple Furniture, Utensils, and Caretakers.

[634] 30:32 "non-priests" - Sadya Gaōn: King David and those of his descendants who were crowned king were the only non-priests who could be anointed with this special holy oil.

[635] 30:34 "ingredients" - Rashē: there were 11 ingredients in all.
Donation of spices is first stated in verse 25:6.
Rashē: A pungent spice was included in the mixture to teach people to include sinners in their prayers.

[636] 30:35 "mixed well" - But Ramban and Ibn Ezra render it: "mixed with salt."

[637] 31:2 "Biżalel" – Also mentioned in 35:30.

[638] 31:2 "Ĥūr" – He had been instrumental in the battle against Amalek (17:10 & 12).

[639] 31:6 "Ahalēav" – He is mentioned again starting at verse 35:34.

[640] 31:13 "shabat" – See note on 16:23 about the occurrences of shabat in the verses.

[641] 31:15 "work for six days" – As stated in the Decaloge. This states the Jewish work ethic. The sages in the Talmud each had professions. See note on 20:9.

[642] 31:17 "rested" – As stated in Brāshēt (Genesis) 2:2-3.

Kē Tēsa - Section 2[643]   - 47 verses

G-D GIVES MŌSHE THE STONE SLABS

2436 903 31:18 After G-d had spoken to Mōshe (Moses) on Mount Sēnī (Sinai), G-d gave to him the two stone slabs, upon which were commandments engraved by G-d.[644]

SOME PEOPLE DEMAND AHARŌN TO FASHION A FORM

2437 904 32:1 The day before Mōshe was scheduled to descend[645] the mountain, some people mistakenly thought[646] that Mōshe should have returned, and thought that he had abandoned them.

Therefore, people said to Aharōn (Aaron):

"Fashion a form that will be with us,[647] because we do not know what has happened to the man named Mōshe[648] who led us out of Egypt."

2438 905 32:2 Aharōn instructed them:

"Forcibly remove the gold earrings of your wives,[649] sons, and daughters and bring them to me."

2439 906 32:3 Some people took off their own gold[650] earrings and gave them to Aharōn.

GOLD STATUE

2440 907 32:4 Aharōn took the gold and fashioned a statue[651] of a calf.

Misguided people proclaimed:

"Jewish people: This is your[652] deity[653] that brought you out of Egypt."

2441 908 32:5 Aharōn saw that these powerful people were serious and not willing to listen to reason.

Therefore, Aharōn built an altar.

Aharōn said:

"Tomorrow[654] there will be a feast to G-d."

2442 909 32:6 Some people woke up early the next morning and offered offerings.

Some people sat down to eat and drink, and then celebrated.

KĒ TĒSA - SECTION 2 - CONTINUED

G-D ORDERS MŌSHE TO WALK BACK TO THE PEOPLE

2443 910 32:7 G-d instructed Mōshe:

"Go down from this mountain.

"Some[655] of your[656] people whom you had led out of Egypt are being misled to sin.

2444 911 32:8 "They are behaving badly.

"They have formed, worshipped, and made offerings to a gold calf statue.

"These people proclaimed:

'Jewish people: This is your deity that brought you out of Egypt.' "

2445 912 32:9 G-d communicated to Mōshe:

"I have seen how some people behave: they are not obedient and do not change their evil ways.

G-D WANTS TO START OVER

2446 913 32:10 "Leave Me alone in My anger that is directed against them so that I can destroy them.

"Instead of them, I will create the Jewish nation from your descendants." [657]

MŌSHE PRAYS FOR THE WELFARE OF THE JEWISH PEOPLE

2447 914 32:11 Mōshe prayed[658] to G-d:

"G-d, why are You so angry against Your[659] people?

"You brought them out of Egypt with powerful deeds.

2448 915 32:12 "Why should the people of Egypt be able to say:

'G-d led the Jewish people out simply to annihilate them.' ?

"Do not be angry.

"Be good to them, and do not do evil against Your people.

2449 916 32:13 "Remember Your servants Avraham (Abraham), Yiẑhak (Isaac), and Yisrael (Israel = Jacob), to whom You had promised and communicated:

'I will make your descendants as numerous as the stars[660] of the sky.

'I will give to them all this land that I have told you about.

'They will inherit the land forever.' " [661]

Kē Tēsa - Section 2 - continued

G-D AGREES

2450 917 32:14 G-d decided not to punish the Jewish people to the extreme.[662]

2451 918 32:15 Then Mōshe turned and walked down the mountain, while holding the two stone slabs in his hand.[663]

> The slabs were engraved on both sides.
>> They were engraved on both front and back.[664]

2452 919 32:16 The stone slabs had been fashioned and engraved by G-d.[665]

YIHŌSHŪA AND MŌSHE HEAR THE NOISE OF WILD CELEBRATION

2453 920 32:17 Yihōshūa (Joshua)[666] heard the people's shouting and said to Mōshe:

> "It sounds like a war going on down there."

2454 921 32:18 Mōshe responded:

> "The noise doesn't sound like winners or losers of a battle.
> "Rather, it sounds like people partying."

KĒ TĒSA - SECTION 2 - CONTINUED

MŌSHE THROWS DOWN THE STONE SLABS AND THEY SHATTER

2455 922 32:19 Once they came close enough, they saw the gold calf statue and people dancing.

Mōshe became angry and threw down the stone slabs from his hands,[667] and they shattered[668] at the foot of the mountain.

2456 923 32:20 Mōshe melted the gold calf and pulverized the gold.

He poured the gold dust into water[669] and forced those people who had sinned, to drink it.

2457 924 32:21 Mōshe asked Aharōn:[670]

"What did these people do to you such that you caused them to commit this terrible sin?"

2458 925 32:22 Aharōn answered:

"Please do not be angry.

"You know how difficult some of these people can be.

2459 926 32:23 "They told me:

'Form a statue for us because the man Mōshe, who lead us out of Egypt, is not here anymore.'

2460 927 32:24 "So I told them:

'Give me your gold.' [671]

"which they did, and I threw the gold onto a fire[672] but the form of a calf took shape."

2461 928 32:25 Mōshe realized that the people were out of control.

Kē Tēsa - Section 2 - continued

Mōshe Calls For The Faithful To Act

2462 929 32:26 Mōshe proclaimed:

"Whoever believes in G-d, come to me."

In response, many people, especially all the men of the tribe of Lāvē came to him.

2463 930 32:27 Mōshe told them:

"G-d communicates:

'Take your swords and punish the sinners.'"

The Tribe Of Lāvē Responds

2464 931 32:28 All the men of the tribe of Lāvē[673] did so.

About 3,000 people were duly punished.

2465 932 32:29 Mōshe told the tribe of Lāvē:

"You have distinguished yourselves as agents of G-d.

"You will now be the spiritual teachers[674] of the Jewish people.

"G-d is going to bestow His blessing upon you today."

2466 933 32:30 The next day Mōshe told the people:

"You have committed a terrible sin.

"I am going back up to G-d and I will beg for atonement[675] for your sin."

Mōshe Returns To G-d To Obtain Atonement For The Jewish People

2467 934 32:31 Mōshe returned to G-d and said:

"People committed a terrible sin by forming a gold[676] statue.

2468 935 32:32 "Please forgive their sin.

"If You cannot forgive their sin, then please give them my merits[677] so that they can be forgiven.

"I am willing to take the consequences and punishment of losing my merits."

2469 936 32:33 G-d communicated to Mōshe:

"Every person is judged solely based on his or her own actions.

KĒ TĒSA - SECTION 2 - CONTINUED

G-D COMMUNICATES THAT A DIVINE AGENT WILL ACCOMPANY THE PEOPLE

2470 937 32:34 "Lead the Jewish people into the land of Israel.
   "I will appoint an agent[678] to accompany you.
   "Eventually, people will be duly punished for this sin."
2471 938 32:35 G-d punished those people who had sinned but who had not been punished by the tribe of Lāvē.

2472 939 33:1 G-d communicated to Mōshe:
   "Lead these people, whom you led out of Egypt, to the land of Israel which I promised to Avraham, Yizhak, and Yaakōv, communicating to them:
   'I will give this land to your descendants.'
2473 940 33:2 "I am authorizing an agent to fight off the current residents:[679] the nations of
   (1) Kinaan (Canaan),
   (2) Ĥāt (Hittites),
   (3) Emôr,
   (4) Pirēz,
   (5) Ĥēv,
   and (6) Yivūs,
2474 941 33:3 "who occupy the land flowing with milk and honey.[680]
   "I will not be with the people because they are difficult, and I would end up destroying them along the way."

KĒ TĒSA - SECTION 2 - CONTINUED

THE PEOPLE STOP WEARING JEWELRY

2475 942 33:4 When the Jewish people were told all that had transpired between Mōshe and G-d, they felt very regretful, and therefore, they did not wear jewelry.

2476 943 33:5 G-d communicated to Mōshe:
"Tell the people:
'Sometimes, you can be a difficult people:[681]
'If I (G-d) would be with you, and you commit a terrible sin, I would annihilate you.
'Therefore, continue to not wear jewelry.
'I still have not decided on the punishment for the gold calf sin.' "

2477 944 33:6 The Jewish people continued to not wear jewelry from then on.

MŌSHE RELOCATES HIS TENT OUTSIDE THE CAMP

2478 945 33:7 Mōshe set up his tent away from the Jewish camp.
He named his tent: the Meeting Tent.[682]
Anyone who needed spiritual guidance walked to the Meeting Tent.

THE JEWISH PEOPLE SHOW RESPECT TO MŌSHE

2479 946 33:8 Whenever Mōshe left the camp to walk back to his tent, the Jewish people stood up until they could no longer see him.

2480 947 33:9 Whenever Mōshe was in his tent, the cloud column appeared at the entrance of his tent.
During those periods, G-d communicated to Mōshe.

2481 948 33:10 When the Jewish people saw the cloud column at the entrance of Mōshe's tent, they stood and prayed.[683]

2482 949 33:11 G-d communicated directly to Mōshe.
Mōshe would travel between his tent and the camp, but his disciple, Yihōshūa,[684] stayed in the Meeting Tent.

Kē Tēsa – Section 2 – Study Notes

[643] Section 2 - This section is one of the few very long sections in Tōra. It is long in order for a Levite to be called to the Tōra for the story that involved the Levites as champions. See the first note in the previous section for more information on this.

[644] 31:18 "G-d gave to Mōshe the two stone slabs, upon which were commandments written by the finger of G-d." See the Table 6 that compares the 2 versions (here, and that in Divarim (Deuteronomy)) of the events surrounding the stone slabs. See also notes on verse 24:12.

[645] 32:1 "scheduled to descend" – Verse 24:18 states that Mōshe was on the mountain for 40 days. However, it is not clear whether anyone had been told that it was planned for Mōshe to be there for 40 days. Tōra Study Bible takes the approach of those commentators who state that the Jewish people had been told. Nonetheless, some people mistakenly thought he would come down on the fortieth day. See verse 32:7 and the note on that verse.

[646] 32:1 "mistakenly thought" – Mōshe was scheduled to come back on the next day. The anxiety of some people, along with the fact that they saw how the top of the mountain burned like a fiery furnace (verse 24:17) caused them to think that Mōshe was no longer alive (verse 32:23).

[647] 32:1 "Fashion a form that will be with us" – According to Ramban, the people had no intention of resorting to idolatry. They simply wanted a tangible object through which to direct their prayers to G-d. This desire may not have seemed sacrilegious because, although the people had not yet been informed of the tabernacle, the sacred box had gold figures on its lid, as stated in verses 25:18-20. Perhaps the gold figures on the lid of the sacred box were a concession to human need for a physical object.

[648] 32:1 "man named Mōshe" – Even though Mōshe had been their leader for over a year, these misguided people suddenly speak of him disdainly as if he were a distant stranger.

[649] 32:2 "Forcibly remove the gold earrings of your wives…" – Aharōn

used this as a stall tactic. He felt that their family members would not give up their gold, which was true. So the men gave their own gold as stated in the next verse.

650 32:3 "gold" – This is the gold they asked for from their Egyptian neighbors before leaving (12:35). Later, for the building of the Tabernacle, the people donated items, including gold (35:22), which showed they regretted the use of gold for the gold statue.

651 32:4 "fashioned a statue" – In verse 32:24, Aharōn tells Mōshe that he took the gold and threw it into the fire. The gold formed itself into the shape of a calf.

652 32:4 "your" – Their use of the word "your" shows that a few evil people tried to convince the majority to accept idol worship.

653 32:4 "deity" – Once they saw the statue, those people who were severely misguided decided that it is the deity that had led them during this entire time. It shows how a few anxious people with little faith can get carried away. The majority of people did not believe them because, among many factors:
 a) the Jewish people had faith in G-d throughout their slavery in Egypt, so they certainly would not stop believing now,
and b) they had recently heard G-d Himself communicate to them "do not form idols" (verse 20:4).
 But the silent moral majority is often overshadowed and bullied by evil people, and enough people fall victim to crowd behavior.

654 32:5 "tomorrow" – Another stall tactic on the part of Aharōn.

655 32:7 "Some" – The verse includes a word that makes it very plausible to translate the verse as "because some of the people." Mōshe would have stayed on the mountain longer had it not been for the gold statue. This translation supports an alternate approach as mentioned in the note on verse 24:18.

656 32:7 "your" - G-d wants Mōshe to take ownership of, and responsibility

regarding, his leadership, rather than just perfunctorily carrying out G-d's commands in a detached way. In verse 34:9, Mōshe finally speaks in a way that shows that he considers himself to be part of the people.

657 32:10 "your descendants" – G-d offers again to do this later in Bamidbar 14:12.

The birth of Mōshe's older child, his son Gârshōm, is recorded in 2:22. The birth of his younger child, his son Elēezer, is mentioned in a veiled manner in 4:24-25 (based also on 4:20), although his name is not mentioned until 18:4.

Interestingly, the sons of Mōshe are never mentioned in terms of their spiritual qualities or leadership potential. They are not even mentioned in the genealogy stated in 6:14-25. This is in contrast to Aharōn, whose all four sons are mentioned in 6:23, and were selected for priesthood (although only the younger two lived long enough to serve as priests (see Vayikra (Leviticus) 10:1-5)). Similarly, in Bamidbar chapter 3, the descendants of Aharōn are listed but not those of Mōshe.

It is interesting that one of Mōshe's grandchildren became a priest to idol worship (Book of Judges (Shōftim) 18:30). See the study note on verse 6:20.

658 32:11 "prayed" – See note on verse 8:8 for other instances when Mōshe prayed.

659 32:12 "Your" - Mōshe refuses to let G-d abandon the Jewish people.

660 32:13 "stars" – Mōshe reminds G-d of His own solemn promise to the Jewish forefathers. Note that nowhere does Tōra state that this promise to the forefathers was ever told to Mōshe. Either G-d or the Jewish leaders had told him. Another possibility is that Mōshe had already written down the first book of Tōra (i.e. Brāshēt (Genesis), and thus he knew all details of the history of the ancestors.

The divine promises to the patriarchs had been stated in Brāshēt 13:16 (like dust), 15:5 (like stars), 17:2, 16:6, 22:17 (like stars and sand), 24:60, 26:4, 26:24, 28:14 (like sand), 32:13, and 35:11.

Although the Jewish people have always been much fewer in number than other nations, the promise made by G-d is that the Jewish people will survive. In addition, the comparison to stars is appropriate when considering that Jewish people have been pivotal in furthering social, scientific, technological, medical, political, judicial, and economic progress of societies and civilizations throughout history throughout the world.

[661] 32:13 "inherit the land forever" - See note on 3:8 for this everlasting promise that G-d made to the Jewish people.

[662] 32:14 "to the extreme" – Although they will not be punished to the maximum, there will be some punishment. Verses 32:28 and 33:3 deal with immediate ramifications of the wrong-doing.

[663] 32:15 "hand" – However, later, when Mōshe describes it to the new generation, he states that originally, he had held the original slabs in both hands (Divarim 9:15). Both Shimōt 32:19 and Divarim 9:17 state that he thrust the slabs down with both of his hands. For the second pair of slabs, all verses state that Mōshe held them in one hand (Shimōt 34:4, 34:29, and Divarim 10:3).

[664] 32:15 "front and back" -
Rashē: The letters went all the way through the stone. It was miraculous that the middle of letters that had dangling parts (such as a circle, i.e., "O"), were suspended without any physical support.
Ibn Ezra: You could read the engraved words correctly when viewing them from either side of the slabs.

[665] 32:16 "fashioned and engraved by G-d" – See notes on 24:12.

[666] 32:17 "Yihōshūa" – See note on verse 17:9.

[667] 32:19 "hands" – See note on 32:15.

[668] 32:19 "shattered" – Mōshe recounts this in Divarim 9:17.
Radak (Rabbi David Kimchi): The broken pieces of the slabs were saved and eventually they were placed in the treasury of the Holy Temple (See his commentary on Kings I 8:9).

⁶⁶⁹ 32:20 "He poured the gold dust into water" – Mōshe specifies that he threw the dust of the pulverized gold calf statue into the river that flowed down from Mount Sēnī (Divarim 9:21). That is the first mention that there was a river on Mount Sēnī.

⁶⁷⁰ 32:21 "Mōshe asked Aharōn" – In Divarim 9:20, Mōshe reveals that G-d had been angry with Aharōn.

⁶⁷¹ 32:24 "Give me your gold" – Note that Aharōn is so overcome with feelings of guilt regarding his misdeed that he doesn't defend himself by mentioning that he had used a stall tactic regarding the gold (see verse 32:2).

⁶⁷² 32:24 "threw the gold onto a fire" – Aharōn had no intention of forming a statue. He had hoped that it would form a lump.

⁶⁷³ 32:28 "tribe of Lāvē" – All (or most) men of Levites as well as some men from other tribes answered the call.

⁶⁷⁴ 32:29 "You will now be the spiritual teachers" –
Rashē: Previously, firstborn men had been appointed as the spiritual teachers (verses 11:5 and 19:22).

⁶⁷⁵ 32:30 "beg for atonement" – Before Mōshe knew the extent of the sin, he succeeded in preventing destruction of the people (32:11-13). Now he needed to achieve atonement for them.
Note, however, that Mōshe does not feel the need to ask forgiveness for having shattered the (first) stone slabs. G-d never considers that to be a wrong-doing. For instance, at the end of Mōshe's life, G-d reiterates that Mōshe cannot enter the land of Israel because he had not sanctified G-d's name at the water of Merēva (Bamidbar 20:13). G-d never mentions or implies that breaking the stone slabs as a problem.

⁶⁷⁶ 32:31 "gold" - Rashē: Mōshe desperately tries to find any possible excuse for the people. He expresses that because they had so much gold given to them by Egyptians, they were reckless in their behavior and cannot be held fully responsible for their action.

677 32:32 "give them my merits" – This is the understanding of the Siforno. Mōshe is still desperately trying to find a path to atonement.

Ramban: Remove my name from the book of life, and I will allow myself to be punished as well.

Rashē: I do not want future people to read that I was unable to save the Jewish people. Therefore, remove my name from this narrative (or perhaps, the entire Tōra).

678 32:34 and 33:2 "agent" – See note on verse 23:20.

679 33:2 "current residents" – Brāshēt (Genesis) 15:19-21 list the following 10 tribes as residents of the land of Kinaan:
1 Ken,
2 Kinēz,
3 Kadmōn,
4 Ĥet (Hittites),
5 Prēz,
6 Rifaim,
7 Emôr (Amorites),
8 Kinaan (Canaanites),
9 Gêrgash
and 10 Yivūsê.
Add to that list the
11 Plishtim (Philistines) (listed in Brāshēt 26:1)
and 12 Ĥēv (Hivites), which is listed here.

680 33:2 "milk and honey" – See Essay 6 and the study note on verse 3:8 about the meaning of milk and honey, and other verses that mention it.

681 33:5 "difficult people" – The literal phrase in the verse is "a stiff-necked people." Traditional sources explain that Mōshe responded to G-d by agreeing, but stating that this same obstinate nature of the Jewish people makes them steadfast in their belief in, devotion to, and service to G-d.

682 33:7 "Meeting Tent" – This is not the Communion Tent that is part of

the Tabernacle.

[683] 33:10 "prayed" – See Essay 7 for instances when the people prayed.

[684] 33:11 "Yihōshūa" – He wanted to learn as much as he could from Mōshe and to serve him as much as possible. See not on verse 17:9 for information about Yihōshūa.

Kē Tēsa - Section 3   - 5 verses

2483 950 33:12 Mōshe (Moses) said to G-d:

"You told me to guide the people, but You did not specify what agent[685] You would provide.

"I request this information because You have told me:

'You are special, and I like you.'

MŌSHE ASKS TO UNDERSTAND THE WAYS OF G-D

2484 951 33:13 "Please inform me how You reward people and how You plan to treat the Jewish people."

2485 952 33:14 G-d responded:

"My presence[686] will accompany you and protect you."

2486 953 33:15 Mōshe said to G-d:

"It would be better for us to reside in the wilderness if You do not accompany us.

2487 954 33:16 "By being with us, other people will realize that the Jewish people have inherited the land of Israel by divine decree, rather than by ordinary conquest.[687]

"And by being with us, the Jewish people will realize that I am their divinely selected leader." [688]

Kē Tēsa – Section 3 – Study Notes

[685] 33:12 "You did not specify what agent" – Mōshe is gently trying to ask G-d to lead the Jewish people Himself. Different commentators explain what the implication is:

Rashbam – Mōshe implies that he wants G-d himself to accompany them.

Ramban – Mōshe is asking whether this agent is the protective agent that was specified previously in verse 32:21, because that agent was not good enough.

See the note on verse 23:20 for an overview of the entire sequence of interaction between G-d and Mōshe on this issue.

[686] 33:14 "My presence" – G-d intends to imbue the agent with more of His divine presence than previously, based on Mōshe' request. See note on verse 23:20.

[687] 33:16 "by divine decree, rather than . . ." – Although the actual verse is in the form of a question, within the context of the interaction between Mōshe and G-d, many commentators take it to be a rhetorical question. This rendition is based on the Siforno.

[688] 33:16 "I am their divinely selected leader" – This is the rendition of Rashbam, who sees this as a second concern that Mōshe has.

Kē Tēsa - Section 4   - 7 verses

G-D AGREES TO REVEAL DIVINE BEHAVIOR TO MŌSHE

2488 955 33:17 G-d responded:
   "I will agree to your request because I like you and have selected you to be the leader."

MŌSHE ASKS TO EXPERIENCE THE GLORY OF G-D

2489 956 33:18 Mōshe (Moses) said to G-d:
       "Please show me Your glory."
2490 957 33:19 G-d responded:
   "I will allow you to hear the sound of my holy name.
   "I will be kind to whom I want, and I will be merciful to whom I want.
2491 958 33:20 "You cannot see Me because no person can see Me and continue to live.
2492 959 33:21 "I have prepared a special protected place on the mountain[689] where you will stand.
2493 960 33:22 "When My glory passes by you, I will place you in this protective area and I will cover you with My presence.
2494 961 33:23 "When I uncover your eyes, you will detect My back, but not My face.

Kē Tēsa – Section 4 – Study Notes

[689] 33:21 "on the mountain" – Rashē, and most commentators, assume all this took place on Mount Sēnī (Sinai). See note on verse 3:1.

Kē Tēsa - Section 5   - 9 verses

2495 962 34:1 G-d communicated to Mōshe (Moses):
"Form two stone slabs[690] that look similar to the ones that you broke.
"I will engrave them[691] with the same words[692] as before.
2496 963 34:2 "Walk up[693] to the top of the Mount Sēnī (Sinai) tomorrow morning.
2497 964 34:3 "No one else should accompany you and no living thing should be on the mountain while you are there."

Mōshe Forms The Second Slabs, And Carries Them Up The Mountain

2498 965 34:4 Mōshe formed the second set of stone slabs.
He walked up the mountain the next morning, carrying the stone slabs in his hand.[694]
2499 966 34:5 The presence of G-d descended onto the mountain and G-d communicated His name.

13 Attributes of Divine Mercy

2500 967 34:6 G-d moved past Mōshe[695] and communicated His 13 attributes of mercy:[696]
   1 "Merciful G-d to people when they plan to sin,[697]
   2 "Merciful G-d to people who sin,[698]
   3 "Wisely powerful,[699]
   4 "Mercifully preventing people from sinning,[700]
   5 "Gracious,
   6 "Slow to punish,
   7 "Good to people,
   8 "Faithful to carry out solemn promises,
2501 968 34:7
   9 "Transfers merits to later generations,[701]
   10 "Forgives premeditated sin,
   11 "Forgives rebellious behavior,
   12 "Forgives accidental sin, and
   13 "Punishes guilty people little by little,
     "but if descendants continue to sin,[702] G-d punishes them."

KĒ TĒSA - SECTION 5 - CONTINUED

MŌSHE BOWS AND PRAYS

2502 969 34:8 As Mōshe listened to the divine message, he bowed, and then he prayed.[703]

MŌSHE REQUESTS THAT G-D STAY WITH THE JEWISH PEOPLE

2503 970 34:9 Mōshe said:

"If you like me enough to listen to my request, although the people are difficult, please be with the people and pardon our sin and accept us[704] as Your chosen people."

Kē Tēsa – Section 5 – Study Notes

⁶⁹⁰ 34:1 "form two stone slabs" – The original stone slabs had been formed by G-d. See notes on 24:12 and Table 6.

⁶⁹¹ 34:1 "I will engrave them" – Verse 34:28 states that Mōshe engraved the second pair of slabs. However, in Divarim (Deuteronomy) 5:19, Mōshe states that G-d had engraved the second pair of slabs.

⁶⁹² 34:1 "same words" – There are some differences in the wording of the Decaloge in Mōshe's lecture before the Jewish people enter the land of Israel (Divarim 5:6-18).

⁶⁹³ 34:2 "walk up" – Mōshe describes how he formed the slabs and carried them up the mountain in Divarim10:3.

According to Ibn Ezra, this occurred on the first day of the month of Elul. It is the start of the third 40-day period (see verse 34:28 and the note on 24:18). Mōshe came down from the mountain on the Day of Atonement. This 40-day period might be the one referred to in Divarim 10:10.

⁶⁹⁴ 34:4 "hand" – See note on 32:15.

⁶⁹⁵ 34:6 "G-d moved past Mōshe" – Mōshe's facial skin took on a radiant splendor, as mentioned in verse 34:29.

⁶⁹⁶ 34:6 "His 13 attributes of mercy" – Later in history, G-d communicated His Supreme Attributes of Divine Mercy to the prophet Mēka (Micah) 7:18-20. Righteous people try to emulate these attributes.
 1. G-d is incomparable
 2. G-d pardons sin
 3. G-d overlooks rebellious sins
 4. G-d especially loves the people who serve Him
 5. G-d does not hold a grudge
 6. G-d cherishes people's acts of kindness
 7. G-d is especially merciful to people who repent
 8. G-d does not let sin override good deeds
 9. G-d sees to it that after a person repents, previous sins are erased.
 10. G-d is compassionate to law-abiding people

11. G-d is kind to ethical people
12. G-s is gracious, even to imperfect people
13. G-d is merciful to people who attempt to be righteous.

See Essays 2 and 4 about the nature of G-d, how people relate to G-d, and the Tōra's concept of serving G-d.

[697] 34:6 "merciful to those who plan to sin" - According to Rashē.
Based on the teachings of Rav Joseph Soloveitchik: This divine aspect applies from the contemplation of sin until a person repents (Holzer, 2013, p. 124).

[698] 34:6 "merciful to people who sin" - According to Rashē.
Based on the teachings of Rav Joseph Soloveitchik: This divine aspect occurs once G-d accepts repentance and re-establishes His relationship with the repentant person. When dealing with the people who repented after believing the negative report of the scouts (Bamidbar 14:18), only one instance of the name of G-d is stated (Holzer, 2013, p. 123).

[699] 34:6 "wisely powerful" - According to Ibn Ezra.

[700] 34:6 "mercifully preventing people from sinning" – According to Ibn Ezra.

[701] 34:7 "Transfers merits to later generations" – This is similar to the statement in the Decaloge, verse 20:6, which is also restated by Mōshe in Divarim 5:8.

[702] 34:7 "punishes . . . if descendants continue to sin" – This is similar to verse 20:5 in the Decaloge, also restated by Mōshe in Divarim 5:9.

[703] 34:8 "prayed" – See Essay 7 about the nature of prayer.

[704] 34:9 "our . . . us" – This is the first time Mōshe identifies himself as part of the Jewish people in a personal way. When G-d demands that Mōshe think of the Jewish people as being his people (see verse 32:7 and the note on that verse), those words take their effect here.

Kē Tēsa - Section 6 — 17 verses

G-D AGREES TO THE REQUEST TO LEAD THE JEWISH PEOPLE

2504 971 34:10 G-d communicated:

"I now make a solemn promise:

"I will[705] perform unique wondrous actions for the Jewish people and they will realize how wondrous these actions are.

2505 972 34:11 "I will displace the people who now inhabit the land of Israel.

2506 973 34:12 "Do not make treaties[706] with those peoples because it will work against you.

2507 974 34:13 "Destroy their idols and cut down the trees that they worship.

2508 975 34:14 "Do not worship any idol.

"G-d demands your faithfulness.

2509 976 34:15 "Do not make a treaty with them.

"They will worship their idols, offer offerings to their idols, ask you to come, and you might eat those offerings.

DO NOT INTERMARRY

2510 977 34:16 "If you allow idol worship, there will be intermarriage,[707] and idol worship will spread.

2511 978 34:17 "Do not form idols.

PASSOVER HOLY FESTIVAL

2512 979 34:18 "Observe the holy festival[708] of matza.

"The holiday lasts for 7 days in the spring time[709] because that is the time of year when you left Egypt.

FIRSTBORN KOSHER ANIMALS

2513 980 34:19 "Because the Jewish firstborn had been spared,[710] you must sanctify your first born kosher animals.

Kē Tēsa - Section 6 - continued

Firstborn Donkeys

2514 981 34:20 "Redeem a firstborn of a donkey[711] with a lamb.
 "If you choose not to do so, then you must kill the firstborn donkey.
 "Redeem your firstborn sons.
 "Each person should offer an offering on the holy festival.[712]

Commandment 110:[713] Rest During Year 7

Sabbath And Sabbatical Year

2515 982 34:21 "Work for 6 days[714] and rest on day 7.[715]
 "Plowing and harvesting are not permitted during year 7[716] (sabbatical year) and these activities should also not be performed just before and just after year 7.

Shavūōt And Sūkōt Holy Festivals

2516 983 34:22 "Observe the holy festival[717] of weeks (Shavūōt festival).
 "Bring the first of the wheat harvest.
 "Observe the holy festival that occurs during the main harvest season (i.e., the festival of huts, Sūkōt festival).

Come To The Central Location Of Worship Three Times A Year

2517 984 34:23 "Men should present themselves to G-d three times a year.

The Land Of Israel Will Be Too Large For People To Come Every Day

2518 985 34:24 "I will displace the nations[718] that currently reside in the land of Israel.
 "I will enlarge the boundaries of your country to such a large extent that you cannot come to the central place of worship[719] all the time.
 "Other nations will fear you such that they will not wage war against you.
 "Appear to G-d three times a year.

KĒ TĒSA - SECTION 6 - CONTINUED

OBSERVE THE LAWS OF PASSOVER

2519 986 34:25 "Do not use leavened grain as part of offerings.[720]
"Do not leave leftovers of the Pesaĥ (Passover) offering[721] after sunrise.

KĒ TĒSA - SECTION 6 - CONTINUED

Commandment 111:[722] Do Not Cook Mixtures Of Meat And Dairy

2520 987 34:26 "Bring the best fruits to the house of worship.
"Do not cook a mixture of meat and dairy." [723]

Kē Tēsa – Section 6 – Study Notes

---

[705] 34:10 "I will" – G-d now agrees to lead the Jewish people, as Mōshe has been requesting. See note on verse 23:20 for details.

[706] 34:12 "do not make treaties" – Verse 23:33 prohibits allowing idol worshippers to live in the land of Israel, and it is commandment 93.

When Yihōshūa (Joshua) entered the land as leader of the Jewish people, for each village, town, and city, the Jewish people sent a messenger giving the native inhabitants choices. If they agree to destroy their idols and give up idol worship, they were welcome to stay in the holy land. If they were not willing to do that, the Jewish people would allow them to safely leave Israel and relocate. Only if the natives were not willing to do either of the two options, would battle be necessary.

[707] 34:16 "intermarriage" – This verse gives a reason why intermarriage is not good. Rambam counts this as a negative commandment of the 613 commandments in Divarim (Deuteronomy) 7:3.

[708] 34:18 "festival" - Festivals are also mentioned in:
    Shimot 23:14-16,
    Vayikra (Leviticus) 23:2, 4-43,
    Bamidbar (Numbers) 28:16-31
    Bamidbar 29:1-39,
and Divarim 16:1-17.

In addition to these 3 central holy festivals, there are the two other Biblical festivals:
    the New Year (Rōsh Hashana)
and the Day of Atonement (Yōm Kipur).

[709] 34:18 "spring time" - Also stated in verse 23:15. See note on verse 13:4 that explains how a leap month is used to keep Pesaĥ in the spring season.

[710] 34:19 "Jewish first born had been spared" –This verse provides the link between the laws of firstborn and the tenth plague. During that plague in Egypt, although other firstborn were punished, Jewish firstborn were not affected. This directive is also stated as commandment 21 in verse 13:12.

See note on verse 11:5 about all the laws of firstborn.

[711] 34:20 "redeem a firstborn donkey" – These laws are also stated in verse 13:13, where they are commandments 22 & 23 as counted by Rambam.

[712] 34:20 "offering on the holy festival" – Also stated in verse 23:15.

[713] Commandment 110 – This commandment is explained by Rambam: in his <u>Mishne Tōra</u>: Book 7: Produce: Laws of Sabbatical and Jubilee Years.

[714] 34:21 "work for 6 days" - See note on verse 20:9.

[715] 34:21 "rest on day 7" – Shabat. This is also stated in verse 23:12, where it is commandment 84 according to Rambam. See note on 16:23.

[716] 34:21 "year 7" – Sabbatical year. Also stated in verse 23:11, where it is commandment 83.

[717] 34:22 "festival" – Stated as commandment 85 in verses 23:14-16.

[718] 34:24 "I will displace the nations" - Mōshe mentions this in Divarim 7:19 when he assures the Jewish people that they will settle the land of Israel.

[719] 34:24 "central place of worship" – See notes on verse 25:8 that explains the role of a temple.

[720] 34:25 "Do not use leavened grain as part of offerings" – In Vayikra 2:11, there is a commandment to not put leaven on offerings. In Vayikra 6:10 there is a commandment to not allow any flour or dough offerings to become leavened.

[721] 34:25 "leftover of the Pesaĥ offering" – As was stated in verse 23:18, where is it commandment 87.

[722] Commandment 111: Book 5: Holiness: Laws of Forbidden Food

[723] 34:26 "do not cook a mixture of meat and dairy" – Verse 23:19, which is commandment 90, is worded the same as this verse, but the oral law renders the earlier verse as "do not <u>ingest</u>". In this verse Jewish people are commanded to not <u>cook</u> them together, even if there is no intention of eating the resulting cooked food. Divarim 14:21 prohibits simply <u>benefiting</u> from mixtures of meat and milk products.

Kē Tēsa - Section 7   - 6 + 3 verses

2521 988 34:27 G-d communicated to Mōshe (Moses):
"Write down these verses, which the people will accept again because the solemn promise which they had made before the gold calf had been formed, must be renewed." [724]

40 Days Without Food Or Drink

Decaloge On The Stone Slabs

2522 989 34:28 Mōshe was with G-d for 40 days[725] and nights, during which he did not eat or drink.
Mōshe engraved[726] the Decaloge[727] on the second pair of stone slabs.[728]

Majestic Splendor Of Mōshe's Face

2523 990 34:29 Mōshe walked down the mountain carrying the pair of stone slabs in his hand.[729]
Mōshe did not know that his face was radiant[730] after he had seen the divine glory.[731]
2524 991 34:30 When Aharōn (Aaron) and the Jewish people saw the radiance of Mōshe's face, they were afraid to come near him.
2525 992 34:31 Mōshe asked Aharōn and the Jewish leaders to come to him.
Mōshe spoke to them.
2526 993 34:32 Afterwards, the Jewish people came to Mōshe.
Mōshe taught them[732] the commandments that G-d had communicated to him on Mount Sēnī (Sinai).

KĒ TĒSA - SECTION 7 - CONTINUED

Kē Tēsa - Last Section

MŌSHE WEARS A VEIL

2527 994 34:33 After he had spoken to the Jewish people, he wore a veil.[733]
2528 995 34:34 When G-d communicated to Mōshe, he took off the veil.

After each encounter with G-d, Mōshe would teach the newly communicated commandments to the Jewish people.
2529 996 34:35 The Jewish people had seen the radiance[734] of Mōshe's face.

Therefore, Mōshe wore the veil until he heard communication from G-d.

Kē Tēsa – Section 7 – Study Notes

[724] 34:27 – The rendition of this verse is based on a combined understanding of Rashbam, Ibn Ezra, and Ramban.

[725] 34:28 "40 days" – See note on verse 24:18 that explain the 3 40-day periods. Mōshe mentions this additional 40-day period in Divarim 9:18 and 10:10. Another 40 days are mentioned in Divarim 9:25.

[726] 34:28 "Mōshe engraved" – In verse 34:1, G-d states that He will engrave them. In line with this, Divarim (Deuteronomy) 10:2 & 4 indicate that G-d had engraved them.

[727] 34:28 "Decaloge" – This is the first time that the number 10 is mentioned in connection with the engraving on the stone slabs. Note that Rambam considers that there are 13 commandments in the Decaloge (see verses 20:2 – 20:14). According to Rambam, rather than call the Decaloge "The Ten Commandments" as is commonly done, Rambam might refer to them as 10 statements.

[728] 34:28 "stone slabs" – See notes on verse 24:12 that explains the role of both pairs of stone slabs. And see Table 6 for a comparison of the two narratives about the stone slabs.

[729] 34:29 "hand" – See note on 32:15 concerning whether Mōshe held them in one hand or both hands.

[730] 34:29 "radiant" – This word is rendered according to Rashbam. Alternatively, it can be rendered as "majestic splendor."

[731] 34:29 "after he had seen the divine glory" – This is mentioned in Rashē. This had taken place in verse 34:6.

[732] 34:32 "taught them" – This is the understanding of this verse according to Rambam, Mōshe held multiple repeat lectures after each of the divine revelations of commandments. First, he taught them to Yihōshūa, then to Aharōn, then to the sons of Aharōn, and then to the leaders. Afterward he would teach them to the Jewish people as a whole.

[733] 34:33 "veil" – According to Rashē, Rashbam and Siforno, Mōshe did not wear the veil while he related the divine communication to the Jewish people. He wore the veil only after he finished teaching the Jewish people, until the next communication from G-d.

[734] 34:35 "radiance" – According to Sadya Gaōn, this facial radiance remained on Mōshe until his passing. According to Ibn Ezra, after Mōshe had finished teaching the latest commandments, the radiance was gone. Mōshe wore a veil so that the Jewish people would not see that the radiance was gone because he was afraid that the Jewish people would not revere him if they saw he did not have radiant skin.

Vayakhâl [735] - Section 1   - 19 verses   (Total: 122 verses)

[There is 1 negative commandment in this portion.]

SABBATH

2530 997 35:1 Mōshe assembled the Jewish people, and said to them:
"These are the things that G-d commands you to do:

Commandment 112:[736] Court Must Not Punish On Sabbath

2531 998 35:2 "Work for six days, but keep the seventh day as a holy shabat (Sabbath)[737] of rest to G-d.
"Anyone who works on shabat will be condemned.
2532 999 35:3 "It is forbidden to ignite a fire on shabat."

MATERIALS FOR THE TABERNACLE

2533 1000 35:4 Mōshe said to the Jewish people as follows:
"These are the things that G-d commands:
2534 1001 35:5 "Donate,[738] of your own free will, special offerings to G-d, of the following types of items:
    1 gold,
    2 silver,
    3 copper,
2535 1002 35:6
    4 "blue wool,
    5 red wool,
    6 wool colored with dye from a crimson worm,
    7 fine linen,
    8 goat hair,
2536 1003 35:7
    9 "ram skins dyed red,
    10 wild animal skins,
    11 acacia wood,
2537 1004 35:8
    12 "pure olive oil for lamps,
    13 spices for the anointing oil,
    14 fragrances for the sweet incense,

Vayakhâl - Section 1 - continued

2538 1005 35:9
    15 "two onyx stones for the apron,
    and 12 various stones for the breastplate.

CRAFTSMEN

2539 1006 35:10 "All talented people should do their part to fashion the items[739] commanded by G-d,

2540 1007 35:11 "namely:
    1 the tabernacle,
    2 its inner covering,
    3 roof,
    4 fasteners,
    5 beams,
    6 crossbars,
    7 pillars,

2541 1008 35:12
    8 "the sacred box,
    9 its carrying poles,
    10 its lid,
    11 the cloth partition,

2542 1009 35:13
    12 "the table,
    13 its carrying poles,
    14 its utensils,
    15 showbread,

2543 1010 35:14
    16 "the menora lamp,
    17 its utensils,
    18 lights,
    19 oil,

2544 1011 35:15
    20 "the incense altar,
    21 its carrying poles,
    22 anointing oil,
    23 incense,
    24 entrance drape,

Vayakhâl - Section 1 - continued

2545 1012 35:16
    25 "the animal-offering altar,
    26 its carrying poles,
    27 its utensils,
    28 wash basin,
    29 its base,
2546 1013 35:17
    30 "hangings for the enclosure,
    31 its pillars,
    32 its bases,
    33 the enclosure entrance drape,
2547 1014 35:18
    34 "tent stakes,
    35 enclosure stakes,
    36 ropes,
2548 1015 35:19
    37 "cloths,
    38 clothing for Aharōn the high priest, and
    39 clothing for his sons, who are the regular priests."

Vayakhâl – Section 1 – Study Notes

[735] "Vayakhâl" - The Hebrew word *vayakhâl* means "he assembled."

[736] Commandment 112 – This commandment is explained by Rambam: in his <u>Mishne Tōra</u>: Book 3: Seasons: Laws of Shabat.

[737] 35:2 "shabat" - Previous mention of Sabbath are:
 Brāshēt: 2:2 & 3;
 Bishalaĥ: 16:25,27,29.30;
 Yitrō: 20:8,10,11 (i.e., Decaloge);
and Mishpatim 23:12.

Here it expresses the fact that building the Tabernacle does not override the prohibition of working on shabat. Talmud Tractate Shabat 73a (Mishna 7:2) derives that the 39 major categories of activities in the preparation of, and construction of the Tabernacle are the major categories of work that Jewish people refrain from performing on shabat. See note on verse 16:23.

[738] 35:5 "donate" – In portion Trūma, G-d tells Mōshe to ask the Jewish people for donations, and then G-d proceeds to specify the construction of the Tabernacle and its furniture and utensils.

In this portion, everything is repeated as a request by Mōshe to the Jewish people. The study notes on chapters 25, 26, and 27 apply to this portion as well. Two items that are specified for the first time after portion Trūma are the incense altar (30:1-6) and the wash basin (30:18).

[739] 35:10 "items" – Interestingly, there are 39 items listed here and there are 39 forbidden activities on the Sabbath. A list of the items that comprise the Tabernacle is found in verses 39:33-41. They also total 39.

Vayakhâl - Section 2 - 10 verses

2549 1016 35:20 The entire Jewish community left Mōshe in order to respond to G-d's request.

THE PEOPLE DONATE

2550 1017 35:21 Each person who wanted to volunteer his or her talent came forward.
 People came who wanted to donate to G-d for the fashioning of the tabernacle, its items, and the clothing.
2551 1018 35:22 Both men and women who wanted to, came and brought jewels set in gold as nose rings, earrings, signet rings, and belts.
2552 1019 35:23 People who had blue wool, purple wool, red wool, fine linen, goat hair, red-dyed rams skin, and special skin, brought them.
2553 1020 35:24 Those people who had silver and copper brought them as an offering.
 Those people who had acacia wood brought it.

SKILLED WOMEN

2554 1021 35:25 Women who were skilled weavers brought blue wool, purple wool, red wool, and fine linen.
2555 1022 35:26 Women who were skilled, spun goats hair.

THE LEADERS DONATE THE PRECIOUS STONES, SPICES, AND OIL

2556 1023 35:27 Nobles brought onyx stones and precious stones for the priest's apron and the breastplate.
2557 1024 35:28 The nobles also brought spices and oil to be used for the lamp, anointing oil, and sweet incense.
2558 1025 35:29 Each man and woman who wanted to contribute, did so.

Vayakhâl - Section 3 — 13 verses

Biżalel

2559 1026 35:30 Mōshe said to the Jewish people:
"G-d has singled-out Biżalel[740] son of Ūrē son of Ĥùr, of the tribe of Yihūda.
2560 1027 35:31 "G-d has gifted him with divine spirit, wisdom, understanding, knowledge, and craftsmanship.
2561 1028 35:32 "G-d has gifted him with skill working with gold, silver, copper,
2562 1029 35:33 "gems, wood carving, and all types of craftsmanship.

Ahalēav

2563 1030 35:34 "G-d also gifted him,[741] as well as Ahalēav[742] son of Aĥēsamaĥ, of the tribe of Dan, with the ability to teach craftsmanship to other people.
2564 1031 35:35 "They trained other gifted craftsmen who are skillful as weavers of blue, purple, and red wool, and fine linen, and various other skills.

2565 1032 36:1 "Biżalel and Ahalēav and other gifted craftsmen and craftswomen should work and form the tabernacle, its furniture and utensils."
2566 1033 36:2 Mōshe spoke to Biżalel and Ahalēav and the other craftspersons.
2567 1034 36:3 They received from Mōshe the various donations.
 The Jewish people continued to bring donations each morning.
2568 1035 36:4 Each skilled person performed the skill that he or she was expert in.

VAYAKHÂL - SECTION 3 - CONTINUED

THE JEWISH PEOPLE BROUGHT MORE THAN ENOUGH MATERIAL FOR THE TABERNACLE

2569 1036 36:5 They reported to Mōshe:
"The people are bringing much more material and items than is needed based on G-d's instructions for the tabernacle.
2570 1037 36:6 Mōshe told the leaders to tell the people:
"Do not bring any more donations."
So they stopped donating.
2571 1038 36:7 The items that the people had brought was more than sufficient for the needs of building the tabernacle.

Vayakhâl – Section 3 – Study Notes

[740] 35:30 "Biżalel" – He is first mentioned in 31:1. He is mentioned as a master goldsmith, silversmith and coppersmith in verse 35:32 and it is apparent in chapter 37 that he was a master at carpentry and cabinetry.

[741] 35:34 "him" – Namely, Biżalel. He was not only a master craftsman, but he also had a talent for teaching others. In addition, verse 38:22 states that he supervised and managed the people he taught. Therefore, although in chapters 37 and 38, the verses state that he, Biżalel, crafted the furnishings of the tabernacle, much of the work was performed by his disciples, as stated in verse 36:1, 4, & 8. However, Tōra credits him with the accomplishment because he taught and supervised.

[742] 35:34 "Ahalēav" – He is first mentioned in 31:6. He specialized in weaving and fabric crafts, as stated in verse 38:23. He also taught and supervised, as indicated in verses 36:8 and 38:23.

Vayakhâl - Section 4   - 12 verses

WALL CURTAINS

2572 1039 36:8 The skilled workers[743] made the 10 curtains of linen, blue wool, purple wool, and red wool.
   They skillfully wove the cherubim into the fabric.
2573 1040 36:9 Each curtain was 56 feet long and 8 feet wide.
2574 1041 36:10 They sewed together 5 curtains, and they sewed together the other 5 curtains.
2575 1042 36:11 For the outermost curtain of each set they made loops made of blue wool.
2576 1043 36:12 Each had 50 loops that were opposite one another.
2577 1044 36:13 They made 50 gold clasps and they connected the two sets of curtains together using the gold clasps around the wool loops.

ROOF CLOTH

2578 1045 36:14 They made a roof of goat hair consisting of 11 cloths.
2579 1046 36:15 Each cloth was 60 feet by 8 feet.
2580 1047 36:16 They combined 5 cloths together and 6 cloths together.
2581 1048 36:17 They made 50 loops on the outer edge of each of the 2 giant cloths.
2582 1049 36:18 They made 50 copper clasps to hold together the roof cloth.
2583 1050 36:19 They also made the middle roof cloth out of ram skin, and the top-most roof covering out of special animal skins.

Vayakhâl – Section 4 – Study Notes

---

[743] 36:8 "skilled workers" – Biżalel and Ahalēav taught craft skills to other capable people and supervised them, as explained in the notes on verse 35:34.

Vayakhâl - Section 5 — 35 verses

WALLS

2584 1051 36:20 They[744] made the wall boards out of acacia wood.
2585 1052 36:21 Each board was 20 feet high by 3 feet wide.
2586 1053 36:22 Each beam had 2 prongs at the bottom.
2587 1054 36:23 There were 20 boards for the south side.
2588 1055 36:24 They made 40 silver sockets that fit into the prongs that are at the bottom of the 20 boards.
2589 1056 36:25 They made 20 boards for the north side.
2590 1057 36:26 There were 40 silver sockets for those boards.
2591 1058 36:27 They made 6 boards for the west side.
2592 1059 36:28 There were 2 boards for the corners at the west side.
2593 1060 36:29 The two corner boards went from top to bottom.
2594 1061 36:30 There were 8 boards with their 16 silver sockets.
2595 1062 36:31 They made 5 bars of acacia wood for one side
2596 1063 36:32 and 5 bars for the opposite side, as well as 5 bars for the west side.
2597 1064 36:33 The middle bar went through the middle of the boards through the length of the wall.
2598 1065 36:34 They coated the boards in gold.
   They made gold rings as holders for the bars.
   They coated the bars with gold.

THE ENTRANCE

2599 1066 36:35 They made the veil out of blue, purple, and red wool and linen.
   They wove pictures of cherubim into the veil.
2600 1067 36:36 They made 4 beams of acacia wood and coated them with gold.
   Their hooks were gold.
   They made 4 silver sockets for each of them.
2601 1068 36:37 They made a curtain made of blue, purple, and red wool and linen, for the door.

Vayakhâl - Section 5 - continued

2602 1069 36:38 They made the 5 columns along with their hooks.
   They coated them with gold.
   They made copper sockets for them.

SACRED BOX

2603 1070 37:1 Biźalel[745] formed the sacred box as 5 by 3 by 3 feet out of acacia wood.
2604 1071 37:2 He coated it with gold.
   He fashioned a gold crown for it.
2605 1072 37:3 He made 4 gold rings for it, two rings on opposite sides.
2606 1073 37:4 He fashioned two acacia rods and coated them with gold.
2607 1074 37:5 He placed the rods into the rings so the box can be carried by them.

LID

2608 1075 37:6 He made the lid for the box out of gold.
   It measured 5 by 3 feet.

STATUES ON THE LID

2609 1076 37:7 He fashioned the statues out of gold, one on each side of the lid.
2610 1077 37:8 The statues were made of a single piece of gold.
2611 1078 37:9 Each statue had a face that faced the other, and wings that spread across the lid.

TABLE

2612 1079 37:10 He made the table out of acacia wood.
   It was 4 by 2 feet, and was 3 feet high.
2613 1080 37:11 He coated it with gold and he made a gold crown for it.
2614 1081 37:12 He made a border for it.
   It was 4 inches high.
   He made a crown for the border.
2615 1082 37:13 He made 4 gold rings and attached the rings to the 4 corners of the feet of the table.
2616 1083 37:14 The rings were positioned near the border.

Vayakhâl - Section 5 - continued

2617 1084 37:15 He made the rods of acacia wood and coated them with gold.
   They were used to carry the table.
2618 1085 37:16 He fashioned all the dishes and utensils for the table, namely, the dishes, pans, bowls, and jars, each made of gold.

Vayakhâl – Section 5 – Study Notes

[744] 36:20 "they" – See notes on verse 35:34.

[745] 37:1 "Biżalel" – See note on verse 35:34.

Vayakhâl - Section 6 - 13 verses

MENŌRA

2619 1086 37:17 He[746] formed the menōra candelabra out of gold.
　All of it was shaped out of a single block, including the base, shaft, cups, knobs, and flowers.
2620 1087 37:18 It had 3 branches on each side.
2621 1088 37:19 Each of the 6 branches had 3 almond-shaped cups long with a knob and flower.
2622 1089 37:20 The center shaft had 4 almond-shaped cups with knobs and flowers.
2623 1090 37:21 There was a knob under each of the 3 branch-pairs.
2624 1091 37:22 The entire menōra was made of a single block of gold.
2625 1092 37:23 He fashioned the 7 lamps, cups and their tongs out of gold.
2626 1093 37:24 The entire menōra along with its cups and tongs was formed from a large block of gold.

INCENSE ALTAR

2627 1094 37:25 He formed the incense altar[747] from acacia wood.
　It was 3 by 3 feet, and 4 feet high.
2628 1095 37:26 He coated it with gold, including the corner protrusions and the crown.
2629 1096 37:27 He formed 2 gold rings under the crown, at 2 opposite vertices, which rods can go through.
2630 1097 37:28 He fashioned the 2 rods out of acacia wood and coated them with gold.

ANOINTING OIL AND INCENSE

2631 1098 37:29 He combined the ingredients of the anointing oil and the incense.

Vayakhâl – Section 6 – Study Notes

[746] 37:17 "he" – Biżalel. See note on verse 35:34.

[747] 37:25 "incense altar" – Although the tabernacle design is specified in chapters 25, 26, and 27, the incense altar is specified starting in verse 30:1.

Vayakhâl - Section 7 — 17 + 3 verses

ANIMAL-OFFERING ALTAR

2632 1099 38:1 He[748] constructed the animal-offering altar out of acacia wood.
  It was 10 by 10 feet, and 6 feet high.
2633 1100 38:2 He formed the knobs at the top corners as an integral part of the altar.
  He overlaid the altar with copper.
2634 1101 38:3 He fashioned all the utensils used for animal offerings out of copper.
2635 1102 38:4 He fashioned a copper screen under the ledge, halfway up.
2636 1103 38:5 He fashioned 4 copper rings, one at each corner, for the rods.
2637 1104 38:6 He made two acacia wood rods and overlaid them with copper.
3638 1105 38:7 He positioned the rods into the rings.
  The altar was hollowed out[749] of a block of acacia wood.

WATER BASIN

3639 1106 38:8 He fashioned the water basin[750] for washing out of copper mirrors[751] that women who came to pray[752] there, donated.

COURTYARD ENCLOSURE – SOUTH SIDE

3640 1107 38:9 He made the structures that created the enclosure of the courtyard around the tabernacle.
  The south side curtain wall was made of linen 200 feet long.
3641 1108 38:10 It had 20 pillars, 20 copper sockets, silver hooks, and silver threads around the hooks.

COURTYARD ENCLOSURE – NORTH SIDE

3642 1109 38:11 The same was true for north side of courtyard curtain wall.

COURTYARD ENCLOSURE – WEST SIDE

3643 1110 38:12 The curtain wall on the west side was 100 feet long with 10 pillars, 10 sockets, silver hooks and silver threads around the hooks.

VAYAKHÂL - SECTION 7 - CONTINUED

COURTYARD ENCLOSURE – EAST SIDE, WITH ENTRANCE

3644 1111 38:13 The east side of the courtyard was 100 feet long.

3645 1112 38:14 The east curtain wall on one side of the entrance was 15 feet long with 3 pillars, each with a socket.

3646 1113 38:15 And the same was true for the curtain wall on the other side of the entrance.

3647 1114 38:16 All the courtyard curtain walls were made of linen.

3648 1115 38:17 All the sockets for the courtyard wall pillars were copper.

The hooks and caps[753] on the pillars were silver.

The pillars also had silver threads around them.

Vayakhâl – Last Section

3649 1116 38:18 The screen for the entrance was made of blue wool, purple wool, and linen.

It was 40 feet long and 10 feet high.

3650 1117 38:19 It had 4 pillars, each with a copper socket, and silver hooks along with silver threads.

2651 1118 38:20 The stakes all around the curtain wall were made of copper.

Vayakhâl – Section 7 – Study Notes

---

[748] 38:1 "he" - Biżalel. See the notes on verse 35:34.

[749] 38:7 "hollowed out" – As had been specified in verse 27:8.

[750] 38:8 "water basins" – Although most of the items for the tabernacle are specified in chapters 25–27, the water basin is specified in verse 30:18.

[751] 38:8 "copper mirrors" – The wives had used these for putting on makeup to encourage their husbands to be intimate during the years of slavery such that the Jewish population increased despite the king's evil decrees (see verses 1:11-12).

[752] 38:8 – "pray" – See Essay 7.

[753] 38:17 "caps" – This is the first mention of silver caps for pillars. It is mentioned again in verse 38:28

Pikūdā[754] - Section 1 - 12 verses   (Total: 92 verses)

TOTAL AMOUNTS OF GOLD, SILVER, AND COPPER

2652 1119 38:21 The following are the totals of materials collected for the tabernacle.

Mōshe put the people of the tribe of Lāvē in charge of collections and accounting.

It was managed by Ētamar son of Aharōn the priest.

2653 1120 38:22 The craft work was managed by Biźalel, based on the instructions given by G-d to Mōshe.

2654 1121 38:23 Ahalēav[755] was a master craftsman weaver who also managed the work.

2655 1122 38:24 Total gold: 29 kēkar[756] + 730 shekel weight.

2656 1123 38:25 Total silver: 100 kēkar + 1775 shekel weight.

2657 1124 38:26 Half-shekel silver coins: 603,550: one from each man at least 20 years old.[757]

2658 1125 38:27 Total silver used for the silver sockets: 100 kēkar weight.

Each socket weighed 1 kēkar.

2659 1126 38:28 Silver used for the silver hooks, caps,[758] and inlaid hoops: 1775 shekel weight.

2660 1127 38:29 Total copper: 70 kēkar + 2,400 shekel weight.

2661 1128 38:30 The copper was used for:

the sockets of the door posts,

the animal-offering altar covering and screen,

the utensils,

2662 1129 38:31 the sockets of the courtyard pillars, and

all the pins.

2663 1130 39:1 The craftspeople used the blue, purple, and red wool to weave the cloth used to wrap[759] the holy objects.

They fashioned the clothing for Aharōn as high priest, as G-d had commanded Mōshe.[760]

Pikūdā – Section 1 – Study Notes

[754] "Pikūdā" – The Hebrew word *pikūdā* can be translated as "the totals of" or "the accounts of."

[755] 38:22 "managed by Biżalel . . . Ahalēav" – See notes on 35:34.

[756] 38:24 "kēkar" – The Hebrew word *kēkar* is a measure of weight that is equal to 3000 shekel measures. It is rendered into English Bibles as "talent." See note on 30:13 for the weight and value of a shekel.

[757] 38:26 "603,550: one from each man at least 20 years old." – Each half-shekel coin represents an adult man, effectively making this a census. Verse 12:37 states that there were about 600,000 adult men who left Egypt. The population count here is about 4 months after the exodus. It took place after Mōshe descended with the second set of stone slabs, as shown Table 3 (which is found at the study note on verse 12:37). There is no indication that the tribe of Lāvē is excluded from the count. However, the census stated at the start of Bamidbar (Numbers) takes place about 8 months after this census. At the start of Bamidbar the population count is 603,550 men for the twelve tribes, plus 22,300 boys and men in the tribe of Lāvē.

Note that there are 12 sons of Yaakōv. Yōsef had two sons, which Yaakōv blessed as each being a separate tribe, thus making 13 tribes. The tribe of Lāvē will be set aside as special, as stated in Bamidbar 1:49 which commands not to include the population counts of Lāvē as part of the overall Jewish population counts, thus accounting for the separate census of the tribe of Lāvē.

[758] 38:28 "caps" – Caps were first mentioned in verse 38:17.

[759] 39:1 "wrap" – This is previously stated in verse 31:10. There are two opinions:
Rashē: These are the clothes of the high priest.
Ramban: These are cloths used to wrap the objects in the tabernacle when transported.

[760] 39:1 "as G-d commanded Mōshe" – This is the first of 18 occurrences of this phrase in this portion. The sages formalized the weekday version of

the central prayer, known as the Amēda (which means "stand" because a person should stand when making a request from G-d), as 18 blessings. One of the reasons that the sages selected 18 as the number of blessings may have been the 18 occurrences in this portion. The Amēda is also known as Shimōne Esrā, which means "18." Later in history, a nineteenth blessing was added. This is possibly based on the similar expression found in verse 38:22.

Pikūdā - Section 2   - 20 verses

APRON OF THE HIGH PRIEST

2664 1131 39:2 The craftspeople wove gold thread with the various wools and linen for the apron of the high priest.
2665 1132 39:3 They fashioned gold into thin plates and cut it into threads so it could be woven with the wools and linen.
2666 1133 39:4 They fashioned the shoulder pieces for the apron[761] and attached the two ends.
2667 1134 39:5 They fashioned a belt of the gold, wool, and linen threads, as G-d had commanded Mōshe.[762]
2668 1135 39:6 They set the two onyx gem stones onto gold bases.
    They engraved the names of the twelve sons of Yaakōv (Jacob = Israel).
2669 1136 39:7 He[763] secured them onto the shoulder pieces of the apron, as G-d had commanded Mōshe.[764]

BREASTPLATE

2670 1137 39:8 He fashioned the breastplate out of threads of gold, wool, and linen.
2671 1138 39:9 It became square by folding it in half.
2672 1139 39:10 The twelve gem stones were set in the breastplate as 4 rows.
    The first row consisted of carnelian, emerald, and topaz.
2673 1140 39:11 The second row consisted of carbuncle, sapphire, beryl.
2674 1141 39:12 The third row consisted of jacinth, agate, and amethyst.
2675 1142 39:13 The fourth row consisted of chrysolite, onyx, and jasper.
2676 1143 39:14 Each gem had one name of a son of Yaakov engraved on it.
    All twelve names were engraved on the breastplate gemstones.
2677 1144 39:15 Braided gold chains were attached to the breastplate.
2678 1145 39:16 They fashioned 2 gold settings and rings.
    The gold rings were attached to the top corners of the breastplate.
2679 1146 39:17 The gold chains were attached to the gold rings.
2680 1147 39:18 The chains were also attached to the 2 settings of the apron's shoulder pieces at the front.

Pikūdā - Section 2 - continued

2681 1148 39:19 They fashioned 2 gold rings for the bottom corners of the breastplate.
2682 1149 39:20 They fashioned 2 gold rings for the bottom of the shoulder pieces at the front and placed them above the apron's belt.
2683 1150 39:21 They laced the breastplate by its rings to the rings of the apron using blue wool.
    This kept the breastplate above the apron's belt.
    All this was performed as G-d had commanded Mōshe.[765]

Pikūdā – Section 2 – Study Notes

[761] 39:4 "apron" – The priest clothes were described previously starting in verse 28:6 (portion Tiżave). See note on 28:6 for a list of the priest clothes.

[762] 39:5 "as G-d had commanded Mōshe" – second occurrence of the 18 (see note on 39:1).

[763] 39:7 "he" – Very likely it was Ahalēav (see notes on verse 35:34). As supervisor, he personally checked the work and performed the critical tasks.

[764] 39:7 "as G-d had commanded Mōshe" – occurrence 3.

[765] 39:21 "as G-d had commanded Mōshe" – occurrence 4

Pikūdā - Section 3   - 11 verses

ROBE

2684 1151 39:22 He[766] wove the blue robe of the apron.
2685 1152 39:23 The opening for the head was in the middle.
2686 1153 39:24 Along the bottom of the robe the craftspeople fashioned decorative pomegranate figures out of blue, red and purple wool.
2687 1154 39:25 They fashioned gold bells and placed a bell between each pomegranate.
2688 1155 39:26 There were alternating bells and pomegranates along the entire perimeter of the bottom of the robe, as G-d had commanded Mōshe.[767]

TUNIC, TURBAN, HAT, PANTS, BELT

2689 1156 39:27 They fashioned the tunic out of linen.
2690 1157 39:28 They fashioned the turban, hats, and pants of linen.
2691 1158 39:29 They fashioned the belt out of linen, blue wool, red wool, and purple wool, as G-d had commanded Mōshe.[768]

HEADPLATE

2692 1159 39:30 They fashioned the headplate out of gold.
   The words "Holy To G-d" were inscribed on it.
2693 1160 39:31 They tied a blue wool thread on each side of the headplate so it could be worn on the bottom of the turban,[769] as G-d had commanded Mōshe.[770]

COMPLETION OF THE WORK

2694 1161 39:32 All the work was completed, and the Jewish people had performed the work just as G-d had commanded Mōshe.[771]

Pikūdā – Section 3 – Study Notes

[766] 39:22 "he" – See note on 39:7.

[767] 39:26 "as G-d had commanded Mōshe" – occurrence 5 of the 18 (see note on 39:1).

[768] 39:29 "as G-d had commanded Mōshe" – occurrence 6.

[769] 39:31 "headplate . . . turban" – See verses 28:36-38. See footnote and drawing in Kaplan, p.429.

[770] 39:31 "as G-d had commanded Mōshe" – occurrence 7.

[771] 39:32 "as G-d had commanded Mōshe" – occurrence 8.

Pikūdā - Section 4   - 11 verses

THIRTY NINE ITEMS FASHIONED

2695 1162 39:33 The people brought all the fashioned items[772] to Mōshe:
    1 sanctuary
    2 its utensils
    3 fastenings
    4 beams
    5 crossbars
    6 pillars
    7 bases
2696 1163 39:34
    8 ram skins for the roof
    9 roof skins dyed blue
    10 partition
2697 1164 39:35
    11 sacred box
    12 its poles
    13 its lid
2698 1165 39:36
    14 table
    15 its utensils
    16 showbread
2699 1166 39:37
    17 menōra
    18 its lamps
    19 its utensils
    20 oil
2700 1167 39:38
    21 golden incense altar
    22 anointing oil
    23 incense
    24 drapes

Pikūdā - Section 4 - continued

2701 1168 39:39
    25 copper altar for animal offerings
    26 its poles
    27 its utensils
    28 washbowl
    29 washbowl base
2702 1169 39:40
    30 cloth walls of the court
    31 its poles
    32 their bases
    33 entrance cloth
    34 tying ropes
    35 stakes
    36 utensils
2703 1170 39:41
    37 packing cloths
    38 high priests' clothes and
    39 priests' clothes.
2704 1171 39:42 The Jewish people fashioned all the parts of the tabernacle just as G-d had commanded Mōshe.[773]

MŌSHE BLESSES THE JEWISH PEOPLE

2705 1172 39:43 When Mōshe saw that the work had been performed just as G-d had commanded,[774] Mōshe blessed all the people who had performed the work.

Pikūdā – Section 4 – Study Notes.

---

[772] 39:33 "items" – There are 39 items listed here. Interestingly, there are 39 items of the sanctuary listed in verses 35:11-19 in the previous portion, Vayakhel. And there are 39 categories of forbidden activities on the Sabbath.

[773] 39:42 "as G-d had commanded Mōshe" – occurrence 9 of the 18 (see note on 39:1).

[774] 39:43 "just as G-d had commanded" – occurrence 10

Pikūdā - Section 5 — 16 verses

INSTRUCTION TO ASSEMBLE AND ANOINT THE TABERNACLE

2706 1173 40:1 G-d communicated to Mōshe:
2707 1174 40:2 "You should assemble the tabernacle on the first day of the month of Nēsan.
2708 1175 40:3 Place the sacred box in the holiest area and put up the curtain as a partition.
2709 1176 40:4 Place the table and menorah in their designated locations.
2710 1177 40:5 Place the gold altar opposite the sacred box on the other side of the curtain.
2711 1178 40:6 Place the altar for animal offerings in front of the sanctuary.
2712 1179 40:7 Place the wash basin between the entrance of the sanctuary and the animal altar.
2713 1180 40:8 Set up the curtain wall around the courtyard and set up the entrance curtain at the entrance of the courtyard.
2714 1181 40:9 Sanctify the tabernacle with holiness by anointing the tabernacle and all its furniture and utensils with oil.
2715 1182 40:10 Anoint the animal altar and its utensils.
    It is very holy.
2716 1183 40:11 Anoint the wash basin and its stand.

INSTRUCTION FOR PRIESTS TO PREPARE FOR INSTALLATION

2717 1184 40:12 Have Aharōn and his sons wash[775] and have them come to the sanctuary's entrance.
2718 1185 40:13 Then Aharōn should wear his high priest clothes.
    Then anoint him as a priest.
2719 1186 40:14 Have Aharōn's sons wear their priest clothes.
2720 1187 40:15 Then anoint them as priests.
    Their descendants will be priests[776] from now on."
2721 1188 40:16 Mōshe performed everything just as G-d had commanded.[777]

Pikūdā – Section 5 – Study Notes

[775] 40:12 "wash" – First mentioned in verse 29:4.

[776] 40:15 "will be priests" – The ceremony is described in Vayikra (Leviticus) chapter 8.

[777] 40:16 "as G-d had commanded Mōshe" – occurrence 11 of the 18 (see note on 39:1).

Pikūdā - Section 6   - 11 verses

TABERNACLE IS ASSEMBLED

2722 1189 40:17 On the first day of the month of Nēsan,[778] the tabernacle was assembled.
2723 1190 40:18 Mōshe set up[779] the tabernacle.
2724 1191 40:19 He spread the roof covering over it.
   It was done just as G-d had commanded Mōshe.[780]

ASSEMBLING AND POSITIONING THE HOLY BOX WITH STONE SLABS INSIDE

2725 1192 40:20 Mōshe placed the stone slabs[781] into the sacred box.
   He then inserted the rods into the rings of the box and placed the cover on it.
2726 1193 40:21 He positioned the box into the holiest area of tabernacle.
   Then he hung the curtain partition that separates the holiest area from the rest of the Tabernacle.
   It was done just as G-d had commanded Mōshe.[782]

POSITIONING THE TABLE

2727 1194 40:22 He positioned the table on the northside.
2728 1195 40:23 Then he arranged the bread on the table.
   It was done just as G-d had commanded Mōshe.[783]

POSITIONING THE MENŌRA

2729 1196 40:24 He placed the menōra across from the table on the south side.
2730 1197 40:25 He lit the lamps of the menōra.
   It was done just as G-d had commanded Mōshe.[784]

POSITIONING THE INCENSE ALTAR

2731 1198 40:26 He positioned the incense gold altar in front of the partition.
2732 1199 40:27 Then he burned incense on the altar.
   It was done just as G-d had commanded Mōshe.[785]

Pikūdā – Section 6 – Study Notes.

---

[778] 40:17 "month of Nēsan" – This month occurs in the spring, usually the month of April. The Jewish people had left Egypt during the previous Nēsan, on the fifteenth of the month.

[779] 40:18 "Mōshe set up" – Tōra credits Mōshe with setting up the tabernacle. He explained, supervised and managed the process. For example, each wall board was 15-20 feet long and would require a number of people to hoist it into position. Verses that use passive verbs, such as "was assembled" (verse 40:17) and "was performed" (verse 40:25) make it clear that the people worked together to accomplish it.

[780] 40:19 "as G-d had commanded Mōshe" – occurrence 12 of the 18 (see note on 39:1).

[781] 40:20 "stone slabs" – These are the second pair of slabs that Mōshe carved at G-d's instruction. See notes on verse 24:12.

[782] 40:21 "as G-d had commanded Mōshe" – occurrence 13.

[783] 40:23 "as G-d had commanded Mōshe" – occurrence 14.

[784] 40:25 "as G-d had commanded Mōshe" – occurrence 15.

[785] 40:27 "as G-d had commanded Mōshe" – occurrence 16

Pikūdā - Section 7   - 6 + 5 verses

HANGING THE DRAPES

2733 1200 40:28 He[786] hung the curtain at the Tabernacle's entrance.

POSITIONING THE ALTAR FOR ANIMAL OFFERINGS

2734 1201 40:29 He positioned the altar that is in the outer courtyard.
    He offered burnt offerings and meal offerings.
    It was performed just as G-d had commanded Mōshe.[787]

POSITIONING THE WASHSTAND

2735 1202 40:30 He positioned the wash basin in the courtyard, between the altar and the entrance of the Tabernacle.
2736 1203 40:31 Mōshe, Aharōn, and Aharōn's sons washed their hands and feet using the water of the wash basin.
2737 1204 40:32 The priests washed in this way each time they entered the Tabernacle.
    They also washed this way whenever they offered offerings on the altar.
    This was all performed just as G-d had commanded Mōshe.[788]

SETTING UP THE COURTYARD WALLS
CONSTRUCTION IS COMPLETE

2738 1205 40:33 He set up the poles and curtains that create the courtyard area, which surrounded the Tabernacle and the altar.
    He placed the curtain over the courtyard entrance.
    Mōshe thus completed[789] all the activities for constructing the Tabernacle.

Pikūdā – Last Section

CLOUD COVERS THE TABERNACLE

2739 1206 40:34 The cloud covered the holy Tabernacle.
    The glory of G-d filled the Tabernacle
2740 1207 40:35 such that Mōshe was not able to enter the Tabernacle.

PIKŪDĀ - SECTION 7 - CONTINUED

WHEN THE CLOUD ROSE, THE JEWISH PEOPLE TRAVEL

2741 1208 40:36 When the cloud would rise from the Tabernacle, it was the divine signal to the Jewish people to travel.
2742 1209 40:37 When the cloud rested on the Tabernacle, however, the Jewish people did not travel.

A FIRE ABOVE THE TABERNACLE AT NIGHT

2743 1210 40:38 The divine cloud remained on the Tabernacle during the daytime, and there was a fire[790] above it during the night.
    This was visible to the entire Jewish people throughout their travels.

Pikūdā – Section 7 – Study Notes

[786] 40:28 "he" – See note on verse 40:18.

[787] 40:29 "as G-d had commanded Mōshe" – occurrence 17 (see note on 39:1).

[788] 40:32 "as G-d had commanded Mōshe" – occurrence 18.

[789] 40:33 "completed" – The dedication ceremony of the Tabernacle resumes with Chapter 8 of the next book, Vayikra.

[790] 40:38 "cloud . . . fire" – See verse 13:22 and the note on verse 17:1.

Made in the USA
Middletown, DE
17 February 2018